The Dialectical Temper

THE RHETORICAL ART
OF ROBERT BROWNING

The Dialectical Temper

THE RHETORICAL ART
OF ROBERT BROWNING

W. David Shaw

Cornell University Press

ITHACA, NEW YORK

LIBRARY

JAN 6 1969

UNIVERSITY OF THE PACIFIC

193697

Copyright © 1968 by Cornell University

All rights reserved. Except for brief quotations in a review, this book, or parts thereof, must not be reproduced in any form without permission in writing from the publisher. For information address Cornell University Press, 124 Roberts Place, Ithaca, New York 14850.

First published 1968

Library of Congress Catalog Card Number: 68-29661

PRINTED IN THE UNITED STATES OF AMERICA
BY THE VAIL-BALLOU PRESS, INC.

To My Mother and

the Memory of My Father

Acknowledgments

My debts are many and various, and I can record only a few of them here. I owe a great deal to my former mentor, Professor F. E. L. Priestley. A sense of intellectual adventure arising from his lectures at University College, University of Toronto, first drew me to Victorian studies. Since that time he has represented for me all that is finest in scholarship and teaching, and his searching criticisms of my manuscript have proved invaluable. I have also benefited greatly from the friendly, if relentless, prosecutions of Professor Park Honan. He has been exceptionally generous and has devoted more time to my work than anyone had a right to expect. I am grateful as well for the helpful reactions of Professor Roma A. King, Jr. In addition to the care with which they have criticized my ideas, I am indebted like every student of Browning to all these scholars' own fine work. I have also benefited from the advice of Professors Jerome Buckley and Douglas Bush, of Harvard University. Though this book bears little resemblance to early drafts, and though all errors of style and judgment are my own, any virtues the manuscript may possess are due to the influence of these five scholars.

For their flashing of light over wide perspectives I owe a more general debt to Professor Reuben Brower, of Harvard University, and the late Professor A. S. P. Woodhouse, of the University of Toronto. Much of the satisfaction I have known in the study and the classroom has come from an attempt to follow their example. I have benefited as well from conversations with colleagues and students at Cornell. Francis Mineka, M. H. Abrams, Judith Anderson, Evelyn Barish, Dean Blehert, Vincent DeLuca, Neil Hertz, Carol Marks, Jean Blackall, and Dorothy Mermin, among others, have produced the kind of atmosphere conducive to creative scholarship.

I also want to thank Professor William Sale for reducing my teaching assignments for a semester. His consideration enabled me to continue my research at a critical stage of rethinking this book.

I am especially grateful, finally, to the editors of Cornell University Press. Without their generous encouragement and advice I know this study would never have been finished.

All quotations from Browning's poems are from the ten-volume Centenary Edition, *The Works of Robert Browning*, edited by F. G. Kenyon (London, 1912).

I wish to thank the editors of *Victorian Poety* and of *The Victorian Newsletter* for permission to incorporate in the text portions of three of my articles that originally appeared in the spring and autumn issues of *Victorian Poetry* in 1964 (II, 127–132, 277–282) and in the spring, 1966, issue of *The Victorian Newsletter* (XXIX, 18–22). The first two have been extensively revised.

W. DAVID SHAW

Ithaca, New York
March 1968

Contents

The Dialectical Temper

THE RHETORICAL ART
OF ROBERT BROWNING

Introduction: The Rhetorical Art of Robert Browning

The rhetorical art of engaging an audience and controlling its responses is of special importance for Browning, who inherits from Shelley views of the poet's high didactic function and who tries to modify his readers' aesthetic, moral, and religious attitudes by revealing the limitations inherent in most ideas and beliefs. The young Browning is a "subjective poet," described in his Introductory Essay to the *Letters of Percy Bysshe Shelley* as a "seer" who writes directly of his own experience. The first part of the present study, "The Subject's Isolation," analyzes the seer's inability to realize his potential. Browning's failure is partly rhetorical—an inability to persuade his readers—and partly an incapacity to view himself critically. Because he is more concerned with addressing God or himself than another auditor, he neglects those responsibilities of his craft which develop a writer's objective authority and his ability to communicate. And since he is incapable of self-criticism, the subjective poet cannot see that every point of view, including his own, suffers from its own limited perspective.

The second section, "The Objective World," shows how Browning's dramatic monologues overcome both limitations. The best way of understanding ideas or beliefs that exist in

1

the objective world is to impersonate a character who embodies them. To appreciate another point of view, we must first place ourselves inside its spokesmen and represent by acts of sympathetic imagination its intrinsic nature. Because the monologues enable Browning to grasp conflicting ideas and beliefs from inside the characters he portrays, he can reveal the contradictions in their attitudes in the very act of representing them. The monologues are the dialectical weapon of a comic philosopher who, in laying siege to many points of view, can educate his readers at the same time he entertains them. By adopting the unique standpoint of his characters, Browning can combine their ideas and beliefs into a single hierarchical system, advancing from the lower "aesthetic" to the higher "ethical" and "religious" stages of experience. Since the speakers in the monologues have to persuade an auditor, who can function as the reader's "friend," the monologues also develop Browning's rhetorical art of engaging an audience and controlling its responses.

The last section of this study, "The Union of the Subject and the World," shows how *The Ring and the Book*, as the goal of Browning's dialectical ascent, combines the objective authority of the dramatic monologues with the subjective poet's ability to write directly of his own experience. By representing and dissolving many points of view before approximating the "central truth" in the monologues of Pompilia, Caponsacchi, and the Pope, the mature Browning is able to speak out of his own personality with an authority that as a young subjective poet he never possessed. Because he has portrayed many conflicting attitudes, he is free from those limitations of perspective that mar his early poetry. Though all points of view are limited, they are true progressively and inclusively. Before Browning can write "R. B.—a poem," a work in which he can reach the "pure white light" and write

directly of his own experience, he must progress through the
full range of aesthetic, ethical, and religious stages.

In analyzing Browning's rhetorical art, I have tried to
come to terms, not only with the figures of speech, but also
with the less tractable logical devices. Since these include the
syllogism and dilemma and since Browning uses the various
fallacies of disputation, they often play as crucial a role as the
figures of speech, especially in the rhetorical art of a "Victorian sage" whom we value, not only for his verbal complexity, but above all for the authority and brilliance, often
the sheer excitement, of his thinking. No critic can treat ex-
haustively a poet's rhetorical art, however, merely by me-
chanically listing the rhetorical figures or the logical forms
that appear in his poems. For this reason, and to make the
analyses easier to follow, I have avoided technical terms.
Rhetoric, in the large sense, is the art of persuasion—not
simply the persuasive art of a speaker in a poem, but the
poet's own art of engaging his readers and controlling their
responses. As John Holloway observes, the Victorian sage
"does not and probably cannot rely on logical and formal
argument alone or even much at all. His main task is to
quicken his reader's perceptiveness; and he does this by making a far wider appeal than the exclusively rational appeal." [1]
The distinctive feature of Browning's rhetoric is not its exposition of a philosophic, religious, or aesthetic "system," but
its dialectical temper, its habit of imitating and rejecting
different attitudes and beliefs, which forces the reader to discover the astonishing (and often disturbing) life of the ideas.
A good example is the rhetoric of Caliban or David, which
invites audience collaboration. Their doctrines are less important than the life represented and the values discovered along
the way. Most of Browning's "truths" can be perceived only

[1] *The Victorian Sage* (New York, 1953), p. 10.

through a constant cooperation of the speaker, the poet, and
the reader in a process of mutual inquiry and response: the
"philosophy" can be understood only as the outgrowth of
joint creative acts.

The reader may question what general interest or validity
this philosophy can have a hundred years after the poems
were written. He may feel that many of Browning's Victorian attitudes are now out of date. We should remember,
however, that a thinker does not have to reflect our own beliefs in order to have significance for us. Much of Browning's
philosophy enables us to define by contrast what is most
modern in our own attitudes. In addition, it has a significance
in its own right. Browning's modernity lies in his dialectical
method; he coordinates traditional values in a new way,
bringing conflicting attitudes together. Most "truths" for
Browning are only points of view, valid but limited, whose
opposites are also true. He lives under an earlier sense of the
absolute, the whole, and the known, but also (and equally)
under a modern sense of the relative, the partial, and the unknown. In almost all his contemporaries one of these two
types of attitudes was dominant. Unfortunately, as soon as
Browning became fashionable, he was read in the same way
as most of his contemporaries. Because few readers could
bear the synthesis of his resolutions, his dialectical temper
was misunderstood: the early Browning societies forgot the
questioning side of him, and later critics forgot the affirma-
tive side. But if as modern readers we find it difficult to share
all of Browning's beliefs, it should still be possible for us to
share his sense of limitation. Religion apart, what exists, as
Browning asks, but "the little mind of man, reduced / To lit-
tleness that suits his faculty?" (*The Ring and the Book*, X,
1321-1322). It is between our uncertainties that the most
profitable exchange between Browning and ourselves may
take place. Such an exchange would be faithful to Brown-

ing's own genius. One aim of the present study is to show that it might even restore a proper appreciation of his dialectical temper. His ironic and resourceful spirit might then help to mature our own point of view by bringing into play attitudes that lie outside, as well as within, the present range of our responses.

The dialectical movement in Browning's poetry depends upon several elements. Rhetoric is only one of these elements, and I do not want to imply that there is nothing else. Browning is most persuasive when he realizes his rhetorical art as something more than his "ideas," as something that originates in the poetry itself; his language then enacts the very truths to be advanced. For this reason I deliberately exclude from my analysis many long rhetorical poems from Browning's later period. Though not all of Browning's work deteriorates after *The Ring and the Book,* many poems of this late period, even when faultless in their logical progression, are devoid of feeling. At this stage Browning simply records his ideas; he seldom realizes them in the act of writing poetry. My interest in rhetoric has therefore been forced into some kind of adjustment with my interest in art. Nevertheless, the essence of good criticism, I take it, is that such adjustment should not become compromise. We should appreciate Browning's art in the poems that we read, and through that art, the truths that they express. Like Wayne Booth, to whose pioneer study, *The Rhetoric of Fiction,*[2] I am deeply indebted, I emphasize what Browning's poetry is made to *do*—how it is designed to communicate itself. Though this interest in what a poem *does* may seem to conflict with the formalist's interest in what a poem *is,* the rhetorical acts that the poet and his readers perform together depend, as I try to show, on the symbols, tone, and idiom—in a word, the

[2] Chicago, 1961.

"poetics"—of Browning's many surrogates and spokesmen. My own approach may not always achieve a proper adjustment of rhetorical and formal elements. But if it is taken in conjunction with the more formal approaches of Park Honan, Roma A. King, Jr., Robert Langbaum, and others, as Browning's dialectical temper requires, then the resultant balance of rhetorical criticism and formalism should help enrich our reading of the poems.

PART I

THE SUBJECT'S ISOLATION

Browning himself provides the clearest description of his early poetry when he lists three tendencies of the "subjective poet" in his Introductory Essay to the *Letters of Percy Bysshe Shelley*. First, instead of addressing other men or "things external," the subjective poet describes the state of his "own soul." Second, because he is a "seer" rather than a "fashioner," his art is less "a work than an effluence." By this Browning means that subjective poetry is confessional rather than dramatic, that it is a continuous process rather than a finished product, and that its emphasis is psychological rather than aesthetic. Third, because he wants to create "what God sees," the seer tries to ascend at once into his visionary heaven. He despises the objective poet's attempt to see in particulars of "independent and unclassed value" tokens of his unattainable ideal, which the seer must perceive instantly and as a whole.

These three tendencies, carried to an extreme, represent the threefold failure of Browning's early poetry: rhetorical, dramatic, and dialectical, respectively. As a result of his first tendency, the poet neglects those rhetorical responsibilities that should confer authority on his work. Instead of controlling his reader's responses, Browning is turned away, so to speak, in a state of self-communion, in which he seems more concerned to utter than address. As a consequence of his

7

second tendency, Browning substitutes for the actual representation of his own experience a form of spontaneous self-
expression. Without dramatic objectivity his early poetry is
willful where it should be authoritative, private where it
should be public. One result of his third tendency is an attitude of intellectual arrogance and moral conceit. Impatient
with the objective poet's particulars, Browning tries to leap
at once into an omniscient role. Unable to view himself ironically, the subjective poet suffers from his own limited perspective. He short-circuits the arduous process by which the
mature Browning, the comic philosopher whose weapon is
dialectic, learns to expose the contradictions inherent in most
ideas and beliefs, ordering these attitudes into a hierarchy
that allocates them to aesthetic, moral, or religious stages of a
man's development.

Because of his threefold failure—rhetorical, dramatic, and
dialectical—the young Browning is unable to make what he
presents actual: objective, authoritative, public. Following
J. S. Mill's criticism of *Pauline*, he tries to remedy his rhetorical and dramatic failings, the results of the subjective poet's
first and second tendencies. Though *Paracelsus* eliminates the
confessional egoism of the earlier poem, its hero still suffers
from his limited perspective. Only at the end does Paracelsus
learn to identify with other points of view. This identification allows the hero to overcome the intellectual arrogance
and moral conceit that arise from the subjective poet's third
tendency. In *Sordello*, Browning tries to use all the advantages of the subjective method while avoiding the rhetorical,
dramatic, and dialectical defects that may result from each of
its three tendencies. Almost all the poem's difficulties can be
traced to Browning's inability to realize the potential advantages of the method without incorporating most of its disadvantages at the same time. In *Pippa Passes* and the plays
Browning tries to redeem his rhetorical and dramatic failures.

He learns to present characters that an audience can understand and to create events that are in some sense an embodiment of actual experience. Browning's ability to identify with points of view other than his own allows him in *Pippa Passes* to rank his perspectives into a single hierarchy of aesthetic, ethical, and religious values. Browning escapes his isolation when he overcomes the subjective poet's three tendencies. He develops into one of the most controlled and individual poets of his age only by learning to master the rhetorical, dramatic, and dialectical dimensions of his art.

I

The Subjective Poet's Problem: Pauline *and* Paracelsus

Pauline (1833) illustrates each of the subjective poet's three tendencies. It provides the clearest example of the rhetorical, dramatic, and dialectical shortcomings of Browning's early poetry: Though the speaker is ostensibly addressing his beloved, his most important auditor is himself; his aim is not to persuade Pauline but to get his own uniqueness uttered. For an actual representation of his own experience, which would be objective and authoritative, the lover substitutes a private confession. Incapable of viewing himself ironically, he draws God, Pauline, and Shelley into his own particular orbit; suffering from an exaggerated sense of his importance, he celebrates his own point of view as the total truth.

Browning's rhetorical failure is a result of his inability to realize Pauline as an actual person. Though he begins by addressing a woman and returns to her at several points throughout the poem, she is only an emanation of his buried life. Her "soft breast," "sweet eyes," and "loosened hair" represent sensuous aspects of Browning's inner being, which is the real subject of the poem. Without having to choose words that would persuade a real Pauline, Browning substitutes a ready-made or preconceived emotion for an emotion that has its life in the poetry itself.

I am made up of an intensest life,
Of a most clear idea of consciousness
Of self, distinct from all its qualities,
From all affections, passions, feelings, powers;
And thus far it exists, if tracked, in all:
But linked, in me, to self-supremacy, . . .
And to a principle of restlessness
Which would be all, have, see, know, taste, feel, all—
This is myself   [ll. 268–279].

To express intensity the speaker repeats the word "all" four times. His language half congeals into excited stammering, then breaks down into ecstatic "word-heaps." Despite *Pauline*'s lavish use of punctuation, including seventy-one exclamation points, Browning has failed to solve the difficult problem of expressing intensity in poetry.

The failure becomes clearer if we pause to consider for a moment three of the ways in which Browning overcomes this problem in his later poetry. In *The Ring and the Book*, for example, where the need to secure some personal advantage from the judges makes the speakers more resourceful, Guido uses violent language to express intense feeling. Much of his rhetoric has the same purpose as swearing. He gives vent to his sense of outrage by breaking moral and religious taboos. More subtly, Pompilia expresses the intensity of her emotion by playing a formal language game in which she calls the priest the "lover of [her] life" even as she repudiates the sexual analogies. She avoids a conventional erotic form while preserving the conventional intention in all its power. In still a third way, Caponsacchi makes emphatic his damnation of Guido by running language back on its tracks. The priest uses the idea of undoing God's creation, not to establish a religious context for his judgment, but only to measure, by means of a traditional idea, the intensity of Guido's de-

structive impulse. This allows the speaker to give to nothingness a linguistic index by unfixing the given limits of being:

> So I lose Guido in the loneliness,
> Silence and dusk, till at the doleful end,
> At the horizontal line, creation's verge,
> From what just is to absolute nothingness—
>
> [VI, 1928–1931].

Without a similar need to persuade Pauline, Browning is
much less inventive in finding ways to express intensity. For
the rhetorical responsibilities of his craft he substitutes the
chaos of mere self-expression. This is the point of J. S. Mill's
criticism: everything the speaker says about Pauline is a pile
"of inconsistency—he neither loves her nor fancies he loves
her, yet insists upon *talking* love to her—if she *existed* and
loved him, he treats her most ungenerously and unfeelingly.
. . . I know not what to wish for him but that he may
meet with a *real* Pauline." [1]

Pauline's dramatic failure is a result of the subjective poet's
second tendency. Because he identifies so completely with his
speaker, Browning cannot reproduce his experience for the
reader to share. Though he may not have known a real Pauline, his difficulty is not, as Mill suggests, a lack of sincerity.
On the contrary, misguided sincerity is what makes effective
definition of his emotion so difficult. Since poetry is a presentation of experience, it can never remain a vehicle for abstract communication, however real the experience may be to
the poet. Browning's rapid succession of metaphors substitutes a ready-made emotion for an emotion created out of
the materials of his poem. The comparison of a "white swan"
to a "moonbeam" (ll. 101–102) or of "words" to "a swift

---

[1] Mill's comments appear in his projected review of the poem for
The Examiner. They survive in the copy of *Pauline* in the Forster and
Dyce Collection in the Victoria and Albert Museum.

wind" (ll. 532, 534) proceeds from the more to the less concrete. The speaker's soul is disembodied and turns into an Arab bird floating over towers and deserts (ll. 479–480). Such metaphors do not "arouse or define emotion." As David Perkins observes of Shelley's symbols, "They are employed rather to receive feelings already generated." [2] Their authority is convincing only to those who are already moved. As the speaker tries to find a last image for Pauline, she is successively compared to a clear heaven, a rainstorm, thin mist, floating clouds, and a brood of white swans (ll. 893–895). These metaphors are less and less apt and dissipate the speaker's own emotion. The figurative language makes Pauline so rarefied that even her "blood," "thinned by kisses," evaporates in a void. Because such comparisons pile themselves up blindly, each defeating the impact of the others, the presentation of emotional experience betrays no structure whatever. The emotion has its life in the poet but not in the poem. It is apparently so much a part of Browning's own experience that he lacks the detachment to make it actual: concrete, objectified, and public.

Pauline's third weakness is the speaker's inability to escape his own limited perspective. Instead of trying to understand other points of view, he identifies God, Pauline, and Shelley with himself. Mistaking his own point of view for the total truth, he believes that the rest of the world should share his experience. Only in a few passages, when he identifies with natural objects, does the speaker show signs of correcting the defect. He represents the forest's rough, clotted textures in words which indicate his acts of sympathetic imagination. In assimilating the swamp's teeming sense impressions, he comes to feel them from inside, like his own pulse and nerves. Though such examples of negative capability are confined to

inanimate objects like the "solid azure waters" or the "Tall
rushes and thick flag knots," the closest reasoning in the
poem also encourages the speaker to identify with many
points of view other than the inanimate, including that of
God himself. The swift, compressed reasoning which leads to
the conclusion that the soul hungers for an external God (ll.
820–821) can be reconstructed to form a logical dilemma. If
the soul rules, it languishes: "Commanding, for commanding,
sickens it." If God rules, then the soul cannot "be first in all
things." Since either the soul or God rules, either the soul
sickens or it accepts the proposition that it cannot "be first in
all things." To escape from the horns of the dilemma, the
speaker must embrace "weakness" in order to be well; he
must disavow the desire to "be first in all things" and must
embrace a God that is external to himself.

〰 1 〰

Stung by Mill's criticism of *Pauline*, Browning tries to
overcome his rhetorical, dramatic, and dialectical failings. He
must precipitate out of his isolated soul a sequence of dramatic relations, not merely between the poet and what ema-
nates from him, but between an idealist like Paracelsus and
other semiobjective characters. By modifying the subjective
poet's first two tendencies—his description of the state of his
"own soul," and his view of himself as a "seer" rather than a
"fashioner"—*Paracelsus* (1835) tries to remedy the rhetorical and dramatic weaknesses of *Pauline*. Festus and Michal,
for example, are not to be confused with the "Sun-treader"
or Pauline as mere emanations from the hero's consciousness.
They are what Henry James would call *ficelles*, characters
who give the reader in dramatic form the kind of help he
needs if he is to understand the story. They are present not
so much as friends of Paracelsus as "friends" of the reader.
Their rhetorical function is to express the audience's resistance to Paracelsus' striving and to help it grasp the hero's

problems. More complicated is the dramatic relation between Paracelsus and his creator. Because the hero has so much in common with the speaker of *Pauline*, with whom Browning has already identified himself, there is the danger of taking *Paracelsus* as another confessional poem. To be sure, Browning shares many of his hero's attitudes. As a clear statement of the subjective poet's first tendency, the young Browning would certainly endorse Paracelsus' belief that "Truth is within ourselves; it takes no rise / From outward things" (I, 726–727). But as F. E. L. Priestley has shown, Browning also involves his hero in a pattern of "true aspiration and ironic attainment followed by ironic or false aspiration and true attainment." [3] Irony requires dramatic detachment and is incompatible with the total identification of poet with hero in a confessional poem.

The most original feature of *Paracelsus* is not rhetorical or dramatic, however, but dialectical. At first the hero shares the subjective poet's third tendency. He condemns the attempt to see in every particular a hint of his ideal. Paracelsus has the towering aspirations of a scientific Tamburlaine and wants to reveal God's plan instantly and as a whole. Frustrated in this desire, the hero oscillates between aspiration and despair. The poem shows that every point of view naturally turns into its opposite.

Browning reinforces this pattern by emphasizing the pervasiveness of opposition. There are many plain statements about opposition, as well as indirect devices which keep the reader aware of it. When Paracelsus discounts the admiration of his followers, he distinguishes between

> Two sorts of knowledge; one—vast, shadowy,
> Hints of the unbounded aim I once pursued:
> The other consists of many secrets, caught
> While bent on nobler prize [III, 923–926].

[3] "The Ironic Pattern of Browning's Paracelsus," *University of Toronto Quarterly*, XXXIV (1964), 68.

Paracelsus rejects the second kind of "knowledge" as the "vest of falsehood," which he would shed like clothing as a concealment of the "truth" (III, 285). Absolute opposites like these "Two sorts of knowledge" obsess Paracelsus: the fire of the hungry Promethean is divine, but, as Festus suggests, it also reveals his "hidden scorn" (I, 262). In seeking a shortcut to the absolute, Paracelsus would wring "some wondrous good / From heaven or earth" (I, 463–464), even if it means that he must perish in the attempt.

The opposition between arrogance and humility, intellectual pretension and despair, runs sharply through the poem. The metaphors Browning uses constantly reinforce it. Paracelsus nourishes "glorious visions of God's love." But because his ideal is too lofty to realize, he keeps sickening on a "gulf streaked with light / From its own putrefying depths alone" (II, 175–176). At times the opposition prevents Paracelsus from going in any one direction. In the ecstasy of his death speech "leering dotards" give place to a "yellow blear-eyed wretch" (V, 177–179); Galen melts into Zoroaster and a lurid "serpent-queen." The wild leaps of imagery confound his auditor, who wonders if Paracelsus is "talking or singing." The situation can be relieved only by synthesis, by the admission of a wider idea which can reconcile Paracelsus' original ambition to encompass the whole truth and its generated antithesis, his contempt for all particular embodiments of this truth.

〰 2 〰

On two occasions in the poem—first at the beginning, when he is describing his friend's garden, and later when he is dying—Paracelsus approaches such a synthesis. In the first passage (I, 24–60) he empathizes with snails and flies, "shy lizards and quick spiders." The garden wall becomes the outwork of his friend's kingdom, which Paracelsus turns into

THE SUBJECTIVE POET'S PROBLEM

a delightful microcosm of the outside world. This glorification of "common life" strikingly anticipates his final solution. He uses the same language as the poet Aprile, who just before his death finds his salvation in a paradise of "birds' down, furs and fishes' skins" (II, 515). But because Paracelsus originally shuns all particular expressions of his ideal, he dismisses Festus' garden kingdom as a "paradise lost."

Only on his deathbed does Paracelsus learn to see in particulars tokens of his own ideal. Though the truth cannot be perceived as a whole, the individual can learn to approximate the whole by identifying with many points of view. As we have seen, Paracelsus speaks for Browning at the beginning in affirming the validity of "an inmost centre in us all, / Where truth abides in fulness" (I, 728–729). But he is mistaken in his original belief that though each man suffers from the limitation of his own perspective, he should overcome the limitation by trying to draw all the other points of view within his particular orbit. Paracelsus reaches the truth only at the end, when he cultivates the genius for paradox that enables him to define the "incomplete," not as a negation of truth, but as its inseparable condition. If each man is finite, it is impossible to reach the truth by vainly struggling to make one's own point of view more than a part. The "incomplete" is the defining human quality, the culmination of a dynamic principle of imperfection diffused throughout the world. In his last great speech Paracelsus reconciles his original sense of purpose and its generated antithesis, his contempt for the particular, in a higher perception of the truth.

҈ 3 ҈

The evolutionary vision of the poem's fifth section, instead of rejecting the particular, implies a dialectical relation between the whole of life and its parts. Comparisons to parts of the human anatomy—the "breast," the "heart," the "wrin-

kled face"—turn the landscape into a universal body, which
is closer to being human than inanimate. Such use of language is what Kenneth Burke calls "the ideal synecdoche," [4]
since "microcosm is related to macrocosm as part to whole,"
and either the "grand result" of nature can be experienced as
intimately as one's own body or the individual anatomy can
be used to represent the transformations of the physical universe as "the earth changes like a human face" (V, 654). Particular objects trap the formless potency of this dynamic
whole, which "heaves" like a "centre-fire . . . underneath
the earth" and sends "The molten ore" bursting among rocks
(V, 655). The imaginative thrust of this vision grows as a
result of opposition, like the evolutionary force itself. It
fights its way through the restraining weight of the mineral,
vegetable, and animal worlds toward "the consummation of
this scheme" in man.

The forces of nature, Paracelsus recognizes, are not controlled by the "perfect knowledge" he originally sought. But
neither are they "put forth blindly," as the materialist asserts.
Paracelsus unifies his climactic argument by transposing the
seasonal harmonies fashioned out of the opposition of "rare
verdure" and "a wintry clod" into a spiritual harmony. In
striking anticipation of David's desire for "weakness in
strength" at the climax of "Saul," the power he celebrates is
"strong from weakness," like a fragile plant "cast on stub-
born soil." Paracelsus can look from the evolutionary cosmos
to the human truth within himself, or look into the smallest
"chance-sown plant" to learn the laws of the spiritual world.
The harmony wrought with "blind, oft-failing, yet believing
love" is an inner transmutation of the union of opposites in
nature and brings the speaker close to a Christian paradox in

[4] "Four Master Tropes," *A Grammar of Motives* (New York,
1945), p. 508.

the mystery of a love that "stoops . . . to rise" ("A Death in the Desert," l. 134).

Though *Paracelsus* is not a Christian poem, its dialectic is a clear repudiation of the subjective poet's third tendency, which is to mistake his own point of view for the whole. In establishing power, knowledge, and love as man's three faculties, *Paracelsus* also anticipates the Trinitarian doctrines of Browning's later religious monologues, and especially the distinction between "What Does, what Knows, [and] what Is" in "A Death in the Desert" (l. 103). In Browning's unique conception of the Trinity, power, knowledge, and love correspond with Father, Spirit, and Son, in that order. The principle of mediation is equated with love, because for Browning it is love rather than knowledge that tempers power and makes it accessible to man. Christ (or love) renders God's power immanent in the world. Only with a doctrine of love, strong from weakness and hence identical with that limiting principle which he incorporates into his evolutionary scheme, can Paracelsus complete the Trinitarian pattern of power, knowledge, love. Browning cannot properly call God power, like Caliban or his own Johannes Agricola, nor can he call him knowledge, like the Gnostics or the ascetic prior of "Fra Lippo Lippi." But he can properly equate God with love, because love represents communion between the other two principles. In a significant modification of the doctrines expressed in St. Augustine's *Confessions*, Christ rather than the Holy Spirit becomes the mediating principle, the pivotal term of Browning's Trinity.

Though *Paracelsus* partly remedies the subjective poet's first two defects—his rhetorical and dramatic weaknesses—its most important contribution is to the third, or dialectical, dimension of Browning's art. Despite the introduction of minor characters like Festus and Michal, whom Paracelsus must in some way persuade, Browning still approaches his hero less through the skill of his rhetorical art than through an intrinsic interest in the Byronic type. Since the modern reader is less inclined then Browning's contemporaries to admire the Byronic hero, he demands more rhetorical and dramatic workmanship than Browning has used. But the poem is still important dialectically, because of the pattern of opposition and union to which it submits its ideas. It reconciles in its new perception of truth Paracelsus' original aspiration with his contempt for the particular. Paracelsus can approach the truth, not by mistaking his limited perspective for the whole, but only by first identifying with other points of view:

> When all mankind alike is perfected,
> Equal in full-blown powers—then, not till then,
> I say, begins man's general infancy   [V, 750–752].

The idealist is mistaken in his original belief that the individual keeps his own peculiar identity in inverse ratio to the extent of his union with the world and other men. He learns at the end that the more selfhood he has, the more intimate the union and mutual participation between himself and all that is outside himself. Paracelsus realizes that in adding love to knowledge, he must add, not the voracious Romantic love, the desire for perfection, which Aprile equates with his mastery of all the arts ("I would LOVE infinitely, and be loved"), but a pre-eminently Christian love which embodies compassion for frailty and imperfection. The Romantic's aspiration for perfection is what Irving Babbitt has called a "parody of grace," an appeal to the heart in protest against the dogma of original sin. As Babbitt observes of Goethe, Browning "saw that the romantic disease was the imaginative and emotional straining toward the unlimited (*Hang zum Unbegrenzten*), and in opposition to this unrestraint he was never tired of preaching the need of working within boundaries."[5] When Paracelsus learns to share other points of view, he discovers that the truth is both near and far away. Though it is as close as the human body, the truth is also self-concealing and evasive. He can approach it only after entertaining and relinquishing many divergent attitudes. Paracelsus sees that this paradoxical fusion of nearness and farness both creates and preserves the mystery. Instead of being something to be totally comprehended in a single flash of vision, the world gains added significance from being incomplete.

[5] *Rousseau and Romanticism* (New York, 1955) p. 274.

The Subjective
Poet's Failure: Sordello

Sordello's problem is also that of the young Browning: the subjective poet's inability to overcome the rhetorical, dramatic, and dialectical failings of his art. But in illustrating their dangers, *Sordello* (1833–1840) uses as the basis of its own form the very elements that result in the threefold failure of most subjective poetry. What potential advantages of the subjective method is Browning trying to realize? What are the limitations of his method? And why can his hero not eliminate the rhetorical, dramatic, and dialectical defects of his art?

~ 1 ~

Sordello carries the subjective poet's first tendency to a new extreme. Instead of trying to persuade an auditor, as in a dramatic monologue or a play, the speaker addresses the reader directly. Since the speaker is not a character in the poem, there is no fictional character he has to persuade who could function as the reader's "friend." Instead of clarifying the story for the reader, the introduction of a speaker has the opposite effect. It keeps encouraging a traffic between the real and the contrived, between what comes into the poem as part of Sordello's objective situation and what comes into it as psychological analysis imposed at the speaker's will. A typical section from the end of Book III will illustrate this process. We begin with an analysis of Sordello's inner state:

> and he found
> Not only that a soul, whate'er its might,
> Is insufficient to its own delight,
> Both in corporeal organs and in skill
> By means of such to body forth its Will—
> And, after, insufficient to apprise
> Men of that Will, oblige them recognize
> The Hid by the Revealed—but that,—the last
> Nor lightest of the struggles overpast,—
> Will, he bade abdicate, which would not void
> The throne, might sit there, suffer he enjoyed
> Mankind   [III, 564–575].

From this invisible inner being we move out, in the natural description of sunlight and Verona's citadel, to the kind of external facts Sordello knows. Then we take another step back, not this time into Sordello's inner state, but to the speaker's own aesthetic problems. When we finally return to the outside world, we discover that we are no longer with Sordello in Verona but with the speaker in Venice:

> Nor slight too much my rhymes that spring, dispread,
> Dispart, disperse, lingering overhead
> Like an escape of angels! . . .
> . . . They sleep, and I awake
> O'er the lagune, being at Venice   [III, 593–615].

There are no rhetorical clues to indicate who is speaking to whom or for what purpose. This lack of direction makes it difficult to relate to objective "reality." Because we seldom know the position of what is "out there" and what its relation is to the speaker's consciousness, we cannot pinpoint exactly where we are. When the speaker goes on to formu-

late aesthetic theories that would be more in character for
Sordello, it is difficult to relate the speaker's consciousness to
Sordello's, or even to remember who is speaking.

A shift in point of view always complicates the relation
between a speaker and his audience. A shift within a shift is
likely to be even more bewildering. The double jumps outside Sordello's point of view are meant to break the illusion
of a situation that is "out there" and a consciousness that is
"within." By breaking the hold of the rhetorical convention,
Browning wants to challenge a naïve empiricism. To make us
aware of the subjectivity of sense perception and the objectivity of more creative acts, the speaker keeps reminding us
that he is narrating a "story." We are not seeing into the life
of objects but into the creative consciousness, framer of its
own world. The poem's subject is not Sordello but the
speaker's consciousness, which is at once theatre and producer. In displaying his genius for contriving, which says of
Sordello's story, "These contents are framed," Browning is
also saying that as the contents of the speaker's consciousness,
Sordello's story is more "real" than a story that is not
"framed."

The inner play of consciousness may be more "real" than
the outer world of objects. But Browning defines this inner
play in such a way that it is not really anything in particular,
but what his own poetic contrivance makes of it. When we
are constantly reminded that the inner play of consciousness
is itself a contrivance, our expectations of artifice will be out
of phase with its disproportionate immediacy. What is under-
mined at such moments is the reader's own identity. Our attempts to find something "real" in the avowedly contrived
makes us self-conscious as readers. We feel we are creating
our own involvement in the story, and this produces a kind
of vertigo. The unstable relations between the speaker, Sordello, and the outside world break down the wall between

subject and object, as Browning intends. But in turning us loose on an alternating current that keeps switching from subject to object and from object back to subject, the multiple jumps outside the speaker's point of view unfix our bearings altogether. The doubtful merit of a lesson in epistemology cannot justify the disadvantage of this method.

᎗᎗ 2 ᎗᎗

The violation of rhetorical convention makes the shifts too difficult to follow. But Browning adds to the confusion by turning *Sordello* into his most radical experiment in the exercise of the subjective poet's second tendency. It is not the finished product of an objective poet but a psychological process, created on the spot out of the events it describes. Whereas a "literature of product" uses regular syntax, *Sordello*, as an example of what Northrop Frye has called "the literature of process," uses free or uncontrolled association.

> . . . Successively sewer, forum, cirque—
> Last age, an aqueduct was counted work,
> But now they tire the artificer upon
> Blank alabaster, black obsidion,
> —Careful, Jove's face be duly fulgurant,
> And mother Venus' kiss-creased nipples pant
> Back into pristine pulpiness   [V, 39–45].

Browning is trying to find language to express those aspects of experience which assault rather than inform the reader. He shocks us with unpredictable alliterations ("blank," "black," "face," "fulgurant") and assonances like those in "kiss," "nipples," "pristine," "pulpiness," which link words by sound rather than sense. Catalogues like "sewer, forum, cirque" and "Blank alabaster, black obsidion" diffuse rather than concentrate the meaning. As unconscious association takes over in mysteriously resonant names—"Mauritanian tree," "Mareotic juice from Caecuban"—the poetry becomes more and more oracular.

To maintain the emotion as though it were continuously present, the subjective poet turns verbal fragments into questions: "See you?"; "His story?"; "Ye believe?" By anticipating the questions that are running through the reader's mind and stating them elliptically, the speaker also gives the impression of thinking on the spot. He even revives the oral modes of primary epic in which the bard has no leisure to arrange his questions syntactically but must encourage audience response by raising his voice at the end of a sentence. Even the multiplication of dashes and the random punctuation invite an oral approach to the poem. In the absence of detailed punctuation that might facilitate the merely visual response of silent reading, *Sordello*, like the primary epic, must often be read aloud to be fully understood. In writing a poem as a continuous process of creating from experience, Browning has carried the subjective poet's second tendency further than any of his contemporaries. But because his experience has too seldom shaped itself into intelligible form, the method's disadvantages are greater than its merits. Like Dr. Johnson, when confronted with the poems of Ossian, few readers can help reflecting that they, too, could write a *Sordello* if they abandoned their minds to it. Instead of making its materials actual, *Sordello* is willful where it should be authoritative, and idiosyncratic where it should be objective.

⟆ 3 ⟅

Besides rejecting rhetorical and dramatic conventions, Browning cultivates the subjective poet's third tendency: the impulse to perceive the truth instantly and as a whole. Impatient with the objective poet's emphasis on a communicated product, which orders its parts into a rational pattern, Browning keeps introducing images which, bringing with them only a diffused aura of their literal use, enable him to include a whole range of meanings he could not otherwise express:

>   Broke
> Morning o'er earth, he yearned for all it woke—
> From the volcano's vapor-flag, winds hoist
> Black o'er the spread of sea,—down to the moist
> Dale's silken barley-spikes sullied with rain,
> Swayed earthwards, heavily to rise again—
> The Small, a sphere as perfect as the Great
> To the soul's absoluteness. Meditate
> Too long on such a morning's cluster-chord
> And the whole music it was framed afford,—
> The chord's might half discovered, what should pluck
> One string, his finger, was found palsy-struck   [VI, 521–532].

I have chosen a passage as representative as possible, which, instead of vaulting into a sphere above ordinary language, orders its images as logically as any argumentative poem. Its metaphoric sequence, though strongly associative, moves systematically from the volcano's "vapor-flag" to the sea's "hoisting winds" and the rising "barley-spikes" in the dale. The progression is from the large and the remote to the minute and the familiar. In addition, the last member of the series completes another pattern by emphasizing in the motion of the barley spikes, "Swayed earthwards, heavily to rise again," a passage from destruction to renewal and even a possible cyclical return of rain to vapor. But the power of the poetry does not depend on the logical ordering of its parts. By proclaiming "The Small . . . as perfect as the Great," it repudiates, so to speak, its own achievement. The mystery comes from a sense of vast meaningfulness which annihilates all such distinctions. Browning has used the associations of a "vapor-flag" with a "sail," of a "sail" with a hoisting "wind," and of "wind" with a "rainstorm" to blur the outline of the whole. The poetry does not so much say what it means as create a prismatic diffusion of ordered parts. It allows the poet to use the unstable language, which is as evanescent as "vapor," "silken . . . spikes," and "rain," to include a whole range of meaning that in any particular image he can only "half" discover.

Instead of playing an "arpeggio," like the objective poet who arranges his parts in orderly sequence, Browning insists on playing the "whole music." But in collapsing the "arpeggio" back into a chord, the seer too often "leaps his medium" altogether. In searching for analogies, he too seldom casts a calculating eye on the resources available in the objects he selects. In looking round for an analogy to Sordello's growth, for example, Browning strikes upon the simile of the spice tree. But instead of illuminating Sordello's situation, the spice tree itself requires explanation. Because he has to introduce the story of the Soldan's daughter to explain the tree, Browning never allows his analogy to recover from the load of explanation it is called upon to bear [II, 964–973].

Instead of using metaphors that have real links with their subject, Sordello's language retires, almost defeated, when trying to express his vision as a whole.

> "Better" (say you) "merge
> At once all workmen in the demiurge,
> All epochs in a lifetime, every task
> In one!" . . .
> Distinguish not rare peacock from vile swan,
> Nor Mareotic juice from Caecuban   [V, 59–66].

The advantage of carrying to a new extreme the subjective poet's third tendency is that it enables Browning to say something outside the range of ordinary language. But the attempt to leap at once to some conceptually unstable whole blocks the usual channels of meaning. Browning finds that even when he wants to communicate a portion of the "whole music" by playing a string, his "finger" has become "palsy-struck." In challenging us to take a new route to understanding by interfering with our automatic processes of getting meaning out of words, Browning has removed too many of the directives for interpretation. He fails to see that if the seer soars to the empyrean, it is only because he has first embodied his visions in metaphors that have a large enough range of specialized meaning to provide illuminating analogies to the whole.

4

While Browning is carrying to a new extreme the subjective poet's three tendencies, his hero is trying to remedy the rhetorical, dramatic, and dialectical failings to which each of these tendencies may lead. Browning wants to show that even though he can use the subjective method to advantage, he is aware of its dangers and knows how to overcome them. For example, although he keeps breaking the rhetorical conventions in order to collapse the wall between subject and object, Browning wants to show that like Sordello in his appeal to Taurello, he knows how to eliminate the subjective poet's rhetorical weaknesses. Browning himself breaks the dramatic conventions whenever he tries to produce the illusion that the art of writing poetry is a continuous process of creating from experience. But he also wants to prove that, just as Sordello can outgrow the confessional weakness of his art after defeating his rival in the poetry contest, so Browning, too, can correct the subjective poet's dramatic failures. And, finally, though Browning himself tries to communicate the truth instantly and as a whole, he also wants to prove that he has the intellectual sympathy that enables him to share other points of view. Just as Sordello can identify with Palma and a suffering world, so Browning tries to show that he can overcome the subjective poet's third tendency: his impulse to despise particulars and to leap at once into an omniscient role.

Unfortunately, whenever Browning breaks the hold of the rhetorical and dramatic conventions, he sacrifices clarity. And his use of Sordello to illustrate his own ability to outgrow his tendencies has an unforeseen effect. Because each of Sordello's attempts to overcome his limitations ends in failure, the hero's defeat increases Browning's own. Sordello's rhetorical, dramatic, and dialectical failure has important implications for Browning's art. Sordello's failings, as they appear in the course of the narrative, are first, his inability to develop a dramatic sense as a young poet; then, his failure as a lover and humanitarian to share other points of view; and finally, his rhetorical shortcomings in his third role as political thinker, especially in his climactic appeal to Taurello, which ends his career.

⁀ 5 ⁀

Sordello's first role, as the young poet of Goito, represents Browning's original conception of his hero. Unlike the objective artist who invests "The lifeless thing with life from [his] own soul" (I, 491), Sordello displays the subjective poet's first tendency. He

> Proclaims each new revealment born a twin
> With a distinctest consciousness within,
> Referring still the quality, now first
> Revealed, to [his] own soul   [I, 525–528].

In "overleaping means for ends" (II, 491) Sordello also illustrates the subjective poet's third tendency, his impatience with particulars. He cannot reduce "the simultaneous and the sole" to "the successive and the many" (II, 594–595). And because his poetry is confessional, its very intensity of self-expression leads him to neglect other considerations. His typical sentence is "One of God's large ones, tardy to condense / Itself into a period" (II, 723–724).

In Book II, after defeating Eglamor in the poetry contest, Sordello tries to overcome this last limitation, his defective dramatic art. To create his meaning for his audience to share, he realizes that it is not enough to feel intensely. The mere expression of intense feeling is not enough to give his poetry aesthetic form. Sordello tries to articulate emotion by using words "from the new speech round him" (II, 576). But he finds that the need to be intelligible "frustrates . . . / His prime design." When he tries to write dramatic poetry, his audience confuses the poet with "his meanest hero." The only way Sordello can understand other points of view is by impersonating characters who embody them. But the audience cannot appreciate the actor's art of hiding behind a character not his own. Sordello wants to shun all particular expressions of his ideal; yet in personifying in rapid succession many different ideas and beliefs, he finds that his audience is unable to distinguish between his true and assumed character. Though the actor is most himself when he is least himself, this paradox is beyond his audience's understanding. It cannot see how Sordello can be all his creations at once, and hence none of them (II, 625–626). It does not understand that precisely because all the roles he plays are intimations of a truth too deep for adequate embodiment, Sordello is willing to experiment with dramatic forms in the first place.

Sordello is shrewd enough to see that poetry is a presentation of experience and can never be a means of abstract communication. The confessional poet may believe that there is life in his language merely because there was a very different kind of life in the emotional experience it represents. But Sordello sees that until the poet can communicate his experience, it must remain an abstract, vague, and essentially private possession. It is indistinguishable from the sense perceptions of the ordinary man. If such experience is to achieve "being," as opposed to mere "existence," it must become intelligible. It is the function of the dramatic poet to make it as concrete, objectified, and public as he can.

> "The common sort, the crowd,
> Exist, perceive; with Being are endowed,
> However slight, distinct from what they See,
> However bounded; Happiness must be,
> To feed the first by gleanings from the last,
> Attain its qualities, and slow or fast
> Become what they behold . . ." [III, 159–165].

Unfortunately, Sordello still thinks that the use of dramatic conventions destroys "The law of his own nature" (III, 40). He is afraid that they annihilate his distinctive habits of feeling and insight. At times Sordello seems to realize that one of the most effective ways in which he can celebrate his own creative powers is by personifying other points of view. But he fails as a dramatic poet because he cannot make "The Alien" turn "Native to the soul" (III, 167). Since his ideal, being symbolically everywhere, is literally nowhere, except inside himself, Sordello can never make his "truths" actual: objective, authoritative, and public. He can never overcome the subjective poet's second tendency, his impulse to confess too insistently.

〽 6 〽

In his second role, as "the lover and warrior of Mantua," Sordello tries to rid himself of the subjective poet's third tendency. Instead of striving to express the whole truth at once, Sordello must first identify with particular expressions of it. He may then redeem his failure as a dramatic poet by using his intellectual sympathy to entertain and renounce many points of view that exist in the objective world.

In Book IV, which was written under the influence of Shelley's liberalism, Sordello tries to reproduce in himself, by acts of sympathetic imagination, the attitudes of the Guelfs and Ghibellines, who are fighting for the "lady-city" of Ferrara. His greatest challenge is to understand opposing points of view. If he can become one with the crowd, Sordello hopes to evolve from the people's conflict a new social order. His aim is to "effect a happiness / By theirs" that will enable him to be "really fused" with all mankind (IV, 251).

But Sordello fails as a humanitarian sympathizer for the same reason that he fails as a dramatic poet. How is he to empathize with ciphers who have vacant "thrush-eggs" for eyes without becoming completely identical with those he chooses to impersonate only to understand and criticize? When sympathetic imagination becomes more than a dialectical weapon, it turns the impersonator into another Taurello. The warrior who has too completely identified with ciphers symbolizes for Sordello the dangers of such identification. Taurello's massive brow has become one with his coats of armor, and though the rigor of his mail does not inhibit his athletic agility, his face has turned to "marble." Even the obliquity of his posture, half-averted and apparently indifferent to observers (IV, 427–428), recalls Sordello's earlier account of the "bard's start aside and look askance" (III, 638), which he interprets as a sign of thwarted purpose.

If Sordello cannot share other points of view as a humanitarian sympathizer, perhaps he can use his affinity with Palma, the woman he loves, as a model for the proper kind of intellectual sympathy. When Palma learns the secret of Sordello's birth, she confesses her love for him, and is bestowed by Taurello as a bride. But Palma represents personal values that supersede the social ones. Since Sordello accepts her as

the object of his quest, he abandons all efforts to search in
the world outside himself and her for an embodiment of his
ideal.

≈ 7 ≈

In his climactic plea in Book V "to bind / Taurello with
the Guelf cause," Sordello appears most clearly in his third
role as rhetorician. His failure as a dramatic poet and humanitarian sympathizer prevents Sordello from eliminating the
subjective poet's second and third tendencies. But perhaps he
can overcome the seer's first limitation by perfecting the
rhetorical art of engaging an audience and controlling its
responses.

If we study Sordello's climactic oration, we find that its
rhetoric lies halfway between prophetic statement and godlike command:

>   Any cave
> Suffices: throw out earth! A loophole? Brave!
> They ask to feel the sun shine, see the grass
> Grow, hear the larks sing? Dead art thou, alas,
> And I am dead! But here's our son excels
> At hurdle-weaving any Scythian, fells
> Oak and devises rafters, dreams and shapes
> His dream into a door-post, just escapes
> The mystery of hinges. Lie we both
> Perdue another age. The goodly growth
> Of brick and stone!   [V, 23–33].

At times Sordello seems outside language altogether. As his
uncontrolled associations proceed to a point of mad abandon
and the sound of "pristine pulpiness" or "kiss-creased nipples" (V, 44–45) replaces sense, Sordello begins to turn
words inside out, as if he no longer shared the human condition. Sometimes he uses words of a double grammatical con-
gruity, as when, in a form of punning syllepsis, his entry into

Rome becomes his entry into the grave: "At last, a city rears / Itself! nay, enter—what's the grave to us?" (V, 36–37). A word like "enter" seems to hold together different meanings, and it is unclear whether other locutions like the "throw[ing]" of "earth" are to be taken literally or figuratively. Sordello also makes abstractions like "mystery" turn, visibly, into concrete objects, into a "door-post" or a "hinge." Rome takes on a special power, driving Sordello to his grave, precisely because it is still only a vision in his mind. As its "goodly growth / Of brick and stone" engulfs its own beginnings, Sordello shows that what can be done with a visionary Rome is much more remarkable than what can be done with cities that are merely "real."

This kind of writing offers advantages to the poet who wants to express a vision that is outside the experience of his audience. But the peculiar violence of Sordello's language makes it difficult to remember just what he is saying.

> "Leave to lead the brawls
> Here i' the atria?" No, friend! He that sprawls
> On aught but a stibadium . . . what his dues
> Who puts the lustral vase to such an use?
> Oh, huddle up the day's disasters! March,
> Ye runagates, and drop thou, arch by arch,
> Rome!   [V, 15–21].

Such a passage carries to a new extreme a technique which Sordello had used earlier in his poetry contest with Eglamor. By setting "loose / . . . many incidents of little use," he invites his audience to create his meaning for him.

> Let men perceive
> What I could do, a mastery believe,
> Asserted and established to the throng
> By their selected evidence of song
> Which now shall prove, whate'er they are, or seek
> To be, I am   [II, 429–434].

There is an important sense in which the poet must involve his reader as a cocreator. As we shall see, the dramatic monologue invites more collaboration than most literary forms. The most perfect rhetoric so enacts its meaning that the reader helps discover it for himself. But at the same time Browning must control his reader's responses. He must determine the kind of meaning he invites the reader to discover. Sordello's appeal to Taurello to "assist the Pope" is a plea for the reader to do the work the poet has failed to do, to complete a vision for which he has given only the expressive outlines. Because Sordello neglects the responsibilities of his craft, his words pile themselves up blindly, often defeating the impact of each other. The account of his emotional experience betrays no structure whatever, and most of his rhetoric defines only a vague feeling of excitement and disorder.

Sordello concludes his oration by intoning ringing party slogans to Taurello: "Extend Guelf domination"; "Change Secular to Evangelical." But as soon as he tries to sway Taurello to a particular course of action, Sordello feels he is fragmenting the "unexpressed and whole" into lies. It is not surprising that such an appeal fails to convert Taurello to the Guelf cause. But if Sordello fails where he hoped to succeed, his argument succeeds where he never thought of succeeding. For his plea moves Taurello to bestow upon the poet the traditional Utopian role of Plato's "philosopher-king" or Shelley's "unacknowledged legislator of the world." Unfortunately, as W. C. DeVane observes, Sordello's "soul is in conflict: ambition and love war on one side; on the other he has sworn himself to be a champion of the masses of mankind. . . . The conflict is between altruism and ambition." [1] Before Sordello can decide what to do, the struggle to resolve the issue kills him.

[1] *A Browning Handbook* (New York, 1955), p. 84.

⟦ 8 ⟧

Browning finds that he cannot use the subjective method in his own writing and at the same time overcome its limitations in his hero. If Sordello is unable to remedy the rhetorical, dramatic, and dialectical failings of his art, it is because Browning is unconsciously afraid that any attempt to make his work more objective would limit his own creative powers. Like Paracelsus and Sordello, he fears that if he has no role to play he will cease to exist, but he equally fears to be only the roles he plays, only a particular Taurello. At the end of the poem, however, Browning half acknowledges the failure of his methods. He announces that the subjective poet must still find an analogue of Christian "incarnation," some principle that will convey the "mystery" to an audience.

> But of a Power its representative
> Who, being for authority the same,
> Communication different, should claim
> A course, the first chose but this last revealed—
> This Human clear, as that Divine concealed—
> What utter need! [VI, 598–603].

Just as God communicates with the world through his Son, so the subjective poet must put on the masks with which his audience can identify. This principle is already implicit in *Sordello*'s doctrine of the "Maker-see," according to which the poet must move beyond the first two stages of merely saying that he has seen or telling what he saw. He must become "the best" kind of artist: one who can "Impart the gift of seeing to the rest" (III, 868). Sordello's own example indicates that the "Maker-see" is really the "Maker-do." His description enables the audience to close their eyes and feel the "strings of blossoms" or the arch of "hazels" that they seem to brush in passing. If the poet who asserts that he has seen is a seer who substitutes preconceived or ready-made emotion for created emotion, and if the artist who describes what he has seen is the objective poet, the "Maker-see" is the accomplished rhetorician. Like the seer, he invites audience collaboration. But unlike the artist who merely asserts that he has seen, the "Maker-see" controls his reader's responses. Though his emphasis is creative rather than mimetic, and is based on participation rather than detachment, the "Maker-see" does not have to appeal to the reader to do the work the poet has failed to do.

The lesson of *Sordello* is that Browning cannot use the potential advantages of the subjective method without multiplying most of its disadvantages at the same time. If he breaks the rhetorical and dramatic conventions in order to collapse the wall between subject and object, or in order to create the illusion that he is writing his poem as a continuous process of experiencing, then he cannot at the same time perfect those rhetorical and dramatic techniques which make their materials actual: concrete, objectified, and public. By carrying the subjective poet's three tendencies to a new extreme, Browning has left himself open to the charge that, though he seems at times to have written a poem of amazing meaningfulness, he has not written it in the English language.

But *Sordello* still plays an immensely important role in Browning's career. Implicit in the poem is the whole course of the poet's future development. After experimenting with many phases of life, the hero hopes to write a work that will "unveil the last of mysteries" and give "Man's inmost life . . . yet freer play." This hope is strangely prophetic of *The Ring and the Book*, especially of Browning's conception of Guido and Pompilia.

> Next age—what's to do?
> The men and women stationed hitherto

Will I unstation, good and bad, conduct
Each nature to its farthest, or obstruct
At soonest, in the world: light, thwarted, breaks
A limpid purity to rainbow flakes,
Or shadow, massed, freezes to gloom   [V, 601–607].

Sordello's plan to personify in rapid succession the various moods, passions, and attitudes of "life's elemental masque" also anticipates Browning's dialectical method. Moreover, by bringing into focus a relation between speaker and auditor, *Sordello*'s doctrine of the "Maker-see" encourages Browning to experiment in *Pippa Passes* and the plays with works to which the poet brings the words and the reader brings the meaning. These various kinds of rhetoric will eventually culminate in the dramatic monologues. Their inbuilt rhetorical principle, which forces the speaker to persuade an auditor, who can then function as the reader's "friend," is the genius of the monologue form, and after the public's rejection of *Sordello* it enables Browning, in other works, to communicate to his audience at least a portion of that poem's meaning.

3

The Search for an Objective Form: Pippa Passes *and the Plays*

Once he recognizes the need to write poetry that is objective, authoritative, and public, in place of the abstract, vague, and essentially private confessions of the seer, Browning begins to search for more dramatic forms. Though the main characters of *Strafford* (1837) and of *Colombe's Birthday* (1844) share several of the subjective poet's defects, Browning now substitutes for the outpouring of spontaneous emotion an actual presentation of experience in dramatic form. But since he finds the drama an uncongenial medium, he must continue to experiment in *Pippa Passes* (1841) and *A Soul's Tragedy* (1846) with forms that are more objective than his early poems but less objective than the stage plays. Through such experiments he comes to realize that the form with the degree of objectivity he desires is the dramatic monologue.

◦◦◦ 1 ◦◦◦

Browning may have sensed an analogy between his own failure to communicate with his public and the inability of Strafford and Colombe to share their ideals with the people. Strafford is a royalist who tries without success to communicate his ideal of kingship to the Cavaliers and Roundheads. And Colombe, the Duchess of Juliers and Cleves, is deposed

40

by a rival because she is so obsessed with the sanctity of her office, which is "Nearer God's Mother than most earthly things" (II, 171), that she neglects the practical arts of governing. If Colombe suffers from the subjective poet's first tendency and is incapable of identifying with any point of view except her own, Strafford displays the subjective poet's third tendency: he tries to realize his truth instantly and as a whole. Colombe overcomes her limitations when she perceives that it is better to be a commoner married to a man she loves than the wife of an emperor she despises. But Strafford is so impatient of the means that might in time have enabled him to influence Parliament and the king that he is destroyed by the very factions he hopes to unite.

2

A stage play's greatest advantage is its capacity to enact experiences in dramatic form. But in writing for an oral medium in which the author must be clearer and more direct than he has to be in print if he hopes to win attention, Browning is also encouraged to concentrate on the rhetorical art of engaging his audience and controlling its responses. To make the play easier to follow, Browning mirrors *Strafford*'s main action from different points of view. The first act dramatizes the failure of the Cavaliers and Roundheads to unite as a nation. It wins sympathy for Strafford and Pym, who rise above factional differences to envision unity from opposite sides. Though the first scenes of the next two acts seem merely to repeat the historical events of the first act, they illuminate the search for unity from new perspectives. If the audience is to retain a proper sympathy for Strafford, it must lose its admiration for Pym. One way to make the audience do this is to demonstrate that Strafford is not responsible for the rift that develops between Pym's followers and his own. Thus the second act portrays the betrayal of

King Charles, and the second scene of Act III shows that in their plan to join forces with Scotland and impeach Strafford, Pym and the Puritans are just as guilty as the King.

In *Colombe's Birthday*, Browning uses similar devices to control our responses. So that we shall not suspect that Valence is a casuist when he presents his case as the advocate of Cleves, Browning first dramatizes such casuistry in the courtiers. When they hear that Colombe may be displaced, these parasites calculate in advance every attitude of feigned horror that, upon official reception of "the bad news," will produce the desired effect. Their attempt to ascribe their own rhetorical cunning to Valence is Browning's most effective way of persuading the audience of his hero's integrity. Later in the play, in case anyone should question Valence's motives as a lover, Browning creates a listless Don Juan in the person of Prince Berthold. His professions of love function as a kind of lightning rod. By grounding insincerity in his own half-hearted lovemaking, Prince Berthold draws away all such suspicions of Valence.

Besides developing his rhetorical art of engaging and controlling our responses, the stage plays enable Browning to experiment with the rhetoric of dramatic argument. In *Strafford*'s opening scene Browning uses the argument from biblical authority to satirize the Puritans' dogmatic judgments. The appeal to the Old Testament examples of Gideon, David, and Goliath anticipates the comic travesty of this device by the two advocates in *The Ring and the Book*. Browning also introduces a number of logical fallacies to characterize the demagogue Vane and the prosecutors in the trial scene:

> But know you wherefore Wentworth comes? to quench
> This last of hopes? that he brings war with him?
> Know you the man's self? what he dares?   [I, i, 100–102].

By firing rapid questions at his audience, each of which requires a different answer, Vane forces a simple assent: "We know, All know." After committing this fallacy, he tricks the Puritans into a false opposition that cleverly limits the alternatives: "Away with all this! Will you have Pym or Vane?" The prosecutors in the trial scene beg the question when they indict Strafford because he is "The enemy of England" (IV, ii, 276). Instead of drawing the logical inference and concluding that the accused is innocent, Pym prides himself on his inability to establish Strafford's guilt. In a form of the argument from ignorance he boasts that the traitor's crimes are so enormous that they defy enumeration.

The play's most dramatic reversal turns upon another fallacy. When Strafford refers to Charles "as one who comes not," Hollis replies, "Whom forgive, / As one about to die." The syntax is deliberately ambiguous; "one about to die" can refer either to the "one who comes not" or the one who should forgive. The irony also proceeds from a logical fallacy: the confusion of the specific and universal applications of a word. Strafford takes the word "die" in a universal sense and sees Charles, like all men, under sentence of death. Hollis corrects Strafford and assures him that he uses the verb in a specific way, to refer, not to Charles, but to himself: "Strafford, YOU must die!"

Two of the most dramatic moments in *Colombe's Birthday* make use of another logical device: the dilemma. As judge of Berthold's claim, Valence realizes that if he finds in favor of Berthold, he will lose his queen and betray Cleves. But if he decides in favor of Colombe, he will lose a wife. Since Valence must support the claim either of Berthold or Colombe, he must either lose a wife or betray Cleves. Berthold helps resolve this dilemma by proposing marriage to Colombe and forcing Valence to declare his own love. But this solution to Valence's problem simply creates a new dilemma for

Colombe. If she marries Berthold, she will become an un-
loved empress; if she accepts Valence, she will lead the life of
a contented commoner. Colombe resolves her dilemma when
she sees that a lover's devotion is not inferior to a subject's
loyalty. If she cannot share her ideals with the people, she
can at least share her life with Valence. To escape from the
horns of her dilemma, Colombe must learn to identify with a
point of view other than her own. The logical dilemma
dramatizes the most important alternatives in the play; it is
Browning's most effective way of winning approval for Colombe's decision.

≈ 3 *≈*

Though the stage plays help Browning to overcome his
rhetorical and dramatic failings, the drama is not a medium
he finds congenial. Park Honan, among others, has observed
that Browning's characters are too intricate for the stage.[1] A
few plays can accommodate characters as complex as Hamlet, but Hamlet is a simple character compared with
Strafford. Despite Browning's attempts to provide his audience with clear repetitions of the main action, no spectator of
a play can grasp so many conflicts on so many planes. Instead
of finding traits that "act" well and giving Strafford only
such traits as suit him for the action, Browning offers a complex psychological study. Without the opportunity to reread,
the spectator of a play is only bewildered by subtleties that
might delight the reader of a dramatic monologue. Because
Strafford is generally confused himself, there is too little
sharpening of audience understanding. Only when the issues
clarify, as in the ritual of the reversed kneeling, where the
king in disguise begs Strafford's pardon, does the action become dramatically effective.

[1] See Park Honan's excellent discussion in "Characters for the
Stage," in *Browning's Characters* (New Haven, 1961), pp. 41–78.

Colombe's Birthday solves some of Browning's problems by presenting a simpler action. It is more successful than *Strafford* in mastering the fragmentation of language and event. But as the realization of Browning's announced intention in the preface to *Strafford*, where he declares that his aim is to represent "Action in Character, rather than Character in Action," *Colombe's Birthday* illustrates the dangers that attend any reversal in the priority attributed by Aristotle to action over character. Almost all the work's difficulties arise from Browning's reluctance to give to his characters only those qualities that are necessary for the action required of them. Having sensed a parallel between Colombe's discovery that her crown has only private significance and his own discovery that he cannot communicate with his public, Browning seems to have piled on Colombe his own character traits. He begins the wrong way round, with his personal limitations rather than the properties in Colombe that would fit her for the action. If the stage plays are unsuccessful, it is mainly because Browning never masters the dramaturgic basis of characterization, which is rhetorical in nature. His concern with intricate psychological studies (and with complicated connections between the characters and himself) disturbs the rhetorical relation between the characters and the audience. Browning must discover a form which is objective enough to control the subjective poet's three tendencies. But it cannot be a stage play, which the spectator has too little opportunity to analyze. Though it has to be more dramatic than a confessional poem, it must be a form that is less dramatic than a play—one that can use the kind of psychological complexity in which Browning excels.

ᗣᗣ 4 ᗣᗣ

Pippa Passes (1841) and *A Soul's Tragedy* (1846) are two of Browning's most ingenious attempts to overcome the rhetorical, dramatic, and dialectical weaknesses of his early poetry. They are more successful than any of his other works, except the dramatic monologues themselves, in combining the advantages of the early subjective poetry with the advantages of the stage plays. But even though *Pippa Passes* and *A Soul's Tragedy* prove that Browning could be highly inventive when searching for alternatives to the form he finally chose, he never repeated either experiment. His apparent dissatisfaction with the disadvantages of each form as a possible alternative to the dramatic monologue is just as instructive for the reader as an understanding of its advantages.

𝕞 5 𝕞

The most unusual rhetorical feature of *Pippa Passes* is the heroine's ability to persuade other characters in the poem without consciously addressing them. In place of the single auditor of a dramatic monologue or of a *ficelle* like Festus, Browning introduces a whole hierarchy of characters who can help us grasp the heroine's importance. He convinces the reader of Pippa's power, not by affirming it directly, but by dramatizing her influence on four other characters, each of whom can function as the reader's "friend."

Critics have objected to the inherent absurdity of Browning's scheme. Is it plausible that Pippa's songs should change the course of seven lives, including her own? Most objections, I think, proceed from a misunderstanding for which Browning himself is largely responsible. Unlike the other characters in the poem, Pippa in her role as artist is never subject to causal laws. The artist is a creator of being, *causa sui*. If we find the scheme absurd, it is because we are using the laws of cause and effect to judge a power of human re-creation to which they do not apply. Because Pippa's songs represent this power in one of its purest forms, they enable the other characters to rediscover it in themselves. The songs do not create anything that is not already present; they merely free what is implicit. To the degree that all artistic creation is a liberating act, Browning can use the songs to represent a potentiality in each of the other characters. The songs are a formal rather than efficient cause of each of the conversions.

⁀ 6 ⁀

The central question is how art becomes for Browning a liberating influence. If our interpretation of his rhetorical scheme is correct, then we should expect Browning to specify what quality Pippa and the other characters have in common. What power that she herself displays is Pippa able to liberate in each of the other characters? Browning provides the answer in the Introduction, where Pippa displays an impulse to personify other points of view. By identifying with the dawn, she tries to reproduce its intrinsic nature as something half human, whose "curled" form and "seething breast" she can touch and handle. Pippa also wants to flow over into other people. She wants to savor the bride's "snow-pure cheek" and "black bright tresses" (l. 137). The heroine prepares for her liberating acts by identifying with other points of view. This negative capability is the source of the poet's power and is the link between Browning's rhetorical and dramatic design.

Before Pippa even appears, each of the characters she converts has already cultivated the intellectual sympathy that enables him to share another point of view. Pippa's songs merely reinforce the power of sympathetic imagination that Shelley calls the indispensable agent of man's moral growth.[2]

---

[2] Percy Bysshe Shelley, "A Defence of Poetry," *The Works of Shelley*, ed. H. B. Forman (London, 1880) VII, 111: "A man, to be greatly good, must imagine intensely and comprehensively; he must

In the first vignette Sebald's negative capability forces him to share the point of view of the man he has just murdered. Whereas his accomplice Ottima can speak of the sun's "blood-red beam" without recalling Luca's "blood," Sebald's sympathetic imagination keeps dramatizing the outrage done to nature. He speaks of bruising the "plant" and transforming morning into "night" with a ghastly "sun" (I, 32). An unimaginative nature like Ottima's alienates itself in inanimate objects; it makes matter the subject and sees the monk as an adjunct of "the wall's self," a "brown cold piece" of its masonry. A histrionic temperament like Sebald's flows over into objects; it tends to subordinate "the plastered wall" of the monastery to the figure who emerges from it.

When Ottima thrills at the prospect of going back to "the deserted house" and holding the "two dead hands" of her husband, Sebald immediately associates the "two dead hands" with the hands he clasped on the hot July night when he first made love to Ottima and everything around them seemed to "die." His dramatic imagination produces the kind of metaphoric disorder associated with Macbeth's guilt-ridden visions of "pity like a naked new-born babe" or of "heaven's cherubim" that in a riot of emotional syncretism ride upon the "couriers of the air" (I, vii, 21–23). Though Sebald is about to embrace evil when Pippa's song breaks the spell of the enchantress, his conversion has in one sense already taken place. It is implicit in the moral imagination that enables him to share the dead man's point of view. Pippa's "God . . . in his heaven" is the "perfect poet" of *Paracelsus*, "Who in his person acts his own creations" (II, 648–649). Since Sebald's intellectual sympathy is an inferior form of God's own ability to observe every point of view, it is fitting that Pippa's

put himself in the place of another and of many others; the pains and pleasures of his species must become his own." Cf. Adam Smith, *The Theory of Moral Sentiments* (Dublin, 1777).

song should recall him to "The law of [his own] nature."

Sebald's sympathetic imagination enables him to see that the murder is not just his event alone. His negative capability illustrates the truth of Shelley's doctrine that sympathy is the agent of moral growth and that the source of sympathy is man's imaginative power. By emphasizing the moral function of the impersonator who can reproduce points of view other than his own, Browning also indicates a new function of his own dramatic art. The scene in which Sebald rejects his enchantress gives evidence of Browning's own potential as a playwright. After Sebald analyzes her, Ottima protests that she is something more than the revolting catalogue of objects that he itemizes: the bloodless flesh, the hair that "Drops, a dead web," the repulsive "morbid olive . . . shoulder-blades." In one of Browning's most dramatic exchanges, Ottima rebels against the analytic temper that fragments her so completely: "Speak to me—not of me!" Her invitation to Sebald to "Lean on [her] breast" reveals a new imaginative dimension. Ottima's parenthetical "—not as a breast" is also touching, because Sebald has just anatomized her and cruelly repudiated such bodily parts in exactly the way she had dissected Luca on the mortuary slab. Sebald's rejection gives Ottima a power of moral imagination that she never possessed before. No longer devoid of intellectual sympathy, she absolves her accomplice of responsibility and takes the blame herself.

The subject of Pippa's second conversion is the artist Jules. Though he has the negative capability that allows him to share Phene's point of view as a painter, his preoccupation with her "rosy limbs," the "pearly gloom" of her halo, and her body's "outline" indicates that he is still the collector of sensuous objects. The artist who "would enlace / Breast, eyelids, hands, [and] feet" is deficient in sympathetic imagination. This deficiency explains the ease with which the students deceive and is also the point of the song which Phene is taught to recite: "I am the painter who cannot paint."

By treating Jules and Phene as objects, the students turn the marriage into a commercial swindle. They trick Jules into buying as firsthand merchandise an object which has long been traded as a human property. The student Schramm is an automaton with gestures, who seems to play by reflex, like a record, and whose only control button is his pipe. When Jules, who has always had more imagination than his fellow students, discovers their deception, Pippa's song frees in him a capacity for intellectual sympathy that has been present all along. The song reminds Jules that he must create his beloved's worth by descending to her level, as Queen Kate did with her page. Art, like love, demands the production of "form" from "unshaped" matter (II, 298). To mature as an artist Jules must use his moral imagination to reproduce the internal nature of his subjects. He will still be a connoisseur, but his range of taste guarantees that with Jules, unlike the Duke of "My Last Duchess," the woman's predilections will not be aggressively stifled. When models like Phene bring no soul with them, he has to create a soul for them. By acts of sympathetic imagination Jules will learn to play Pygmalion and make his Phene a second Galatea.

Luigi, the subject of the poem's third conversion, is capable of more intellectual sympathy than either Sebald or Jules. He identifies so closely with the people's suffering that he is prepared to die in order to free Italy from imperial rule. But as his mother observes, Luigi is myopic and far-sighted at the same time. If he has sympathy for the people, he shows little affection for his fiancée, Chiara. And in trying to find a shortcut to the absolute, he is guilty of the idealist's characteristic pride. When pressed to state his case against the tyrant-king, Luigi first digresses to the subject of spring, and then, as his language breaks down, he is forced to admit his ignorance of the proof: "He has . . . they have . . . in fact, I understand / But can't restate that matter" (III, 142–143). When Luigi is about to yield to his mother's persuasion, Pippa's song restores his original sense of purpose. In a flash of revelation Luigi apprehends the tyrant as "The Python . . . on the throne." With a final appeal to divine authority the hero's sympathy for Italy asserts and completes itself: " 'Tis God's voice calls: how could I stay? Farewell!"

Intellectual sympathy also enables Monsignor, who is the subject of the poem's final episode, to make the act of moral imagination necessary to understand his niece's point of view and resist the treachery of his intendant, Ugo. The bishop's younger brother, now dead, had commissioned Ugo to assassinate the child of a third brother in order to succeed to his estates. Ugo has hidden the child and blackmailed the younger brother. He is now prepared to bargain with Monsignor. He will have the rightful heiress seduced by Bluphocks and then pass her off as a prostitute: "once Pippa entangled!—you conceive?" (IV, 221).

The bishop unnerves Ugo at the beginning by digressing to the story of Jules, in which the Intendant discerns some devious design. Instead of treating his model as though she were Ruskin's "servile ornament," subservient to his own ideal, Jules will treat her as "constitutional" and affirm Phene's independent worth. The bishop perceives in the same way that he must protect his niece's rights. Instead of treating her as a pawn in an ecclesiastical transaction, he must affirm instead her independent value as his brother's child. When the Intendant makes the fatal slip of revealing the heiress' identity, Pippa's song stimulates the bishop's moral imagination. It reminds him that often, before men can realize an ambition, death removes them from the scene. Conscious of his own approaching death, the bishop resolves to free himself from his family's "whole centuries of sin." The

moment he acts is the moment of his own liberation, when he
orders the Intendant gagged and bound hand and foot.

≈ 7 ≈

The actor's art of understanding other points of view contributes to the moral development of each of the characters.
Pippa's sympathetic imagination is a secular analogue of
grace and is the "formal cause" of all these acts of moral
growth. The intellectual sympathy which the poet's understanding of another point of view requires explains why art,
in Browning's view, is a liberating experience. No longer
deficient in reverence for others, the artist's moral imagination frees a capacity for intellectual sympathy that is already
present in each of the characters whom Pippa converts. This
original conception of the moral imagination, which relates it
to the dramatist's negative capability, makes Browning's rhetorical scheme far less absurd than we may first think.

Besides evolving a new relation between its rhetorical and
dramatic designs, *Pippa Passes* also contributes to the third,
or dialectical, dimension of Browning's art. By presenting the
internal nature of his characters, the dramatic poet invites us
to criticize these people from within and to combine them
into a hierarchy of lower aesthetic and higher ethical and
religious types. The negative capability that enables Pippa to
become what she beholds reverses itself at the end by passing
from empathy with human, to empathy with natural, forms
of life. By identifying with the wildlife and the birds, Pippa
introduces a diminuendo to balance the opening crescendo in
which she moves from the interior of natural objects to the
interior of "the Happiest Four" in Asolo. The whole structure of the poem is hierarchical, and from the sensual, physical love of Ottima and Sebald, it passes to love with an idealistic basis in Jules and Phene, then to love of country, mother
love, and, finally, the love for God. Phene acquires for Jules
the value of the saintly prostitute, who seems to symbolize

for him the very essence of the hierarchic order, just as Queen Kate does for the page. But in the sight of God, who transcends such a hierarchy, "all service ranks the same." The spiritual reversal of ranks, where "there is no last nor first," couches a revolutionary social pattern in theological terms. This reversal is illustrated in the way that Pippa's spiritual integrity, which abolishes concepts of rank altogether and which ascribes no value to property, ironically brings her the rank and property she repudiates. She will wake up next morning one of the wealthy citizens of the town.

The design of *Pippa Passes* anticipates the interlocking structure of *The Ring and the Book*. As late as February 26, 1845, Browning confided to Elizabeth Barrett that he preferred the poem to anything else he had yet written.[3] At the center of both *Pippa* and *The Ring* Browning places the "privileged" points of view that represent the "formal cause" of the action as a whole. But it is surely significant that he never repeated his rhetorical, dramatic, or dialectical experiments in precisely the form he used in *Pippa Passes*. By resorting to the meretricious neatness of the well-made plot, which involves Pippa melodramatically in Ugo's scheme, Browning encourages the reader to judge his work by the irrelevant criteria of efficient causality—by the standards of the one-act thriller or the Jacobean melodrama. This is the greatest weakness of *Pippa Passes*. By introducing stage contrivances, Browning has obscured his most original achievement. If we miss the ingenuity of his rhetorical design, he has mainly himself to blame.

◌◌ 8 ◌◌

The most unusual feature of *A Soul's Tragedy* (1846) is its selection of only two sets of events from contrasting periods in Chiappino's life. Browning finds it easier to control

---

[3] *The Letters of Robert Browning and Elizabeth Barrett, 1845–1846* (New York, 1899), I, 28.

his reader's responses by substituting for the complicated, interlocking structure of *Pippa Passes* a single inversion of ideas and roles, neatly dramatized at the end of the first act when Chiappino and his rival exchange clothes. In the first act Chiappino insists that Luitolfo's murder of the tyrannical Provost is the act he himself was born to commit: "I would have struck it, and could not: he would have done his utmost to avoid striking it, yet did so. I dispute his right to that deed of mine" (II, 296–298). The exchange of clothes enables Chiappino to play the emancipator's role. After the fall of the old regime, Luitolfo reaps all the loss of the exchange and Chiappino all the gain. As an idealist Chiappino is powerless; when he becomes politically influential, he is so seduced by the casuistry of Ogniben that he acquiesces in the execution of the real Luitolfo.

Because this two-part structure subordinates action to character, it is a more appropriate form than a stage play for a study in spiritual disintegration. The second part allows Browning to uncover the contradictions of the first part. As an ironic method, it anticipates Browning's exposure of Mr. Sludge, "the Medium," who presents the real and more vicious side of his character only at the end of his monologue. As Park Honan has noted, the two parts of *A Soul's Tragedy* also anticipate Guido's two monologues in *The Ring and the Book*. The full meaning of Guido's first monologue becomes apparent only in his second, when his real motives are suddenly visible from behind his mask. Similarly, we cannot properly assess Chiappino's contempt for means in the first part till we see in the second how the idealist's impatience is only the reverse side of the reactionary's indifference.

The two-part structure is an ideal form in which to make these dialectical relations clear. Its ironic contrasts help Browning dramatize in terms of social revolution *Pippa Passes'* theological principle that first shall be last. The scapegoat of the old order is the hero of the new, to whom the Pope's legate, Ogniben, must appeal for power. At first Chiappino tries to turn the Pope's legate into a reactionary scapegoat like the Provost, upon whom it will be ritually gratifying to load abuse with his idealist's vocabulary. But Ogniben cleverly affirms an identity of interests with Chiappino. He accepts his opponent's political definitions, and without changing their emotive meaning, tries to equate them with his own. The reactionary's desire to rise above the people, which Chiappino deplores, is, he argues, only a less refined form of the idealist's own goals. In his superior understanding Chiappino is just as much a "king" in the eyes of the populace as if he exercised force over them in the despotic manner of the Provost. There is as much "truth" in his reactionary "falsehood" as there is "falsehood" in Chiappino's idealistic "truth." The ideologies that Chiappino has "falsely" opposed as political polarities are merely different proof of "the soul's nobility," a demonstration that both idealist and reactionary are on the side of "kings."

If the two-part form of *A Soul's Tragedy* offers such rich resources for irony and inversion, why did Browning never repeat the experiment? One answer is that *A Soul's Tragedy*, despite its simplified structure, is still too close to the stage plays. The reappearance of the real Luitolfo in Act II, for example, is an unconvincing stage contrivance. Though Luitolfo must die if Browning is to dramatize the full extent of Chiappino's decline, the execution itself is peculiarly out of place in a psychological study, however fitting it might have been in a Victorian melodrama. A dramatic monologue like "Mr. Sludge, 'the Medium' " can exclude every external action that fails to illuminate directly the speaker's own condition. Though *The Ring and the Book* has to introduce the Pope's judgment in order to account for the change between Guido's first and second monologues, the Pope has already been dramatized in his own right, and the sentencing of Guido does far more to deepen Guido's character than the sentencing of Luitolfo does to illuminate Chiappino's. While intended to mark the low point of his career, Chiappino's sentencing of Luitolfo is not a consciously depraved act at all. Since it is merely the result of a trick, the sentencing tells us more about Ogniben's casuistry than about Chiappino's decline. The ironically contrasting portraits of the same character make *A Soul's Tragedy* Browning's closest approach to the dramatic monologue among the works so far discussed. But its semidramatic structure still forces him to invent a melodramatic action. As in *Pippa Passes*, the stage contrivances prevent the poet from exploring fully the psychology of his characters. To perfect his rhetorical, dramatic, and dialectical art, Browning must turn in the future to a different form.

PART II

THE OBJECTIVE WORLD

Some critics have argued that Browning turns to the dramatic monologue because it enables him to be more objective than other forms and therefore more noncommittal. But their use of the comparative "more" turns their otherwise innocuous tautology into a misleading distortion. For the dramatic monologue is not a more objective form than the stage play; it is a less objective form, and by 1840 Browning has already been writing plays for some time.

The stage plays help Browning remedy the rhetorical, dramatic, and dialectical defects of his early poetry. The confessional poet of *Pauline* had regarded himself as a personality with something to say. But after Mill's criticism and the failure of *Sordello*, Browning has come to realize that dramatic experience is distinct from personal experience, which should not enter directly into the work of art (an idea he expresses in the poems in *Pacchiarotto* entitled "House" and "Shop"). The confessional poet had invited a curious public to apply to the publisher for a ticket to his peep show. The new dramatic poet, thanking his public, must decline such patronage. His poetry must be a shop where he sells through the window and lives unseen at the back of the premises.

Though the stage plays make what they handle actual— objective, authoritative, and public—Browning's desire to rep-

57

resent "Action in Character, rather than Character in Action" prevents him from analyzing the action of each actor as an analogue of the main action and fitting him for his proper place in the whole. Unlike the accomplished playwright, Browning is not sufficiently aware of an audience's impulse to rebel against the postulates of his work. In *The Ring and the Book*, where he treats his characters rhetorically—less as living people with real problems than as a means of controlling our responses, which is the basis of all dramatic art—a number of speakers voice this rebellion against the purity of Caponsacchi and Pompilia. The unsavory qualities of such speakers subtly rebuke the audience for its own resistance and later make it willing to suspend its disbelief. In his stage plays, on the other hand, Browning too often determines his characters' conduct by their real-life psychology rather than by the kind of action that the play requires of them.

Pippa Passes* and *A Soul's Tragedy* are moves in the right direction. In *Pippa Passes*, where he abandons the "novelistic" approach to his characters, Browning introduces the prose interludes to present the basic heresies against the spiritual force of Pippa as artist, the postulate on which he builds his poem. By using "low" characters to voice his readers' own resistance, Browning disarms the opposition before it can become articulate. If the audience can be persuaded that the postulates of the work are not inherently absurd, it can be invited to fill in for itself whatever further traits are necessary for rounding out the characters. But *Pippa Passes* and *A Soul's Tragedy* cannot meet all the poet's needs. Though they are less objective than the stage plays, they are still not sufficiently liberated from melodramatic stage conventions to allow Browning to explore "Action in Character" as fully or complexly as he wants.

The fact is that for the best display of his genius, which is neither purely lyrical nor dramatic, Browning requires a poetic form that is more dramatic than the early subjective poems but less objective than the stage plays. The literary form which best meets these requirements is the dramatic monologue. It enables the confessional poet of *Pauline* to conceal himself behind characters who are not himself. Like a versatile actor he must constantly rehearse new parts. At the same time he can explore various roles with a psychological complexity impossible to achieve in the dialogue of a play. An actor must control his introspection in the act of addressing others on the stage. But the complexity that is fatal in a long play, which depends for its success on simpler action and clearer characterization than a novel or a poem, may be highly effective in a short dramatic monologue. In such a form, with no longer any need to portray the interactions of characters on a stage, Browning can focus his attention on a single speaker thrust into the foreground of the poem.

4

The Rhetoric
of the Monologue

In searching for a new dramatic form, Browning must begin, not with a complicated personality or idea, but with a structure that will enable him to achieve an intended effect, to make an impact on an auditor, who can then be enlisted as the coauthor of his poem. The literary form in which this collaboration is most active is the dramatic monologue. It forces Browning to begin with the rhetorical effect upon the speaker's imagined auditor, then to invent speech that will make the desired impression on the listener, who can function as the reader's surrogate or "friend." The monologue's silent auditor has much the same relation to the speaker as the reader has; he is the reader's friend because he shares the same perspective. Since the speaker must in some sense persuade his auditor, he must also communicate his meaning to the reader. Though the introduction of a silent auditor is an ostensibly dramatic move, it is essentially rhetorical. It is dictated by the effort of a Victorian Joyce to help the readers who were bewildered by *Sordello* to grasp his future work.

The "rhetoric of the monologue" requires the speaker to persuade an auditor. When either the auditor or the speaker's persuasive intent is missing, the poem ceases to be a dramatic monologue. If an auditor is lacking, or if he is present but not listening, the speaker may still be the object of his own rhetoric, like the Pope in *The Ring and the Book* or like Andrea del Sarto. But if an auditor is missing and the speaker is not trying to persuade himself, the monologue turns into a mere mask, like "Soliloquy of the Spanish Cloister" or "The Confessional."

A poem also ceases to be a dramatic monologue when an auditor is present but the speaker makes no attempt to persuade him. An example would be David's climactic prayer of love in "Saul." Instead of trying to convert Saul to a particular course of action, David presents his vision—"See the Christ stand!"—for its intrinsic interest. Unlike the speaker of a dramatic monologue, he seeks no personal advantage in addressing his auditor. In contrast to the lover's plea for sexual favors in "Two in the Campagna," where the speaker is trying to secure some personal advantage from the woman, David's persuasion is disinterested.

Though a speaker's attempt to gain some kind of advantage from his auditor is the distinctive feature of the dramatic monologue, most of Browning's mature monologues also contain an element of disinterested persuasion. By acts of sympathetic imagination the speakers in these monologues reproduce the internal contradictions of many attitudes and beliefs, which Browning can then rank hierarchically. One of the best ways of justifying and demanding such a hierarchy is by having a speaker reveal the limitation of his own point of view. A speaker can do this by introducing in the course of his monologue a higher motive that interferes with his original attempt to secure immediately an advantage from his auditor. This higher motive is what converts the sensual Fra Lippo to the ethical life, then enables him to pass beyond its contradictions to the religious stage. The interference of disinterested persuasion with a speaker's attempt to secure some kind of personal advantage enables him to grow in stature.

When judged according to the standards of Sludge's self-seeking "courtship" of his patron, or of those sensual and merely rational satisfactions of the hedonist and the ethical man, with which many of the dramatic monologues begin, the pure courtship of Caponsacchi and Pompilia may seem like a sheer frustration of the lovers' immediate purposes. But only by revealing the internal contradictions of the attitudes he personifies can Browning justify a distinction between the "lower" aesthetic and the "higher" ethical and religious stages. If there is a single reason for Browning's mastery of the monologue, it is his happy presentation of Christian dialectic in a literary form which keeps enacting the interference of disinterested persuasion with a speaker's attempt to gain some personal advantage from his auditor. Such interference can expose the limitations of most ideas and beliefs and can serve as a means of transition and growth.

Critics have praised Browning's individual portrayals, but have failed to trace any dialectical advance through the whole range of his creations. I believe that by treating these monologues as a dialectic of aesthetic, ethical, and religious stages, we can gain the richest and most unified indications of the poet's development, if not as a philosopher and theologian, at least as a moral and religious sage.[1] Browning's earli-

---

[1] Readers will detect the influence of Kierkegaard's thought in my treatment of Browning's dialectic. Kierkegaard recognizes three stages: the aesthetic, ethical, and religious. The prototype of the aesthetic man is Don Giovanni, the hedonist whose final limitation is boredom or despair. The exemplary ethical man is Socrates; and the limitation of the ethical stage, comparable to boredom at the aesthetic stage, is guilt or sin. According to Kierkegaard, irony is the overlapping of the ethical life with the aesthetic, and humor the overlapping of the religious life with the ethical. Of course, there is no evidence that Browning was familiar with Kierkegaard's work; indeed, given the language barrier, there is little likelihood that he would have been. Whenever I use Kierkegaard's ideas in the following pages, minimal importance is attached to the accidental historic

est monologues present a stage of immediate extroversion where man lives in bondage to his senses. At this aesthetic stage, the characters live in a kind of highly theatrical Hollywood, where bizarre dramas are enacted and spectacular crimes reconstructed. The inner limitation of the aesthetic stage is boredom or despair. As the aesthetic man perceives the irony of his condition, he may momentarily cease to seek his own advantage. Such interference can work in two ways. After the initial advance it can either reduce the rhetoric to the original "aesthetic" state or raise it from the ethical to the religious level. The limitation of the ethical life comparable to boredom and despair at the aesthetic stage is a result of guilt or sin. Just as Cleon's irony is the manifestation of the aesthetic man's despair, so Fra Lippo's "humor" is in the overlapping of the religious life with the ethical. A monologue like "Fra Lippo Lippi" rapidly escalates the reader from an aesthetic, to an ethical, then to a specifically religious, level of awareness; then once the spiritual persuasion seems to be succeeding, it abruptly returns him to its original level of aesthetic persuasion. If there is no return at the conclusion, then the monologue must either end beyond the

fact that Browning and Kierkegaard were contemporaries. I am using Kierkegaard's analysis only as a heuristic device; much of it may be mere scaffolding, to be knocked away when Browning's own dialectical structures are in clearer view. At the same time, we might remember Sainte-Beuve's advice to ask ourselves as critics what the author himself would think of our description of him. In Kierkegaard's power of concrete illustration, as he moves from thesis over to antithesis and then into synthesis, it is not fanciful to suggest, I think, that Browning would recognize the same psychological depth and balance of thought that enable the poet, in reconsidering the premises of orthodox theology, not so much to discard as to enlarge and renew them. Moreover, Browning would certainly be familiar with a comparable dialectic in *Sartor Resartus:* Carlyle's passage from the "Everlasting No," through the "Centre of Indifference," to the "Everlasting Yea" parallels Kierkegaard's passage from the aesthetic, through the ethical, to the religious stage of experience.

stage at which it began, as do "Two in the Campagna" or "A Toccata of Galuppi's," where the new "ethical" persuasions seem to convert the speakers permanently, or else it must set up higher principles of "interference," as in the successive elevations in "Saul." When these "interferences" cannot be overcome, then the dramatic monologue is transformed into something else. David's original attempt to persuade the king gradually eliminates or absorbs those intellectual and rhetorical devices by which the poem undertakes to reach its highest levels. The rhetoric finally abolishes itself by turning into an inspired visionary utterance by Browning himself. With each upward "interference" the poetry takes on a new dimension of insight. These advances, when repeated often enough at the religious stage, lift the content to universal terms. This dialectical method, which forces all ideas and beliefs to exhibit their internal contradictions and arrange themselves in a hierarchy of aesthetic, moral, and religious stages, is, I believe, the instrument of transition and growth that serves as the basis of Browning's rhetorical art.

5

Rhetoric at the
Aesthetic Stage

To criticize behavior at the aesthetic stage, Browning must first understand it from inside. The art of the dialectical critic is like that of an actor: he must identify with the characters he wants to portray. Most of the "aesthetic men" whom Browning presents are too self-centered to address an auditor, and when they do, their speech is seldom part of an interchange, but merely a reaction to a person or event. Their theatre is a petty scene of icons, an art gallery of nominalism, shrunk to one dimension from the Shelleyan heaven of the subjective poet, the "Sun-treader's" realm in *Pauline*. But the curators of this bizarre museum are nominalists who find it difficult to name anything. Without the capacity to use metaphors or symbols, they can seldom infuse their particulars with larger meaning. By personifying their point of view, Browning reproduces its internal contradictions. His sympathetic imagination is an instrument of moral growth. It enables the comic philosopher to discredit the aesthetic man far more effectively than if he simply tried to portray him from outside.

◈ 1 ◈

The serious and the rollicking elements of Browning's art unite in the best of these early masks. In "Soliloquy of the

Spanish Cloister," for example, which he probably wrote in 1839, the poet's zest for what is colorful and lively is inseparable from his criticism. The poem begins as a growl, slowly ✓ evolves into intelligible speech, and is reabsorbed at the end into another growl. This tantrum rhetoric—private and childlike—is apparently the monk's normal mode of speech. According to Jean Piaget, public discourse attains importance for a child only when he reaches the age of seven or eight.[1] The reader soon becomes aware that the monk's description of the surface of objects is more than mere description. His eye sees, but his mind cannot judge. Emotionally and intellectually he is still a child.

As a sensualist whose holy concepts have hardened into formalisms, the speaker drinks his "watered orange-pulp" in "three sips," in order to confute the Arians. Unable to project real meaning into objects, he has a superstitious habit of finding God in everything. He substitutes the rituals of dining for religion and equates theology with the laying of his "knife and fork" in a "Cross-wise" position. At first his outburst seems to be nothing but an overflow of Machiavellian high spirits. But it also reveals the misapplied ingenuity of his intrigue with Satan.

> Or, there's Satan!—one might venture
> 　Pledge one's soul to him, yet leave
> Such a flaw in the indenture
> 　As he'd miss till, past retrieve,
> Blasted lay that rose-acacia
> 　We're so proud of! *Hy, Zy, Hine* . . .
> 'St, there's Vespers! *Plena gratiâ*
> 　*Ave, Virgo!* Gr-r-r—you swine!   [st. IX].

The opening words explode from him with all the ecstasy of demonic inspiration. The announcement of his plot to sign

---

[1] *The Language and Thought of the Child* (New York, 1926).

the pact with Satan, then to counterfeit his signature, is punctuated with a raucous *"Hy, Zy, Hine,"* apparently a formula of Satanic invocation. But the line's impact has nothing to do with the meaning of the individual words. It is an obsessive gesture of the monk, made from the syllables of his spell, but intensified into a half-throttled cry. The most entertaining and dramatic meanings are enacted in gestures of imbalance and hysteria, which Browning cannot express through the dictionary meanings of words. Because he is incapable of using language conceptually, the jealous monk who thinks that sex and marriage are evil does not realize that in damning Brother Lawrence as a Manichee, he is damning himself as well. One of the poet's purest rhetorical patterns is his enlistment of the reader as a partner in jokes made at the expense of the practical joker who damns his victim for the very sin of which he himself, in lusting for Dolores' "Blue-black . . . tresses," is guilty.

Merely by confining us to the thoughts and sensations of the hedonistic monk, "Soliloquy of the Spanish Cloister" achieves an intensity of expression that is impossible in the semidramatic poems and plays. In contrast to these early works, where the emotions and ideas are too complex, the dramatic mask selects only those simple emotions which can "act" well. In poems like "Soliloquy of the Spanish Cloister," "The Laboratory," and "Porphyria's Lover," Browning can communicate the touch and feel of jealousy with an immediacy that would have won the admiration of earlier writers like Donne. Instead of portraying "incidents in the development of a soul," Browning locks a sensualist's hungry desires and envy within the closed cycle of a passion that is concrete and repetitive. To be sure, the contrast of infernal flames and flowerpots, like the nipping of buds from his rival's plants, reduces his hostility to a childlike level. But the song-like stanzas of "Soliloquy of the Spanish Cloister" still compose an incantation of hate, and the monk's curious blend of spleen and sensuality betrays a preoccupation with sex to the point of imbalance. As in Robbe-Grillet's novels, the nakedness of the sensations represents more than a stylistic device; it is due to a way of seeing life. The reader begins with an instant perception of a certain attitude, and the repetition of this attitude from instant to instant clarifies and deepens Browning's meaning. The lighter elements of the poem both interpret and make more transparent the elements which are in earnest.

☞ 2 ☜

In "The Laboratory," another of his early poems (1844), Browning adds a silent auditor in the person of the chemist from whom a court lady is procuring poison to murder her rival. By leaving the reader to infer the character and reactions of the chemist, Browning can still lock the reader completely inside the speaker's point of view. But by introducing an auditor whom the speaker has to persuade, "The Laboratory" becomes, instead of a mere mask like "Soliloquy of the Spanish Cloister," a full dramatic monologue.

The lady can perform her present task well, but she never seems to contemplate its effect on her lover. Her inability to see such connections when the situation demands them produces a childish self-absorption. There is an incredible superficiality in the literalness of her imagination. She is the girlish sorceress who would transfix her enemy with the evil eye, and is baffled when her efforts fail: "she fell not." At the same time, by transforming the accidental into the absolute, she has discovered what Kierkegaard calls "the whole secret of arbitrariness." She allows the realities of life to split upon so arbitrary an interest as the precise taste and color of the poison. Her consistent specifications show she is a true artist, and the insignificant details accidentally offer rich material for the reader's own amusement. The more arbitrarily precise she is in holding fast to such details, the more exquisite are her inscrutable repose and sadist calm: "The delicate droplet, my whole fortune's fee!"

Because thinking of the lovers' exultation turns the knife in the wound, the speaker's ritual of buying poison affords her intense pain as well as pleasure. But the whole action is one which she is apparently powerless to resist. Her ritual before the chemist is a currently staged obsession, like the Duke's play acting before the envoy in "My Last Duchess." It repeats an all-important scene in which she has been involved with the lover and her rivals. Now, before the chemist as the lover's surrogate, she tries to escape her rivals' scorn, which is expressed in the fantasies of the second stanza: "While they laugh, laugh at me." As in most obsessional conditions, only one course of action is open to her: instead of one silly idea—the expenditure of her whole fortune on a droplet of poison—she can adopt another, of slightly milder character. This she does when she bestows her favors on the grisly old chemist, a lover whom she can at least control.

Her whole ritual of buying the poison is a way of repeating the scene with her lover, which she is now continuing and correcting. Besides bringing about the slow and painful extinction of her rivals, she also transforms the past into what it ought to have been. The chemist functions as the lover's surrogate, and the lover, in the person of the chemist, now kisses the lady instead of her rivals. The more we are intrigued by a gesture like the kiss, the more meanings it seems to include. The kissing by the chemist has the same purpose as the Spanish monk's signing of the pact with Satan. The monk is a kind of Faustus of the cloister who sells his soul for vengeance. Marlowe's Faust seals his fate when he kisses Helen. The court lady is a Helen who seals her own destiny by casting the chemist as the Faustus of "this devil's-smithy."

He sells his soul when he becomes the instrument of her revenge and assents to that role by bestowing the kiss. A dramatic monologue like "The Laboratory" enlists the reader as a coauthor. It forces him to look for or imagine a situation capable of causing such behavior. A gesture like the kiss is especially beguiling, because we realize as we consent to it that Browning has invited us to shape its meaning for ourselves.

₥ 3 ᴧᴧᵥ

The traumatic moment when the victim of priestly intrigue in "The Confessional" (1845) witnesses her lover's execution is like the moment of the woman's blurring of consciousness in "Count Gismond." Because the victim's words pile themselves up blindly, only a vague feeling of disorder is defined:

> It is a lie—their Priests, their Pope,
> Their Saints, their . . . all they fear or hope
> Are lies, and lies—there! through my door
> And ceiling, there! and walls and floor,
> There, lies, they lie—shall still be hurled
> Till spite of them I reach the world!   [st. 1].

The very intensity of self-expression prevents her from communicating. The rest of the poem records her attempt to stand back from her experience—to replace the thrill of indictment with an orderly prosecution. Her recounting of the priest's deception has the same function of controlling trauma as the Spanish monk's careful arranging of his utensils, the court lady's punctilious preparations in "The Laboratory," and the woman's willed focusing upon the tercel in "Count Gismond."

The speaker shifts the "sin" from the lovers to the confessor, "the old mild father" whom she confuses with the hangman. The priest ranks with Ogniben, the Pope's legate in *A Soul's Tragedy*, as the most memorable of Browning's early casuists. He induces the girl to participate in the religious forms and includes within her "angel's fate" the disclosure of her lover's plans. He uses indirect reasoning to catch her on the horns of a logical dilemma. If she fails to inform on Beltran, she will not only miss the chance to be a saint but will also damn her lover's soul. The confessor leaves the girl to deny the consequents, which he brings together by establishing a causal connection between being saintlike and saving her lover's soul. By prodding her into denying the single antecedent, he leaves her to conclude that she must now supply him with a full report on Beltran's plans. The priest's success depends upon his agility in playing with double meanings. He uses the verb "purge" in an absolute, or eschatological, sense, but with the knowledge that the girl will understand it in a qualified, or metaphoric, sense. The equivocator can always argue that he has not lied, that even after executing Beltran, he will still fast and scourge himself for the sake of the departed soul. But like Ogniben, the Duke of "My Last Duchess," or Guido Franceschini, the confessor ought to have a bad conscience. He is a priestly Polonius, and his sententious formulas—pointed, epigrammatic, antithetically balanced—are obviously too carefully patterned to be trusted.

After she has finished telling her story, only the girl's hatred of the priest, like the Spanish monk's envy of Brother Lawrence, can renew for each instant the operation of the one before: "Lies—lies, again—and still, they lie!" It is not the meaning of the words that counts, but the overtones of hysteria that repetition, in the given situation, makes them take on. The confessor's throne is the scaffold, and instead of redeeming man by sacrificing God, the priest puts Beltran on the rack and sacrifices man in God's name. Instead of prolonging life, such a God holds over man a threat of vengeance and annihilation. The victim's exchange of functions transfers the aesthetic mask from herself to the confessor. The priest is a hangman, and the mask of his religion turns out to be a death mask.

⤬ 4 ⤬

Since the speaker in a dramatic monologue has to persuade an auditor who can function as the reader's "friend," Browning can use this auditor to convey an intended effect to the reader as well. This practice of starting with an intended effect is also the method of the mystery story, in which the writer tries to achieve a maximum predetermined impact of shock or suspense. By beginning with an intention to move the reader in a specific way, the monologue form enables Browning to achieve a similar effect of surprise in "Count Gismond" (1842). The speaker's indirection suggests that Browning is trying to narrate a medieval mystery story from the point of view of the guilty person, but in order to secure the maximum shock, he decides to withhold knowledge of the woman's guilt till the end of the poem. When Browning tries to backtrack, step by step, from the desired effect to the events he must introduce to reach it, he achieves mystery only at the expense of clarity and irony. If he wants us to discredit the narrator, he has not made it clear enough that she is tricking her friend into accepting her account of events. If, on the other hand, he expects us to believe her story, why does he expand "Count Gismond" from a mere mask like "The Confessional," in which the girl's solitary confinement eliminates all motives for lying, into a full dramatic monologue? Why do the secret exchanges that pass between the speaker and her auditors come to assume so sinister and baffling a dimension?

At first the noblewoman seems to be a much more reliable narrator than the overwrought prisoner of "The Confessional." She betrays no inability to think conceptually. On the contrary, she would have us believe that the thwarted sensuality of the aesthetic stage is less evident in her than in Count Gauthier and her cousins. Just as the confessor exchanges his priestly mask for the hangman's mask, so Gauthier switches roles at the critical moment during the tournament, when he accuses the speaker of committing fornication. She portrays the tournament as a courtly ceremony in which the villains deck her out as "queen" of the beauty contest, then strip her of her regal trappings at a given signal. The elaborate ritual is a form of play acting, and the woman insists that she would gladly have renounced the dramatic role in which the cousins and Count Gauthier had cast her: "they should have dropped / A word, and straight the play had stopped" (ll. 17–18).

The closest analogue to "Count Gismond" is *Colombe's Birthday*, which illustrates that the duchess' real power, hitherto only an illusion, consists of one man's love for her. The producers of the ritual in "Count Gismond" allow their Colombe to sing her "birthday song quite through," then humiliate her publicly. Count Gauthier's staging her as "queen" is a compulsive act, a form of obsessional neurosis, in which he parades her forth as the spectacular beauty he would like to possess. He represents as actuality what is merely a sexual fantasy. The only way he can gratify this fantasy is by making his outrageous charge against her: "Shall she whose body I embraced / A night long, queen it in the day?" Such an interpretation accounts at once for the ritual of his play acting and his otherwise motiveless accusation. The speaker wants her friend to believe that Gauthier's malignity springs, as do the obsessional neuroses of the Spanish monk, of the court lady of "The Laboratory," and of the Duke of "My Last Duchess," from the sensuality of the aesthetic stage.

But the woman's image of the bloody sword which swings against her from Count Gismond's hip and her final statement to her husband, which we know to be a lie, compromise rather than confirm her innocence. At first the reader assumes that feminine sensitivity, as well as the secrecy which belongs to the mystery of love, prevent her from reporting what Gismond had told her after the rescue. When she lies to Gismond about the subject of her present conversation, she may be implying, like the speaker in *La Saisiaz*, that her whole monologue has moved only at the level of surface meanings: "Least part this: then what the whole?" (*La Saisiaz*, l. 618). But what if the lie is literal? Would it not then invite an opposite interpretation? According to this other reading, her son's "black full eye" would remind her of Gismond's scorn, as her husband exchanges with her the dark glance of sinister knowledge. Gismond is behind her before she realizes, and the significant communications are all non-verbal. The husband senses not only that she is lying, but also that she knows this; the reactions are multileveled and reflexive. Instead of responding to her husband, she betrays a love of violence by concentrating on the tercel. Sometimes only a less sharply defined gesture can imply the most deeply felt experience. It is because her responses explain so little that they reveal so much.

By trying to shock the reader with a final intimation of the woman's guilt, Browning only confuses him. The difficulties are a result of the poem's simultaneous moral and psychological plunge. Instead of reinforcing each other, the speaker's moral charge against Count Gauthier and the psychological interplay between herself and her two auditors prevent a unified response. If Browning wanted the woman's indictment to persuade the reader, he should not have cast the poem as a dramatic monologue. The interaction with her two auditors—first with Adela and later with her own husband—introduces a psychological complexity that undermines her charge against Count Gauthier. If, on the other hand, Browning intended to dramatize the speaker's guilt, he should not have sacrificed to the shock effect of a last-minute revelation the sustained irony which an earlier disclosure would have produced. Detective stories have been written by so many inferior writers that Browning's attempt at mystery writing also seems inferior to his achievement in other poems. The dialectical critic can realize his potential only in poems like "My Last Duchess" or "The Bishop Orders His Tomb," in which the moral probing and psychological depth, instead of nullifying each other, work together to achieve the more satisfying effects of comic irony.

〰 5 〰

A dramatic mask like "Porphyria's Lover," which Browning wrote as early as 1836, offers no such problems as "Count Gismond." By remaining deliberately shallow in the moral dimension, this one-act thriller enables Browning to achieve the kind of psychological shock that produces incongruous effects in the other poem. In contrast to the situation in "Count Gismond," there can be no doubt about the speaker's guilt. Instead of bewildering the reader, every detail is like the "close-up" in a movie. The speaker has just caught his highborn mistress in a rare moment of submission, and to freeze her into an attitude of perfect beauty, he decides to strangle her. When the court lady of "The Laboratory" invites the chemist, who is socially inferior, to kiss her on the mouth, her invitation is not primarily sexual at all but a means of social intercourse, based on the communication between classes. In "Porphyria's Lover" the strangler's scheme for prolonging sexual submission is a grotesque perversion of the same principle. It inverts the social reverence which an inferior owes to a member of a higher social order, the kind of reverence Kenneth Burke has seen as one of the chief motives of courtship.[2]

The strangler's anatomy of Porphyria recalls Sebald's fig-

[2] *A Rhetoric of Motives* (New York, 1952), pp. 267–268.

urative dismemberment of Ottima in *Pippa Passes*. His inventory of sense impressions becomes a kind of autopsy. He perceives her first in terms of "the dripping cloak and shawl," "the damp hair," and "little throat." He sees her, not as a person, but as a "smooth white shoulder" and cascading "yellow hair." The joy of conquest represents the lyric sense that possesses every criminal who truly imagines his crime, if only for an instant, before he actually commits it.

> at last I knew
> Porphyria worshipped me; surprise
> Made my heart swell, and still it grew
> While I debated what to do   [ll. 32–35].

In its promise of liberation for the lover, the possibility of murder becomes the necessity for murder. Just as he has strangled Porphyria to preserve the good moment, so the rhetoric seems to arrest the violence and preserve the action in a framed picture. After the lover recounts the strangling, he enumerates in the same dispassionate tone the expressionless gaze of Porphyria's "blue eyes without a stain" and her drooping head, limp upon its neck like a rose upon a broken stem.

By ascribing joy to his victim over the enforced fidelity which she was too promiscuous to maintain in real life, the lover now allows himself to enter Porphyria's mind:

> The smiling rosy little head,
> So glad it has its utmost will,
> That all it scorned at once is fled,
> And I, its love, am gained instead!   [ll. 52–55].

This one act of sympathetic imagination reveals how little sympathy the speaker has, for he now convinces himself that Porphyria is glad he strangled her. He has re-created his mistress in his own image, in the figure of a death mask, which is what every aesthetic mask must finally become.

With the return of silence at the close, the strangler's entrancement, as he waits for God to speak, contrasts with the tempestuous sounds of the opening. Once again his eye sees and his ear listens, but his mind withholds its judgments. His inability to penetrate objects continues to exert a strange fascination. Without the power of sympathetic imagination, the lover remains in bondage to his senses. His constant use of "and," which seems to put every emotion on the same bizarre level, achieves a myopic focus that is too suggestive of insanity to be amusing.

𝆕 6 ∿

Though "Porphyria's Lover" enables the reader to experience intensely the reactions of a homicidal maniac, we may question whether the dialectical critic has to imitate a point of view whose aberrations are so obvious. For a more searching exploration of imbalance the reader must turn to "Johannes Agricola in Meditation." Browning wrote this poem the same year as "Porphyria's Lover," but instead of remaining shallow in the moral dimension, it shows how religious ideas, no less than persons or situations, may be perverted and grotesque.

The poem's greatest rhetorical shaping takes place in the disparity which Browning creates between the values implied by the sanctifying terms "God" and "bless" and the values actually served by their use. The word "bless" acquires its force through a process of association with "bloat" and "blast," and also by its placement among innumerable cases of damning. Browning uses alliteration for two purposes: as a persuasive device to group words like "wax and wane" so that their intellectual point cannot be missed, and as a satiric device to make the relation between contradictory terms like "blast" and "bless" strike our attention as forcibly as possible. In the present poem, this second use of alliteration is more important. It is one of the earliest examples of a rhetorical technique which Park Honan has skillfully analyzed in his discussion of Guido's monologues, and which Browning develops to a high degree of perfection in *The Ring and the Book*.

Another example of this rhetorical shaping is in Agricola's constant association of himself with God. Every time the word "God" appears, it is in conjunction with the pronoun "I" or "me," and the reader soon realizes that Agricola is using them interchangeably. The speaker deviates into blatant antitheses in which "love" becomes "anger," "bless" becomes "damn," and "God" becomes a kind of macrocosmic Agricola. John Holloway has analyzed Matthew Arnold's use of a similar device for discrediting "false propositions," by showing how they are "born of [a] mental temper which Arnold condemns." [3] Instead of preserving the emotive meanings of his prize words and shifting their descriptive meanings, Johannes reverses both kinds of meaning. Browning converts all Agricola's claims to their opposites and exposes his beliefs as various forms of self-deception.

Agricola stands on privileged terms with God, and his self-satisfied convictions give him a sense of power. This self-assurance extends to his rhetorical manner, where the patterns of repetition, the compulsive "Yes, yes" and greedily reiterated "me" accurately reflect his egoism. At first his language sounds prayer-like. But the strident repetitions, blatant and self-assured, do not coincide with the mood of devotion. He begins with a most enchanting lyrical passage: "There's heaven above, and night by night / I look right through its gorgeous roof." From this cosmic vision he shifts to a self-complacent largo movement in which his witty hypotheses introduce incongruous reversals of the high style, then to something approaching physical horror; yet all the

[3] *The Victorian Sage* (New York, 1953), p. 217.

parts form a consistent whole by virtue of his egoism, which glints through, everywhere. The ebullient rhythms, which constitute a real defect when used seriously in a poem like "Rabbi Ben Ezra," become a wonderfully ironic way of converting an ostensibly pious argument into blasphemy. This process of reversal works primarily through antithesis: the contrast between Agricola's complacency as a smiling Epicurean deity and the torments of the damned who swarm below him "in ghastly wretchedness." Rhetoric and theology begin to jar, and the clash becomes audible in the constant shifts from piety to egoism, from devotion to hysterical delight, as Agricola begins to gloat over the miseries of the damned.

There is a magnificent irony in his complacent assurance that his fate is like "a tree's," ignorant of "The law by which it prospers." What if this ignorance of "The law" should include the ignorance of his own fate? He praises God because he cannot understand Him, as though the inability to argue the validity of his position is itself a proof of its truth. In an outrageous prostitution of the argument from authority, Agricola turns God himself into his approved author: "I have God's warrant." In keeping with this habit of code-book definition, he names with great precision each variety of religious aspirant. But he has the rationalist's analytic temper without the rationalist's ability to make connections. His climactic indictment—"undone / Before God fashioned earth and star"—affirms a will that is rationally unknowable, though terribly immanent in its effects.

If Agricola's God exhausts the freakishness of arbitrary caprice and deceives those who think that they are saved, He is sure to damn Agricola. Once again, as in "Porphyria's Lover," Browning parodies the way in which the aesthetic man tries to escape his bondage to the senses, to the precariousness and transience of his life without duration. This bondage is dangerous enough in itself; it is made worse in Agricola by a tendency to hasten God's work and to supply, on his behalf, the tortures which he thinks God's inscrutable patience has too long postponed. Though he assumes a religious posture, Agricola is "splendor-proof" in a way he never understands. Indeed, he can never ascend to the religious stage at all, for his leap to God requires, not the salvation, but the damnation of his rivals; and despite his rejection of economic bargaining, his whole theology institutes an atomistic economy of competing souls.

Johannes perverts theology by locating its dialectic entirely outside himself. His vision of God's external decrees confuses the religious condition with the religious process. He fails to see that righteousness is the internal condition of the righteous man and becomes a principle of external or antithetical wrath only after it has been violated as the inward condition of religious life. Because he turns an inward condition into an outward perception and sees God only externally, as divine despot, Agricola illustrates the truth of Meredith's observation that "the life of comedy is in the idea." His beliefs are more bizarre than the court lady's envy or the Spanish monk's hysteria. Tenacious to the point of fanaticism, he holds his ideas as rigid frames to limit experience as far as possible so that he may vote upon a cause which is between God and other men.

If "Johannes Agricola" is a comedy of ideas, Browning's most important dialectical weapon in revealing the absurdity of these ideas is his method of dissociation. Agricola contaminates the idea of piety with such a host of hateful and envious motives that he enables Browning to break religious "truths" apart, showing that their factual, sadistic aspect has no logical connection with their professed, ideal aspect. As we have already seen, this process is illustrated in the fate of individual words like "bless," "bloat," and "blast." The revealing sound associations are Browning's most striking device, a demonstration of the kind of mild schizophrenia whereby Agricola is made to speak of cruel things blithely. Beneath this comedy of ideas lies the failure of all egoists at the aesthetic stage. They are usually less schizophrenic than Johannes, but all too ready to detect the irony of some inexorable decree, unaware of the profounder irony of their own self-deception.

When he imitates a point of view to reveal its aberrations, Browning discovers that his dialectical method is also an instrument of comic irony. The mounting fervency of Agricola's rhetoric, as he is more and more carried away with it, assumes the whole grand tone of comic opera. Because it achieves a more genuine integration of high spirits and conviction, "Johannes Agricola in Meditation" is, I think, the most successful of the short poems Browning wrote before "My Last Duchess" and "The Bishop Orders His Tomb." It illustrates that when ideas or beliefs take a rigid mold too soon and begin to work against the world, good sense, and their own object, they may be even more grotesque than situations or persons. Only when the reader finishes the poem does he appreciate the reason for the grandeur in which Browning invests Agricola's ideas at the beginning. The cosmic splendor of the speaker's theological conceptions has much in common with the mock-heroic. By uncovering those aberrations of belief that kindle "thoughtful laughter," the comic philosopher can fashion an argument irresistibly shaped to debase those bigots whom it fits.

꙰ 7 ꙰

Among the dramatic monologues that have produced the greatest division of critical opinion are those which use the convictions conveyed by a narrator at the aesthetic stage to control the reader's reaction to people like the grammarian in

"A Grammarian's Funeral" or the poet in "How It Strikes A Contemporary"—men who pass beyond the aesthetic life to the ethical or religious stage. The speaker's responses introduce ironies at the expense of the subject which would not be present if Browning chose to impersonate that subject directly, through the use of a social or religious mask. But because the speaker has much the same relation to his subject as Browning has to the speakers in most of his dramatic monologues, the sympathetic imagination that enables the speaker to identify with his subject is inseparable from his criticism. Whatever the speaker says to discredit his subject, he can never destroy his own excited curiosity, that intellectual sympathy which the monologue presents directly to the reader. If ethical or religious subjects can command the admiration of speakers who move at a "lower" level, Browning can command a fortiori the enlightened reader's own assent.

The disciple who narrates "A Grammarian's Funeral" (probably written in 1853 or 1854), though able to appreciate the ethical and religious levels on which the grammarian moves, seems confined himself to the aesthetic stage. This clash of contrasting levels accounts for much of the poem's irony, for the grammarian seems somewhat absurd by aesthetic standards. The disciple and his fellows can attend to what Kierkegaard calls "both-and," the reconciliation of living and knowing. But for the grammarian, "knowing" has become the exclusive means through which he relates to God: "This man decided not to Live but Know." To put knowing on the same plane with all the rest of living is to change into a "both-and" Kierkegaard's "Either / Or" distinction between aesthetic idolatry and ethical freedom.

At the moment his youth is over the grammarian renounces the "rotation method" of the aesthetic life. Instead of substituting "New measures, other feet anon," which is "the world's way," he escapes the transience of the aesthetic man by enunciating a doctrine of moral and intellectual preparation for an "Actual life" hereafter. When the disciple adds that another man would have said, " 'Time to taste life,' " he is no doubt thinking of hedonists like himself. But the readiness of such "another" man to undertake a defense of the grammarian is Browning's device for overcoming our resistance to the values he wants to confer upon the scholar.

In defending his master, the disciple keeps contrasting the grammarian's persuasive definitions with the unthinking exhortations of the community. The word that undergoes successive definition is "life." In response to the hedonist's cry, "Time to taste life," the grammarian tries to redirect attitudes. The word "life" is one of praise which he seeks to bestow on the qualities of his own choice. The rest of the poem gives the word greater precision within the boundaries of its customary vagueness; the process of constantly relating new conceptions of life to popular views is of great importance in clarifying what is meant by "Actual life." [4] In the scholar's opinion the transient moments in which the hedonist wants him to live are merely an interval in which he can prepare for the life that follows. The reader, like the hedonist, has been in the habit of regarding his education in the art of living as a part of living. But the grammarian's resolution "That before living he'd learn how to live" implies that the two are separable. It forces the reader to attend to new distinctions. By giving "living" a more precise meaning, it with-

---

[4] Here, as elsewhere in this study, I am indebted for my analysis of emotive and descriptive meaning in persuasive definitions to Charles L. Stevenson's discussion in *Ethics and Language* (New Haven, 1944). Although I agree with many of W. K. Wimsatt's criticisms of Stevenson (see "The Affective Fallacy," in *The Verbal Icon* [Lexington, Ky., 1954], pp. 22–25), my rhetorical analysis commits me in advance to some of the affective "heresies" Wimsatt condemns. I have tried, however, to avoid the more radical dualisms of emotive and referential meaning which formalists like Wimsatt rightly criticize.

holds the word of praise from those hedonists who urge, "Live now or never!" It narrows the meaning of the key word to emphasize differences between the "preparations" of the aesthetic man for a life of immediate pleasures and the intellectual's philosophic and ascetic disciplines which render his whole life probationary.

The grammarian, all too aware of the transience of his own life, grants the validity of the hedonists' observation that "time escapes." But without changing the descriptive meaning of the fragmentary instants they both call "now," he shifts their emotive meaning. The "now" of the temporal life to which the sensualist is bound is fit for only "dogs and apes," while "Man has Forever." The disciple shocks the reader by insisting that not the ascetic grammarian, but his life-loving critics, have discounted "life." The paradox depends on the shifting meanings of the term. When the grammarian says, "Hence with life's pale lure!" he is using "life" only in his critics' sense. This meaning returns in the epitaph at the end of the poem: "This man decided not to Live but Know" (l. 139). In contrasting "living" with "knowing," the disciple is using "living" only in the sense of the "low man's" apelike existing from one moment to the next as he receives his pleasures in installments, fragmented and discrete.

To understand the grammarian's point of view, Browning must reproduce it in his poem by an act of sympathetic imagination. But to emphasize the disparity between the poet's true and assumed character, the monologue introduces a speaker who is dramatized in his own right as a personality as unlike the grammarian as Browning is. The speaker's intellectual sympathy does not imply approval. The scholar's "knowing," though admirable as a preparation for some future life and as an example of his fortitude and resolution, is still a fragment of that ideal state in which thought and ac-

tion are one. The sympathetic imagination that enables
Browning to adopt the grammarian's unique standpoint is a
dialectical weapon. For not till he has grasped his subject
from within can Browning show that the grammarian is
another victim of Renaissance disintegration. He is shaped by
the same forces that produce the flashy agility of the priest in
"The Confessional," who is a specialist in cunning, of Porphyria's lover, the professional in erotic sensations, and of
Johannes Agricola, the expert in personal election. With the
breakdown of medieval society, man has been "metamor-
phosed," as Emerson observed, "into many things. . . . The
state of society is one in which the members have suffered
amputation from the trunk, and strut about as so many walking monsters—a good finger, a neck, a stomach, an el-
bow"—dismembered adjuncts of a human being, "but never a
man." [5] In such a world "the scholar is delegated intellect,"
no longer a man knowing, but a Renaissance pedant. He
lacks the rational fullness that would enable him to see the
connections between his own discipline and the rest of life.

Just as his grammatical studies break down language into
particles and enclitics, so the scholar is personally fragmented. Browning reinforces this disintegration by distinguishing between the senses—in particular by focusing on the
visual attributes which characterize the grammarian and the
technology of printing. His burial place is a sparkling citadel,
his time of day is morning, and his features are those of
"lyric Apollo," the sun god. While the rest of the community is still sleeping in a feudal village nestled on the bosom
of the plain, the Renaissance grammarian has "gathered all
books had to give." His place of burial is marked by shooting
meteors and loosened lightnings, celestial fireworks that emphasize the visual.

[5] Ralph Waldo Emerson, "The American Scholar," *Works*, ed. J. E.
Cabot (Boston, 1895) I, 85–86.

Browning's sympathetic imagination first uncovers the in-adequacy of the disciple's attitudes; then the poet portrays the grammarian's beliefs in order to discredit *them*. Since every point of view is limited, nothing can escape Browning's dialectical scourge. But this method of imitating and rejecting different attitudes is also an instrument of transition and growth. Though more one-sided and just as absurd, the grammarian's ethical freedom represents a dialectical advance over the aesthetic idolatry of his disciple. The undercutting of the grammarian's values does not proceed as far as one might think. Whereas Tennyson uses Ulysses as a symbol of resolution and fortitude, it is characteristic that the erudite Browning should choose a pedant as his symbol. There has to be incidental satire, since everything that suffers from the illusion of its own perspective is at least potentially absurd. But, as I have tried to show, the principal irony is not at the grammarian's expense. This irony is inseparable from the manifestations of the higher ethical and religious lives as they overlap with the lower aesthetic stage to which Browning's choice of the disciple's point of view necessarily confines us.

◊ 8 ◊

"How It Strikes a Contemporary" (1851 or 1852) views a poet's ethical and religious life through a gossip who is even more deficient in his insights than the grammarian's disciple. When the gossip tries to indicate the poet's moral or intellec-tual qualities, he can merely enumerate surface impressions like the aquiline nose or formidable brow, metonymic signs of resolution and intelligence. His frankness first appeals to the Philistines in Browning's audience and wins their confi-dence: "Well, I could never write a verse,—could you?" But in case the familiarity of the gossip's tone seduces the reader into sharing his point of view, Browning must expose its limi-tation. At the end of the poem he blows up the whole delusive structure by having the speaker characterize himself as a shallow dandy: "Bless us, all the while / How sprucely we are dressed out, you and I!" Because the speaker is even more limited than the grammarian's disciple, he can draw to himself more of the absurdity attaching to the poet in the monologue than the disciple can draw from the grammarian. In addition, the gossip's very inadequacies make his praise of his subject more convincing. If such a lightweight is prepared to concede the poet's eminence, then the reader, unless he is willing to be more intolerant of artists than is an acknowledged Philistine, must consent a fortiori to the poet's merits.

After discrediting the external splendors of the ruler, the gossip delineates, with his customary concern for detail, the attributes of the contemporary poet who dines on a crust in an old coat, seemingly far removed from the centers of influence. Though the eccentric poet is an object of amusement, he is less absurd than the grammarian. Since everything is included in his nightly letter, the poet serves as the exchange center for all transactions between God and man, and in service to his temporal lord he is an "unacknowledged legislator." Whereas the speaker must rotate the round of his pleasures—"Let's to the Prado and make the most of time" —the poet's service to "our Lord the King" will dramatically reverse at death the misplacement of attributes: "A second, and the angels alter that."

The speaker perceives that there are adequate resources of irony behind his subject's mask. His difficulty in describing "the Corregidor's" ironic features reveals that the poet has assumed the customary incognito used by man at the ethical stage:

> Oh, you might smile! there wanted not a touch,
> A tang of . . . well, it was not wholly ease
> As back into your mind the man's look came

[ll. 47–49].

Since the "poet's affair is with God," as Browning had said in one of his letters, the inwardness of this relation forbids any outward expression which would make recognition easier. Instead of performing extraordinary acts of piety or devotion, this "knight of the hidden inwardness" passes his time by resting his foot upon his dog's back and playing cribbage with his maid. The more public his profession, the more grotesquely it tends to resemble the egocentric devotions of Johannes Agricola or the Spanish monk. To match his neutral personality, the poet's dwelling is neither a monastery nor a palace, but "that new stuccoed third house by the bridge, / Fresh-painted, rather smart than otherwise!" The poet's eccentricities are only superficial. In the essential matters his views resemble Browning's own. Like the ironic philosopher of the dramatic monologues, he realizes that admiration for his art is enhanced by a recognition of the disparity between his true and his assumed character. Like a versatile actor, the poet indeed is most himself when he is least himself. He is a king in disguise, whose acts of intellectual sympathy, if honestly performed, are acts of moral judgment of the world.

ᗰ 9 ᗰ

"How It Strikes a Contemporary" and "A Grammarian's Funeral" use an aesthetic point of view to command the reader's assent to a higher ethical stage, which is itself subjected to varying degrees of criticism. A fable like "The Statue and the Bust" reverses this process. It shows that a conventionally moral attitude, when it suffers from the limitation of its own perspective, can be just as ridiculous as an aesthetic point of view. Moral pretension, no less than sensual indulgence, is a comic extravagance. To overcome such limitation, Browning has to employ the sensualist's own value of licentiousness in sex.

In formulating a doctrine of individual freedom that opposes social convention, Browning, of course, is also indulging his love for making out a rhetorical case—for arguing his point from an extreme instance. Though he sermonizes only in fun, he implies through his joking that perseverance in one's aspirations is the real mark of character. To establish a new "morality," which the reader is not to confuse with the sensual bondage of the aesthetic stage, Browning must first discredit conventional conceptions of virtue and vice. If the poet felt that his Victorian audience, like most of his present-day readers, would accept licentiousness as a matter of course, he would never have introduced so many arguments in its favor, and half the brilliance of his rhetorical indirection would be lost.

But even in the twentieth century the relation of love and sex cannot be taken for granted, and it is no accident that Browning casts the moral of "The Statue and the Bust" as a riddle. Its enigma is designed to satisfy the pleasure of deciphering, which is one of Browning's ways of enlisting the cooperation of his readers. He is not merely recommending adultery, which might be just as ridiculous as the behavior he is criticizing. The human mind is incurably idolatrous, and he does not want the reader to substitute one kind of idolatry for another. The narrator's final sidelong glance as he is about to take his leave of the reader ("De te, fabula!") is an ironic reminder that, although he is using certain unorthodox views to free the reader from his own biases, the illicit love that might have been proper for the duke is not necessarily a solution in the reader's own case. The folly of mistaking a particular point of view for total truth is just what Browning's dialectical method singles out as proper material for its comic art.

The attempt to prod the human mind to reach beyond the concentric circles in which it moves is also the purpose of another fable, "The Glove," which was probably written in 1845. Like "The Statue and the Bust," it tries to liberate the reader by reversing the terms of the usual equation. It identifies aesthetic idolatry with worship of conventions, and ethical freedom with a violation of the rules. In her attitude toward the courtly conventions, Browning's emancipated heroine, like Shakespeare's Beatrice, is disengaged and juridical. She explores the delicacies of a courtly-love situation by asking what it would mean to take literally the conventional offer of Don Giovanni, the prototype of Kierkegaard's aesthetic man, to die for the lady's sake. Her rhetoric is an ingenious example of special pleading, and she justifies her deed as a brilliant variant of the deed Beatrice demands of her professed "servant," Benedick: "Kill Claudio!" Later the narrator himself clinches the argument against conventions by showing how the lady's disregard for them prepares her for her happy marriage to a commoner. The gallant and dashing De Lorge, cuckolded in married life, is ironically destroyed by the very conventions he upholds.

⚘ 10 ⚘

"The Statue and the Bust" and "How It Strikes a Contemporary" warn the reader against mistaking the relative for the absolute. They show how even conventionally proper attitudes may suffer from the blindness of their own perspective. Other poems like "Protus" and "Sibrandus Schafnaburgensis" make the same point by using the opposite device. They lock us so firmly inside an obviously deficient point of view that we feel at times like shouting to be freed.

"Sibrandus Schafnaburgensis" is a close-up of a "primitive" who keeps focusing upon the crawling side of nature. He sees the world in terms of the spider's arms and water beetle's face, and even uses sexual metonymy to transfer to the body of nature parts of the human anatomy. When he would be private and "spend / Hours alone in his lady's chamber," he takes refuge in the plum tree's "crevice" with its "lap of moss" and "lip of gum." The farrago of the polyglot who mixes Latin with his double entendres and who sprawls on the grass roaring "Over a jolly chapter of Rabelais" mingles incongruously with the aseptic purities of "sour John Knox." The toadstool growing in Sibrandus' sixth chapter and "the live creatures" that "Tickled and toused and browsed" his book all over advertise the speaker's hilarious revolt against pedants like the grammarian. But even in discrediting the pedants, the extravagance of the speaker's own high spirits becomes itself an object of comedy. As another example of Browning's dialectical irony, it exposes the aberration of any merely sensual point of view.

Equally immediate in its close-up on sensuality is Browning's dramatic mask "Protus" (1855), which transforms the robust comedy of the earlier poem into ceremonial pageantry. It portrays the will to power of a barbaric usurper who rules with mailed fist till his heir poisons him. John the Pannonian, with his gross facial features, is the incarnation of brutality, and the use of one subject with many verbs gives cumulative force to the account of his stride to power: "Came, had a mind to take the crown, and wore / The same for six years." The rough-hammered granite bust evokes the "Great eye, / Gross jaw and griped lips" of the "blacksmith's bastard" as a heroic presence, something which compels our wonder. One can readily see, in the proto-Fascist John, how Browning is developing synesthesia, from its innocuous use in Keats, into the instrument of that Carlylean will to power which will culminate in the rhetoric of a Fascist Pound. John the Pannonian's sculptured head is the mask of the "imperial voluptuary" whom Kierkegaard takes as one of the prototypes of the aesthetic man. Kierkegaard explicitly identifies this aesthetic mask with Nero, an emperor from the same historical period as John: "They call his glance an imperial glance, and the whole world trembles before it, and yet his inmost nature is anguished dread." [6] Since John is poisoned by his son six years later, we can easily appreciate the cause of the emperor's dread. As the paradigmatic sensualist, the "crown-grasper" is a brutalized version of the Duke of Ferrara or Count Guido Franceschini. They are all examples of the aristocratic voluptuary whose "glance becomes so flashing that it terrifies," and who is finally enigmatic even to himself.

〽 11 〽

The Duke of "My Last Duchess" (1842) occupies the same position in Browning's canon as Hamlet does in Shakespeare's. His power as a dramatic character resides in his endless suggestiveness, in the play of enigmatic forces that continue to seduce and inspire his subtlest critics. With the Bishop of St. Praxed's and Count Guido Franceschini, he is Browning's most convincing portrayal of the aesthetic stage. His complexity arises from the accuracy with which Browning reproduces the baffling contradictions of the aesthetic man who, in attempting to shock and entertain the envoy, is also trying to make his existence durable to himself.

Some of the best commentators on the poem believe that the Duke delivers his speech as a warning which he wants the envoy to convey to his future wife. Professors E. K. Brown and J. O. Bailey summarize this view when they state that the Duke "expects from his bride single-hearted, worshipful loyalty, and will tolerate no less. He tells the story of his last duchess as a subtle means of making this point." [7] But other

[6] Sören Kierkegaard, "Equilibrium," in *Either/Or*, tr. Walter Lowrie (Princton, 1944), II, 157.

[7] *Victorian Poetry*, ed. E. K. Brown and J. O. Bailey (New York, 1962), p. 774.

critics have objected that the Duke is more interested in obtaining a dowry than a submissive wife, and if the envoy were to report this speech to the Count's daughter, it is unlikely that the dowry would be forthcoming. It is possible, of course, that the daughter would have no choice in the matter, since Italian women of the sixteenth century were still treated as chattels on the marriage market. But if the daughter has no choice, there is even less reason to suppose that the Duke is delivering his speech as a warning. For him to do so under such circumstances would be to grant the possibility of an unruly chattel and to suggest that the marital rights of a duke are only nominal. On the other hand, the Duke is too adroit and sophisticated to indulge in plain effrontery. It would not be in character for the Duke crudely and openly to challenge the envoy to report the Duke's story if he dared.

Thomas Assad argues that the Duke stoops to reveal a domestic frustration because the revelation enables him to demonstrate his knowledge of art. But the role of art is not as important in "My Last Duchess" as it is in "Fra Lippo Lippi" or "Andrea del Sarto." One cannot help feeling that Mr. Assad has mistaken a subordinate theme for the primary one. After all, could a mere taste for appreciating art make the Duke do what "he claims he never chooses to do, and that is to stoop?"[8] Neither B. R. Jerman's thesis that the Duke is witless[9] nor Robert Langbaum's hypothesis of the Duke's insanity[10] can explain convincingly why the Duke should volunteer all the shocking information that he does. As in a portrait of Pontormo, there is a presumption of superiority in the Duke's manner that will accept no question from the out-

[8] "Browning's 'My Last Duchess,'" *Tulane Studies in English*, X (1960), 117–128.
[9] "Browning's Witless Duke," *PMLA* LXXII (1957), 488–493.
[10] *The Poetry of Experience* (London, 1957), p. 85.

side world nor admit any satisfaction of our curiosity. Indeed, the usual roles of speaker and reader are reversed: the reader, like the envoy, feels that he, and not the Duke, is being inspected. The critic's inquiring gaze at the Duke is at first rejected; nor does it perceive any simple explanation of his motives.

I believe that the clue to this mystery lies in an area which other critics have indicated, but which no one seems to have explored at length. Commentators have sensed that the Duke is staging a "show" for the envoy by drawing and closing curtains and speaking rhetorically. George Monteiro, in particular, has stressed the dramatic basis of the Duke's speech: "Virtually a libretto, the Duke's monologue sustains a central metaphor of drama and performance." He begins his play with a curtain, and "sees himself in a dramatic light." [11] But because most critics have paid too little attention to the Duke's language and gestures, they have not generally recognized the full extent to which he is involved in a drama of social pretension—of ceremonious posturing, play acting, and verbal artifice. The ceremony is part of the stagecraft. He was like the producer of a play till life, in the form of his Duchess' admirers, moved into his theatre and set up its counterplay. Isolated by the greedy idolatries of his producer's art, the Duke's theatrical self has fiercely willed the extinction of every other self. Now, in the perfect theatre of the dramatic monologue, with the envoy as his captive audience, the Duke must restage the uneven drama of his domestic life in the form most flattering to his producer's ego. He is at last ready to give the faultless performance which, as we gradually infer, he has never had the absolute mastery to stage in real life.

The opening lines have a sweep of godlike omnipotence.

[11] "Browning's 'My Last Duchess,' " *Victorian Poetry*, I (1963), 235.

The Duke's lordly gesture "calls" into being, as though by a fiat of divine creation, an acknowledged "wonder":

> I call
> That piece of wonder, now: Frà Pandolf's hands
> Worked busily a day, and there she stands   [ll. 2–4].

The paratactic syntax sounds impressively oracular. Like Belinda's echo of Genesis in "The Rape of the Lock" ("Let Spades be trumps! she said, and trumps they were"), the very grammar invites a biblical parody. The Duke has dazzled his auditor with a magnificent opening, and fully conscious of the effect he has made, he can now afford to descend from this plateau of ceremony, with its operatic pointing at the picture, to a drawing-room atmosphere of mere formality. In extending his civilities to the envoy, this autocratic spellbinder, while choosing "Never to stoop" himself, becomes a subtle social parody of the Christian God of Browning's St. John, who "stoops . . . to rise . . . Such ever was love's way" ("A Death in the Desert," l. 134). The Duke pretends to "stoop," not out of love (for his melodramatic pretensions exclude the imagination of love), but only out of a selfish desire to dramatize his own importance.

The speaker is producing a play in which the envoy must act his proper role. Thus the profession of feeling in "Will't please you sit" is offset by the Duke's self-important quotation of himself ("I said") and by the studied artifice of his "by design." Feeling is further displaced by the classificatory instinct evident in the phrase "Strangers like you" and by the placid rationality of the causal "for," as though the envoy were simply another statistic, his response a calculated theatrical effect, something which the Duke has already predicted with scientific accuracy. Instead of speaking of the Duchess' "deep passion," he uses hendiadys ("The depth and passion of its earnest glance") to give an increased formality and an

emphasis in keeping with the Latinate elegance of "that pic-
tured countenance." An austere note enters with the aggres-
sive insolence of the first parenthesis: "(since none puts
by / The curtain I have drawn for you, but I)." Its audacity is a theatrical triumph which further accentuates the
displacement of tone in the slightingly acrid "Strangers like
you," and which reaches a minor climax in the insolent
threat—"if they durst"—he casually tosses off. His lofty
rhetoric corresponds in the social realm to the sublime in the
aesthetic: each is tinged with as much terror as dignity. The
use of first-person pronouns ("As they would ask me," "But
to myself they turned"), the studied indifference of the
parenthesis, which is really a stage direction, and, above all,
the frightening brevity of the arresting "if they durst,"
which owes half its power to its appearance as a careless
afterthought, all enable the Duke to glory in an authority
which the Duchess' spontaneity never allowed him to possess
while she was alive. The very disparity of meaning between
the rhyming words "breast" and "West," which the heroic
couplet brings into one web of sense, confirms our suspicion
that the Duke lacked this kind of mastery in his married life.
The rhymes, which are irrational satellites revolving round
the rhetoric, imply that, like "the dropping of the daylight,"
the Duchess' "breast" had indeed become for him a sinking
sun. In order to dramatize his complete possession of the
Duchess' "smile," the Duke in his little play takes keen delight in turning that smile on and off, merely by pulling a
rope, with all the absorption of a child with a toy. But from
what he proceeds to say we gather that the Duchess would
never have allowed the curtain to be drawn over her in real
life.

What is most repulsive in the Duke's manner is the callous
precision of an insane rationalist. The Duke casts his critique

of the instinctive and humane into the brainlessly analytic
mode of a social geometer:

> "Just this
> Or that in you disgusts me; here you miss,
> Or there exceed the mark"   [ll. 37–39].

The speaker has the hypersensitive nerves of an infallible
producer and rejects as vulgar any rational discussion with
his star performer. His moral calculus transforms the rationality of the Duchess into the impudence of a saucy school-
girl, "plainly" setting "Her wits to [his]," as though chop-
ping logic with her master.

By way of a transitional "Oh sir," as though to anticipate
and forestall the mingled outrage and amazement of his auditor, the Duke passes to a fleeting reminder, in the two words
"she smiled," of the Duchess' instinctive humanity:

> Oh sir, she smiled, no doubt,
> Whene'er I passed her; but who passed without
> Much the same smile?   [ll. 43–45].

The jealous producer finds intolerable the spontaneous
warmth of an actress who dares move beyond the role in
which he has cast her by extending to others "Much the
same smile." The third and final use of "smile" communicates
in a lightning stroke the full extent of the Duke's despotism:
"This grew; I gave commands; / Then all *smiles* stopped together" (italics mine). The account of the march to power
of this conqueror, whose use of asyndeton resembles Caesar's
"I came, I saw, I conquered," shifts at once from the height
of cruelty to a producer's sensitive appreciation of the Duchess' portrait, valued by the Duke now, in his theatrical performance before the envoy, as his most striking stage property. The impresario remains polished and unperturbed; his

dissociation of brutality from the usual signs defines a peculiarly intense animus and contempt for everyone around him.

The Duke's assurance that he is more interested in obtaining a wife than a dowry is a transparent deception. Hedged round with double negatives and alliterating Latinisms, the indirection of the grammar reflects the indirection of the Duke's motives, which are precisely the opposite of what he avows. His condescension, as he steps back to allow the deferential envoy to accompany him, as a social equal, out of the room, is devoid of feeling: it is a subtle theatrical trick, a way of affirming the pride it seems to modify. Only the arrogant aristocrat who chooses "Never to stoop" can afford to stoop at all without loss of dignity. Hence the weird feel of the social play acting; everything moves by mysterious theatrical convention. The envoy and the Duchess are puppets controlled by unseen machinery, and even the Duke, in extending civilities to a menial he despises, seems to be speaking through a ventriloquist. By rhyming "rarity" and "me," the last couplet reminds us that the Duke is a unique specimen and can properly be connected only with a "rarity." The very task of relating several of the terms placed together makes the reader aware of new combinations. The "fair daughter's self" will never be as "fair" as the more concretely described statue or as any of the other works of art that her dowry will allow the Duke to buy. By concentrating meaning into the pure forms of marital property and financial obligation, abstractions like "fair daughter's self" and "known munificence" admit sharp contrasts to the speaker's lively appreciation of his art.

The final picture of the Duke, pointing with a grand gesture to his statue of Neptune boldly "Taming a sea-horse," brings to mind the contrasting picture of the Duchess, riding round the terrace on her mule. The mule and the sea horse are superficially appropriate to the Duchess and the Duke, respectively. But if the Duke identifies himself with the lusty Neptune mastering the unruly beast, it is the Duchess herself who must figure as the sea horse; submissive only in death, as the sea horse is in art, she has always been indomitable in real life.

The final images carry a great weight of meaning, once we make relevant associations with the earlier "fool" and "mule." The images are sufficiently generalized to effect a reversal unobtrusively, but suggestive enough to accommodate Browning's own indictment of the speaker. When the Duke refers to his statue of Neptune's taming a sea horse, a lurking suspicion that the Duke is indulging in wish fulfillment leaps suddenly to attention to assert its primacy. For, as we have seen, the Duke reveals just enough about the Duchess to indicate that she would not allow the curtain to be drawn over her while alive. His wife's picture is the Duke's "hang-up," in both a literal and Freudian sense.[12] By reducing his frustrations to the theatrics of social play acting, the Duke's speech is a means of re-enacting, and thus of artfully discharging, the real humiliation which he suffered in his last marriage, and which has been revived on the present occasion by the distasteful act of having to "stoop" to negotiate another marriage—to a mere Count's daughter—and with a social inferior at that. Browning has not chosen his auditor casually. The envoy on his marriage mission is precisely the person to revive the Duke's memories of his last marriage. As an emissary of a count, he is important enough to give the Duke a sense of power in manipulating his responses, yet at the same time he is insignificant enough to remove any of the Duke's fears that his puppet might take on independent life. The envoy's mission revives traumatic memories from the Duke's past. But they are memories which, once revived, the

---

[12] I am indebted for this observation to Professor Dean Blehert.

Duke can amplify and correct before a submissive auditor who enables him to transform the past into what it ought to have been.

The Duke's theatrical indirection is really evidence of his psychological complexity, suggesting Freud's profoundly dramatic notion of compulsive or obsessive behavior that attains expression by theatrical subterfuges designed to evade traumatic psychological experiences, often sexual in their origin. The Duke's behavior conforms precisely to Freud's classic analysis of the obsessional neurosis.[13] It transforms and corrects the domestic situation giving rise to his obsession. The ceremonious rhetoric, matchlessly contrived to secure, from the first lordly gesture to the final impudent levity, a breath-taking progression of dramatic shocks, keeps suggesting that the Duke is play acting, and that however reprehensible he may really be, he is not Satanic in the grand Miltonic way he would like the envoy and the reader to believe he is. As Robert Langbaum finely says, the last ten lines "produce a series of shocks that outstrip each time our understanding of the duke, and keep us panting after revelation."[14] It is almost as though the Duke is afraid to be dull and must keep up a rapid succession of dazzling paradoxes and ever more violent shocks, which a less inwardly disturbed or compulsive rhetorician would be content to let lapse. One keeps sensing that the Duke is trying to evade the threat of personal catastrophe by building a fence and by constantly busying himself with doing something. According to Freud, "The actions performed in an obsessional condition are supported by a kind of energy which probably has no counterpart in normal mental life."[15] The Duke makes a

---

[13] Sigmund Freud, *A General Introduction to Psychoanalysis*, tr. Joan Riviere (New York, 1960), pp. 268–283.
[14] *The Poetry of Experience*, p. 84.
[15] *A General Introduction to Psychoanalysis*, pp. 270–271.

tyranny, not only within his own domestic life, but also within the theatrical domain of art. The Duke resembles Browning himself in relation to the reader, and calculates every phrase and gesture that will force his own will or aesthetic intention on the envoy.

Like most victims of obsessional neurosis, the Duke occupies himself with such matters as the envoy's sitting and rising, which do not really interest him. Freud observes that such people "perform actions which . . . afford [them] no pleasure"—like the Duke's telling of his wife's attentions to Fra Pandolf, for example, which must be painful to recall but which he is compelled to talk about. The behavior of the neurotic may, according to Freud, be "absolutely silly," as the Duke's revelations would seem to be in view of his negotiations for another wife. Though such apparent "silliness" has led critics like B. R. Jerman to call the speaker "witless," the Duke seems more the obsessional neurotic as Freud describes him. He is "originally always a person of a very energetic disposition, often highly opinionated, and as a rule intellectually gifted above the average."[16] Laurence Perrine's excellent analysis of the Duke's shrewdness, a valuable antidote to theories of his witlessness, emphasizes this aspect of his character.[17] The Duke is overconscientious and more than usually correct in extending his courtesies to the envoy. In keeping with Freud's diagnosis, the Duke's genius in controlling the responses of the envoy and his skillful use of rhetoric are evidence of superior intellect. But he devotes these powers to such ostensibly "silly" ends that, as Freud observes of the neurotic, "it is a sufficiently arduous task to find one's bearings in this maze of contradictory character-traits and morbid manifestations. . . . Only one thing is open to him . . . instead of one silly idea he can adopt an-

[16] *Ibid.*, p. 271.
[17] "Browning's Shrewd Duke," *PMLA*, LXXIV (1959), 157–159.

other of a slightly milder character." [18] This is precisely
what the Duke does at the end of the poem, when he identifies himself with the lusty Neptune and sees the woman as
the mule. He "can displace his sense of compulsion, but he
cannot dispel it." He must repeat and correct the traumatic
domestic situation that has given rise to his ceremonial compulsion.

The Duke forgets the nominal purpose of his interview
and substitutes a fantasy of sexual seduction for the immediate rhetorical "seduction" of the envoy. His monologue is a
grotesque form of social courtship, involving as it does communication between hierarchically related orders. Verbal
"courtship" of an inferior embodies the hierarchical principle
of which the Duke is so conscious, and it is a surrogate for
the rhetoric of sexual courtship, much of whose "mystery"
likewise proceeds from inequalities in social status. "The
Bishop Orders His Tomb" offers a similar parody of courtship when the old ecclesiastic turns his death bed into a
satyr's bed and acts out in fantasy a kind of sexual seduction
of his late mistress but fails in his "courtship" of the heirs.
But whereas the Bishop's failure is largely a result of the disparity between the two kinds of "courtship," the Duke's
substitution of a verbal and dramatic mode of "seduction"
provides him with a vicarious thrill. His private satisfaction is
to that extent a "mystery" and admittedly more important to
the Duke than the purchase of a dowry, as he himself avows,
though without ever understanding in what sense his repudiation of the financial motivation is valid. His rhetoric is a
parody of disinterested persuasion, designed less to sway an
auditor than to gratify that psychotic need of dominion and
ownership which compels him to treat the envoy, like his
"last Duchess," as another stage property.

The Duke's spellbinding performance before his auditor

18 *A General Introduction to Psychoanalysis*, p. 277.

enables him to glory in what Kenneth Burke has called "an aesthetic of crime which is infused, however perversely, with the 'mystery' of aristocracy." [19] He represents "aristocratic vice," criminality that has the appeal of dramatic style. This is because Browning has cast the Duke as the outrageous producer of a social play which must bring into harmony with the prejudices of the speaker's own taste every spontaneous action of the Duchess. The Duke's theatrical sense, finely adjusted and revealing no more than a shadow of concern with the nominal purpose of his interview, results in the removal of the speaker from the reader and in the willed isolation of his person. He is the compulsive producer who must re-enact on a stage flattering to his thwarted ego the drama of his past domestic life, and who, with all the craft of the spellbinder's art, deliberately sets out to control the responses of the envoy. The Duke's treatment of his auditor is strikingly rhetorical; he gives evidence of what Burke would call a "pantomimic" morality always on the alert for slight advantages. Even his self-abasement before his visitor is a form of self-exaltation, "the first 'stratagem' of pride."

Thus, to see Browning's Duke as a theatrical producer is not to suspend our moral judgment of him. The intellectual sympathy that allows Browning to understand a point of view so different from his own also allows him to uncover its internal contradictions. Beneath the surface brilliance lies the doom of Auden's "intellectuals without love." The poem's last phrase, "for me," re-establishes the whole proprietary nature of the Duke and rules out any possibility of a final redemption before he disappears forever by descending the staircase into what is at once a literary immortality and an insolently courted hell of personal damnation. The speaker is as surely imprisoned by his senses as any inhabitant of Dante's Inferno. Only an interpretation of this kind can account for

[19] *A Rhetoric of Motives*, p. 145.

the complex moral and aesthetic response which Browning's Duke arouses. The present reading enriches existing ideas about the poem by linking a disciplined attention to rhetoric with the hypothesis that the Duke is staging a "show" which enables him to transform his domestic past into what he believes it should have been. The Duchess, of course, may be the victim and the envoy the stooge, but only the Duke, in his bland amorality, is duped. The craft of the producer, whose theatrical self fiercely wills the extinction of every other self, becomes a metaphor for the damnation of all self-deceived and egocentric men.

⟡ 12 ⟡

If the Duke of "My Last Duchess" is a frustrated sensualist, the cleric of "The Bishop Orders His Tomb at St. Praxed's Church" is a satisfied and indulgent one, who is frustrated only by approaching death. He uses his trite moral tags in the same way that the Duke employs conventional social gestures. The Bishop's platitudes enforce upon himself conventional religious ideas, whose real meaning is outside his experience. He is full of practical wisdom, a wisdom of saws and proverbs founded on concrete examples, but like the Duke, he can grasp nothing beyond his senses.

Though the dying Bishop tries to prolong his sensuous life, his inability to do so is Browning's final comment on the futility of the aesthetic stage. As an object of Browning's irony, the Bishop is incapable of irony himself. Deluded by his own partial vision, the Bishop in his idolatry shows just the kind of warped perspective that the dialectical critic likes to imitate and discredit. There is no remedy for the Bishop's despair. The closest he comes to a cure is at the end of the poem, when he accurately appraises his heirs' indifference. But because he is incapable of raising himself to the higher ethical stage, his end is marked by a return to sensuous enjoyment, and the moment for transformation is lost. He has alienated his soul in a love for sensuous objects, and his incapacity to exist even in this life makes his desire for immortality doubly pathetic.

Only physical sensations can penetrate the Bishop's mind. One reason why Gandolf keeps entering the poem is that the speaker is always viewing his rival's "onion-stone." This paltry tomb stimulates the Bishop's delusions and turns him into a grotesque Faustus of the senses. Like much baroque sculpture, the tomb he envisions is a metaphysical conceit in stone. The erotic Pan jammed in between St. Praxed and Moses becomes a stereoscope for envisioning ideas. Because it provides outrageous or unusual bases for analogy, it is also a fertile source of conceits. The anticlimax arrives with a severe alliterative jolt: "Saint Praxed in a glory, and one Pan." The point of shock comes with the twitching of the nymph's last garment. The possible religious analogy breaks down with the recognition that this is not the mighty Pan of Milton's ode on Christ's Nativity, but a satyr. The juxtaposition of the decapitated Jew's head and the Madonna's breast is also a source of wit. By mixing religious and erotic elements, the Bishop turns all his powers to an act of self-celebration, in emphatic parody of the lavish use of gifts which Ruskin extols in Gothic ornament. His playful, half-irrelevant fancy of the "sunbeam" sure to "lurk" in the "aery dome" approaches Ruskin's "sportive grotesque." But as he strips the human anatomy into dismembered "nape," "head," "breast," and "heart," the physical parts begin to clash outrageously with his architectural conceits. Even the religious patterns, instead of transferring their dignity to him, have more in common with the mock-heroic and turn him into a kind of Epicure Mammon quoting the Book of Job.

The Bishop wants to use God's name to give authority to his own schemes. But in his delirium he reverses the direction of the transfer, and instead of passing from himself to God, he arrogates to himself the function of God in the Eucharist. Unable to use the word "mass" to denote a religious mystery, he reduces it to a form of cannibalism ("And see God made and eaten all day long"), which feeds into his own demonic parody: "Will ye ever eat my heart?" Unalleviated by any interpreting mind, such savagery enables the reader to share the very touch and feel of sensuality. Stripped and prepared for the cannibal feast of his tormentors, the Bishop melodramatically identifies himself with the sacrificial body of God and sees himself as food for his heirs.

As the speaker begins to waver into fantasy, the very grossness of his perceptions denies the stability of his world. The paratactic syntax achieves an effect of delirious ecstasy and breaks down the Bishop's logical connections in a frenzy of descriptive detail:

> Your tall pale mother with her talking eyes
> *And* new-found agate urns as fresh as day,
> *And* marble's language   [ll. 96–98—italics mine].

Beginning at line 80, the conjunction "and" multiplies at an alarming rate. It ceases to be a genuine compounding word and becomes instead an index of greed that fractures rather than joins meanings. But though the logic is at fault, there is still a confused limpidity. The climactic delirium redramatizes former motives and gives resonance to the startling details. The lightness of logical connections gives the passage its surprises. All the terms are misplaced, with a total disregard for their earlier contexts. But the associations, no longer rationally controlled, are as revealing as the derangements of Lady Macbeth's sleep-walking speech.

The broken energy of the language, interspersed with dashes and ellipses, recalls the Bishop's grotesque praise of his lump of lapis lazuli—a swollen rhapsody, coarsely amplified and alliterated, then grammatically suspended. At the height of his delirium, the brief clauses, logically unconnected, recall the earlier staccato passages, where the words seem to jump with malicious agitation: "For Gandolf shall not choose but see and burst!" He jolts crookedly from one detail to the next in myopic pursuit of the sensual satisfaction closest at hand. The decadent Latin is a delightful parody of the Bishop's earlier instructions for a Ciceronian epitaph, whose language he now confuses with the postclassical Latin of Ulpian. The rhetorical inversion of the trite religious tag ("Evil and brief hath been my pilgrimage") is an echo of the pseudopoetic "Swift as a weaver's shuttle fleet our years." Even the greedy request for a tomb of "Peach-blossom marble" is confused and becomes a demand for "All lapis, all." The most revealing lines join deceptively similar grammatical and rhythmic forms with sharp conflicts of meaning. He telescopes his former pictures of St. Praxed and Christ into a vision of "Saint Praxed at his sermon on the mount," then confuses them both with the "tall pale mother with her talking eyes." These dislocations are calculated means of discrediting the Bishop. They force us to reorder his confused and deficient moral attitudes with new insight.

In his climactic delirium, as the Bishop's true motives surge to the surface, the beliefs that lie deepest are enacted in swelling delusions of avarice and lust. His sensuality becomes an irrational compulsion that turns his words into weapons of greed. His grammar has always been active; even the ejaculation "Ah God, I know not" seems to rearrange itself into the damaging formation: "God [whom] I know not." All along the Bishop has shown himself to be garrulous and repetitive. But now the double entendres become more extravagant and betray the full extent of his compulsion. The punning syllepsis of his "praying . . . mistresses" recalls the way he has "preyed" on Gandolf for his sensual satisfactions. As he

imagines his repose, while he folds the great laps of the bed-
clothes and is thrilled by his mistress' glittering eyes, his sanctified tomb becomes a kind of satyr's bed; his sons' cannibalism mocks the very seat of their begetting.

Depth psychology has shown that contradictory meanings
often coexist at the unconscious level. The Bishop's halluci-
nations are now bringing these contradictions into focus, like
repressed material under psychoanalysis. The active grammar
and the puns function as "counterlogical elements," to use
W. K. Wimsatt's term. Though the counterlogical character
of double entendres and puns has little, if any, aesthetic value
by itself, Wimsatt has argued that such elements "save the
physical quality of words." [20] In Wimsatt's new version of
the critic's role, there should be a "marked correlation not
between poems and contemporary poetics but actually between poems and contemporary anti-poetics." [21] This is particularly true in Browning's case, especially when the grossness of his speaker forces him to stress the physical elements
of words.

The Bishop's whole ritual of ordering his tomb is a form
of wish fulfillment, a way of transforming his grave into a
satyr's bed adorned with the emblems of Bacchus, which
brings to a climax most of the poem's earlier motives.
Throughout the poem the alliterative binders have exaggerated the physical qualities of "God" and "gritstone," "leisure" and "leers," "twitch" and "tables." Ordinarily, the
experience of making contact with sensuous reality is a rare
event in reading poetry, which the very nature of language
denies us. But "The Bishop Orders His Tomb" enacts more
of its meaning than most poems. Alliterations like "Big . . .
blue . . . breast" keep achieving that feeling of enactment

[20] "One Relation of Rhyme to Reason," *The Verbal Icon* (Lexing-
ton, Ky., 1954), p. 166.
[21] "Rhetoric and Poems: Alexander Pope," *The Verbal Icon*, p. 185.

which proves the sensuous meaning of the words upon our pulses:

> Some lump, ah God, of *lapis lazuli*,
> Big as a Jew's head cut off at the nape,
> Blue as a vein o'er the Madonna's breast   [ll. 42–44].

Just as the Bishop has prodded us into associating the block of jasper with the New Jerusalem, the alliteration of "pure" and "pistachio-nut" comes to his aid as a humorous binder. As in the unlikely linking of incoherence and mechanism with religious mystery ("mutter," "mass," and "made"), so the humor here depends upon the incongruity inherent in the coupling. The religious and erotic couplings of "Pan" with "Praxed," of the "popes . . . and priests" with the "pale mother," have implied some logical connection between the pagan god and the Christian saint; the joke is that we know there is none. But we are well on the way to believing it; the alliteration is at least a *fait accompli*. The Bishop's association of himself with "Pan / Ready to twitch the . . . last garment off" his mistress culminates in his vision of a bed-like tomb, decked out with thyrsus crowned with grapes, the special emblems of Bacchus and his satyrs. He thinks of the tomb as part of his physical body, and he feels himself into the "impoverished frieze" and "starved design" of the sculpture, which like its lusting inhabitant, requires "grapes" to sustain it. The Bishop's concept of God acquires its force only through a process of gradual association with words like "curse," "lump," "made," and "eaten" and with the "Gritstone" all "a-crumble"—an association which depends for its shock effect on the sheer, emotional impact of the oozing of the corpse through "Clammy squares."

In the closing scene the picture of the dying Bishop, crushed and humiliated, deepens momentarily into a vision of terror. The thwarted rhetorician, who would be the first to appreciate the irony of the word "orders" in the title, experiences a final break in his ties to humanity. In the arrested motion of his strategically placed participle ("and, *going*, turn your backs / . . . like departing altar-ministrants"—italics mine), the Bishop rhetorically exaggerates his heirs' ingratitude. His philosophic "Ay" and solemn repetition ("And leave me in my church, the church for peace") recapture the meditative rhythm of the opening line: "Vanity, saith the preacher, vanity!" But what he once mouthed as a mechanical formula he now actually feels. The Bishop is a master of gesture, of a theatrical eloquence beyond vocabulary. With this enactment of the speaker's meaning, Browning has exerted all the moral stress the poem will bear. The poseur must not be allowed to deepen into a tragic figure. It seems inevitable that the poet will transgress his bounds and pass beyond the sensualist's warped perspective. But with a last quick flourish the poet regains his balance. The closing lines galvanize this mock-pathetic languor into energetic life and comically redramatize the bases of the Bishop's savage animus, his grotesque hatred and outrageous lust.

Near the beginning of his monologue the Bishop asks for a definition of life. Though he never offers a formal reply, the rest of his speech provides his answer to himself. Life, for the Bishop, is an endless stream of physical sensations. Because nothing connects these sensations, his moral and philosophic platitudes set up no kind of commerce between his momentary existence and eternal existence. He is fast sinking into a stupor and is a little pathetic, because all his efforts to gratify the senses are only ineffectual gestures without duration.

The Bishop's conception of life turns out to be Browning's definition of death. There is a reversal in meaning, confirmed by the question "Do I live, am I dead?" which is twice repeated (ll. 13, 113). The Bishop, like the Duke, is implicated as a hell figure and assigned to a kind of negative eternity.

There is thus unconscious irony in his opening reflection: "And thence ye may perceive the world's a dream." The world is always a "dream" for the aesthetic man. At the height of his delirium, when everything becomes confused as in a nightmare, he recognizes the unreality of that sensuous world which he has spent his life in celebrating. As the lights go out and Gandolf begins to leer ominously from his darkened tomb, vistas of futility open on all sides, and we have, in spite of the comedy, a scene of nightmare and a close approach to something demonic. Because its pictorial brilliance and vividness, far from destroying the moral criticism, do much to clarify, and even deepen, its impact, "The Bishop Orders His Tomb," like "My Last Duchess," is as perfect a poem as any Browning wrote. As one of the most faultless presentations of the sensualist in literature, it provides an inexhaustible source of comedy. And since the Bishop's sensations are so sporadic and so frequently in danger of disintegrating, Browning can perfect his dialectical method by using this potentially tragic life to reveal the internal contradictions of the aesthetic stage.

13

We have seen that the aesthetic man's ennui renders him highly impressionable. Without any mediating mind, his masks are like negatives on which images are permanently printed. Deprived of all the devices of the subjective poet, these early monologues avoid potential monotony and exert a strange fascination, in the manner of Robbe-Grillet's novels. The speakers see and hear, but their minds cannot judge. Though they celebrate the power of sensuous objects, the speakers cannot project significance into these objects and cannot compare one object with another, for fear of suggesting a connection that does not exist. Because nothing is altered by the observer's attitude toward objects or by his conception of them, these monologues seldom use figurative language. When a speaker like the Duke of Ferrara commits the extravagance of using an adjective, it is usually as a chemist would, to convey precisely a conception of a physical property by an appeal to sense experience.

The boredom that characterizes such speakers, far from signifying a deficient imagination, may arise at times from an excess of that "make-believe" which exhausts the Duke's sense of power or the Bishop's sensual satisfactions. The ennui that mesmerizes Johannes Agricola into looking "night by night" at heaven is pathological and ends in violence. Whereas the genuinely religious Pompilia has the courage to will repetition instead of novelty in her constant celebration of her "soldier-saint," the aesthetic Agricola finds that through repetition the interesting grows stale unless he can continually excite himself with gratuitous touches of Gothic horror. Johannes has the artistic temperament without being an artist. Such men are dangerous. Just how dangerous we can see in "Porphyria's Lover" and "The Laboratory," which are, in essence, stories of artists without a medium. In his extreme form, in the Duke of Ferrara and later in Andrea del Sarto, the aesthetic man, unable to give vent to his impulses in satisfying creations, derives a perverse pleasure from frustrating his pleasure.

This complexity of motivation is partly a psychological defense: it is a protection against the intrusion of uncongenial minds, a dramatic correlative of Browning's own strategy of noncommitment, which will not allow the critics of *Pauline* to uncover his own attitudes. But his way of writing also conveys a view of life. In such enigmatic performances, ranging from the kind presented in the animated-cartoon world of "Protus" to Count Gauthier's highly melodramatic kind, the lighter and more entertaining elements of Browning's art both deepen and render more concrete the elements which are critical. The sense of caricature is deliberate. We feel ourselves looking at a world of gesticulating marionettes, going through their grotesque motions as some hidden puppeteer pulls the strings. Agricola's violence, the court lady's jealousy, and the Bishop's greed all lead to states of hysteria, in which the real world is transformed into a comic nightmare, reminding us, a little strangely, of a horror cartoon. The reader soon becomes aware that Browning's description of the surface of objects is more than a way of using words. Awareness of objects enters the speakers' minds only as sense perceptions. A style that will not allow the mind to invade the self-sufficiency of inanimate objects stresses the aesthetic man's bondage to the physical world. It enables Browning to explore with unparalleled immediacy and range the method of rotating pleasure by which the sensualist, caught in a closed cycle of frustrated passion, tries without success to evade boredom and despair.

6

Rhetoric at the Ethical Stage

If early poems like "The Confessional" and "Porphyria's Lover" are not as weighty and give expression to Browning's moral views more or less fitfully, his monologues at the ethical stage are the work of a Victorian sage who writes in the light of an insight and a group of moral ideas, with the discipline that comes from them. "Sibrandus Schafnaburgensis" is little more than an overflow of animal high spirits; and however delightful, it cannot compare with "Johannes Agricola in Meditation" or "The Bishop Orders His Tomb," where Browning combines entertainment with a deeper and more interesting moral significance. Though the aesthetic masks present roles with sharpness and immediacy, as early as February 11, 1845, in a letter to Miss Barrett, Browning refers contemptuously to "these scenes and song-scraps," which "*are* such mere and very escapes of [his] inner power." The valuable qualities of the early monologues are all qualities of a well-managed surface—which is not to say that such virtues are superficial. They impose on the poet a necessary discipline but fail to communicate to his readers even a small portion of his own values.

To mature as a dialectical poet, Browning must add to the sensational immediacy of his early masks a rhetorical signifi-

114

cance that enables him to develop his reader's moral and religious attitudes. Without retreating into the private symbols of a second *Sordello*, he must lay bare the issues basic to all significant conduct and, by dramatizing the factors present in all moral choice, force his readers to judge the inadequacies of life at the aesthetic stage. Browning is a dialectical poet who exposes the limitations that characterize most ideas and beliefs in order that his readers may mature and grow. One of the difficulties in reading such a poet is what Wayne Booth has called an attitude of "dogmatic neutrality" on the part of modern readers. Browning ridicules whatever is one-sided or absurd in the aesthetic state. But because many of us live at this stage ourselves and are accustomed to twentieth-century literary norms which present this state for our approval, we may resist Browning's appeal to overcome its limitations. By using irony to release the sensualist from aesthetic idolatry, Browning's major monologues make their speakers aware of social obligations and human bonds. Their Socratic dialectic makes the egoist conscious of other points of view less biased than his own. Moral criticism of the Victorian kind perhaps overstressed judgments and led to misreading. But "dogmatic neutrality," though less obvious, is equally dangerous to an understanding of Browning's ethical stage, and is certainly the greater danger among modern readers trying to interpret such monologues.

ᔅᔆ 1 ᔆᔅ

The love poems contain Browning's fullest account of the limitations that afflict the aesthetic man and eventually lead him to social or religious awareness. In "Love among the Ruins" (1852), which begins as an attempt to differentiate love from other activities at the aesthetic stage, the lover ends by discovering similarities never suspected, which he still only indirectly acknowledges and finally evades. "The Last

Ride Together" (1855) is a rationalization of the "rotation method," the sensualist's habit of passing from one pleasure to another. It mocks the excessive subtlety of the lover's logic and the futility of his false ascent. The most searching of the love poems, "Two in the Campagna" (1854), converts the Shelleyan plea for free love advanced by an argumentative Don Juan into a recognition of his own isolation and despair. Though it looks forward prophetically to the "Infinite passion" of the ethical and religious lives celebrated in the Epilogue to *Ferishtah's Fancies* and "Prospice," the "finite hearts that yearn" remain in bondage to the senses. At the aesthetic stage the "good moment" may be a moment of love, but it is still love in anguish. This despair, most honestly acknowledged in "Two in the Campagna," appears as agonizing doubt in the Epilogue to *Ferishtah's Fancies*. But where the lover cannot annihilate himself before God there can be no dialectical advance. Browning cannot restore the reader's experience of belief without restoring his experience of unbelief at the same time. We should not celebrate Browning as the apologist of Victorian theology without remembering the anguish of his own resolutions. It requires such despair to catapult the ethical man into the higher religious sphere. "Prospice" (1861), in which the lover completes his dialectical ascent, is a much more moving poem if read as the culmination of this process. Only by tracing the drama of Browning's own advance can we feel the full impact of his final affirmations.

The speaker in "Love among the Ruins" implies that he and the girl should repeat the triumphs of the teeming grass and blooming houseleeks, the incontinence of a prolific natural order. By confining transience to Roman hedonism, he wants to confer a delusive duration on his own "good moment." But the shift in tenses involves the present in the folly of the "king" who "looked, where she looks now" (l. 59).

The lover participates in that hedonism, and its voluptuousness is still going on. The sensual motives which the lover tries to liberate are precisely those attitudes which he finds transient in the past. The real analogy is not between the lovers and nature—a realm of "undistinguished gray" which, in contrast to the girl with the "eager eyes and yellow hair," cannot achieve even the dignity of consciousness. The important connection is between the speaker and those ardent "charioteers" of old whose "soul" caught fire "For [their] goal." The voluptuousness of the imperial past, at first introduced as a minor detail, leaps to attention. The "emancipation" which the lover seeks is a form of sensual bondage; the life he celebrates, another pagan death.

The final affirmation, "Love is best," is not a declaration that Browning makes himself. It is an attempt at persuasive definition by the speaker, who reaffirms the traditional emotive meaning of the term "love" as one of value. But because it might normally be associated with "the monarch and his minions and his dames"—a species of "love" that has just been discredited as "folly, noise and sin"—he shifts its descriptive meaning. Convinced of the uniqueness of his own adventure, the lover is trying to narrow the prize word's connotation and to redirect attention to differences between his own love and "the monarch's." The difficulty is that the poem will not support this redirection. His metaphors have established too many links between the girl and the Roman voluptuaries for him to disavow the connections now. The lover is a victim of his own language, trapped in a symbolic matrix of his own making. Browning's method is related to the practice of Victorians like George Eliot and Carlyle; and John Holloway has shown the enormous importance in their rhetoric of redefining or manipulating terms.

A recent critic, William Cadbury, has called "Love among the Ruins" a failure, because its unreliable narrator uses

spurious arguments in enunciating a doctrine of love's worth
—a belief which Browning formulates seriously in other
poems, and so apparently intended us to accept here. "Instead of a lyric about love we have an anti-lyric about a
narrator," says the critic, and concludes that "the failure of
the poem is [therefore] a failure in basic strategy." [1] Cadbury's argument is a shrewd one but illustrates, I think, the
danger of working with only two categories. Unlike a
"lyric," "Love among the Ruins" is not merely an overflow
of powerful feelings. But unlike the early masks, it is not
simply a picture of static characters either. In their mature
form, the monologues are a record of the dialectical process
by which a character comes to *realize* his attitudes. At the
beginning of the poem the lover is trying to secure some personal advantage from the woman. But by revealing the
absurdity of the seducer's role, the poem invites the speaker
to discard his sensuality for a set of attitudes that can discover, spread, and multiply significance.

The lover is about to make this advance when his perception changes. His final affirmation that "Love is best" is a
statement of truths for which there are no large words,
truths which must, to be apprehended at all, be invested in
common language. But this dropping of rhetorical artifice
should not mislead us. The lover's statement carries little
conviction, because it is really an evasion. We should not
reduce it by sentimental quotation to an attitude which
Browning offers solemnly for our approval, for it is inseparable from the disturbing revelation that love is itself a kind of
death:

> Oh heart! oh blood that freezes, blood that burns!
> Earth's returns

---

[1] "Lyric and Anti-Lyric Forms: A Method for Judging Browning,"
University of Toronto Quarterly, XXXIV (1964), 66.

For whole centuries of folly, noise and sin!
Shut them in,
With their triumphs and their glories and the rest!
Love is best   [ll. 79–84].

Though his thought keeps maturing, the contradictions of the aesthetic life are too painful for the lover to face. A mystery is present, but its solution is not the discovery that "Love is best." As the goal of Browning's own quest, the resolution of this mystery includes all the ironies of human life. Because it can be approached only by one who has first experienced "Earth's returns / For whole centuries of folly, noise and sin," the lover's relation to this mystery is, at most, heuristic. Here we meet the disturbing insight at the center of Browning's much debated "philosophy of imperfection." Though Browning had defined it as the poet's task, not even his own poems succeed in "putting the infinite into the finite." There is present here a Carlylean sense of emerging from the inane, hastening stormfully across the astonished earth, then plunging again into the inane. The speaker is deeply aware of the terrors as well as the sanctities of time, of the undertow of oblivion flowing just below the surface of history itself. For the "blood that freezes" and the "blood that burns" the total truth is like physical death. This is its excitement, promise, and terror—that no one can experience it without being destroyed.

ɷ 2 ɷ

The sensuous ecstasy in which the speaker of "Love among the Ruins" seeks refuge is marked by a transience which raises the question: In what kind of experience is it possible to possess one's life? "The Last Ride Together" (1855) is Browning's criticism of the romantic solution. It exposes to ridicule the boast of a lover that, in taking possession of his beloved, he is taking possession of all time.

The speaker is master of just enough rhetoric to make his lament following the lady's rejection of him sound heroic. His life has been broken in the middle, and can reform itself only out of "memory" of "the hope [she] gave." The opening prepares for a rebuke; instead, after four lines of lament, we get the most lavish compliment. The noble lover appears to do with no trouble at all what we should expect him to do with great difficulty. In celebrating his own forgiving nature, he is celebrating the very egoism which is the enemy of self-criticism. His heroic statements emphasize only the make-believe and transience of his "instant made eternity."

Everything hinges on the lady's acceding to his trivial last request. "With life or death in the balance," his plea to go riding with her travesties the kind of awe the religious man should feel only before God. It is quite clear that the mistress is indifferent; there is nothing reciprocal, and hence nothing real, about this adventure. Instead of allowing him to mature and grow, this failure prompts the lover to assess the comparable failures of poets, sculptors, and musicians. Since little escapes Browning's criticism, it is fatal to follow Santayana in taking the idea of a heaven in which the lovers can ride forever as the poet's own concept of love. The more the speaker protests his assurance, the less we are meant to believe it. The distance separating price and prize—"I gave my youth; but we ride, in fine"—keeps laying bare the gap between promise and fruition. The lover's "heaven" is only a fiction, and his "eternity" an "instant." The romantic "solution" lacks the anonymous authority of a moral tradition. Its consolations are willful where they should be authoritative, self-deluded and eccentric where they should be objective.

3

The most dialectical of the love poems, "Two in the Campagna" (1854), clarifies the limitations of the aesthetic point of view presented in "Love among the Ruins." The speaker is a scholastic Don Juan who begins by celebrating the erotic life, like Donne's lover in "The Ecstasy." But the coda overcomes these limitations by dramatizing the lover's sympathetic identification with the pain and mystery of all human life.

The speaker is the victim of his own analogies, and in using repulsive spider and beetle imagery, he does not "come out" where he had planned to. "The grassy slope," "brickwork's cleft," and phallic "towers" are erotically alluring. But the five beetles groping in the honey-meal suggest a kind of sexual mounting of the small orange cup and a teeming promiscuity that is unexpectedly hideous. A psychological critic like Betty Miller, who builds up an interesting case against Browning's overly assertive masculinity,[2] would probably explain such imagery as his disguised revulsion against bodily contact. In such words as "primal" and "naked," as in many pictures of the Golden Age, including the depiction of Eden itself, there is a sense of being close to moral taboos. The strident anaphora ("*Such* life," "*Such* miracles," "*Such* . . . forms," "*Such* letting"—italics mine) is fiercely exultant, and his Shelleyan inference that he and the woman should love as freely as nature becomes explicit in his next simile: "As earth lies bare to heaven above!" If "heaven" is the "unashamed . . . soul," then the "earth" that "lies bare" to it must be the body. Though the metaphysics of his attempt at seduction recalls the scholastic argument of "The Ecstasy," this plea marks the turning-point of the little drama, not its climax. The invitation to descend to physical satisfaction brings a contradictory revulsion, which surges to consciousness in his question: "How is it under our control / To love or not to love?"

The disquisition that follows is the climax of the poem.

[2] *Robert Browning, a Portrait* (London, 1952).

The movement is still lyrical, but there is now a counter-pointing rhythm that resists any impulse to ecstatic song. The lover wants to possess his life in the erotic instant, but even if "the good minute" were to bring him in a lightning flash the intense experience he seeks, he realizes it would be a moment without duration. His possession of "the good minute" immediately becomes a dispossession that ends in the feeling of a loss renewed: "Already how am I so far / Out of that minute?" The language sets up a disturbing tension between the warm and familiar ("soul's warmth," "touch you close") and the cold and remote ("stand away," "Onward, whenever . . . winds blow"). The spiders' "thread" and "thistle-ball" are at once present to the witnessing eye. As in "Love among the Ruins," the truth to which the poem points has a nostalgic quality, a depth of brooding introspection, that cannot be reached, and perhaps could not have been borne by Browning if it were. The speaker loves the woman "more than tongue can speak." But he also feels a pang of the soul's incurable loneliness—what Yeats called the "tragedy of love," the "perpetual virginity of the soul." With complete candor the man tells her that she means "just so much" to him, "no more." This process of reversal is carefully prepared for and works even at the level of single words, as in the reduction of a lover to an insect. At the moment of separation Don Juan himself becomes a beetle in a hideous Kafka-like metamorphosis. His inability to complete the argument confirms our suspicion of his growing revulsion. We witness the irony of a rhetorician's twisting logic to his own seductive purposes but using a contradictory kind of image that deviates from the original line of reasoning and arrives symbolically at an opposite conclusion.

Because he inherits with Don Juan's role a sensual point of view that he is already outgrowing, the speaker finds it hard to express his discovery in words. This is the paradox "he

seemed about to learn," but which his assumption of a seducer's attitude prevents him from communicating. His
amusement at his own failure to follow the argument—his
sense that he has lost "the thread"—seems at first to refer to
his Shelleyan plea for free love. But he has not really lost that
"thread," for he states the conclusion of that line of reasoning only to reject it. The lost "thread" must be the need for
a moral displacement of the seducer's attitudes. By establishing contact with other "finite hearts," the sensualist is trying
to outgrow his original responses. The "Infinite passion" that
brings all men together is not a mere evasion, like the complacent reflection that "Love is best." The speaker's ironic
acceptance is inseparable from the effort of communal love,
and even "Infinite passion" includes the irony of "finite
hearts that yearn," the lostness of the unfinished man and his
pain. The nostalgia for the infinite must increasingly pre-
occupy the lover in view of the hopelessness and brevity of
his life. Love seeks to accept this burden of despair and is not
adequate. The speaker refuses to counterfeit his certainty;
and as the argument unfolds, Browning assimilates new perceptions to discredit the point of view he began by imitating.
The direct facing of inner loneliness exposes the absurdity of
the seducer's role. But because it enables the speaker to grow
in awareness, Browning's dialectical method enriches rather
than violates the structure of the whole. The integrity of the
close depends on the honesty of recognizing the lostness, and
by that very recognition maintaining control.

*** 4 ***

Instead of consigning its victims to sensual bondage, love
can also motivate a dialectical ascent. In the Epilogue to
Ferishtah's Fancies (1883) it allows Browning to substitute
for his aesthetic life, when he "boylike sulked or whined," an
active enlistment in the ethical fight of battling it "like men."

Love also prepares for his final religious ascent in response to "God's 'Come!' " But in a moment of Shelleyan reverie, when the poet sees the world revealed in moonlight as a splendor of "good and beauty, wonder crowning wonder," a paralyzing doubt forces him to ask whether all such ascents are "mere fool's-play." Browning dramatizes the dark foundations of belief, the voids beneath the affirmations of theology. All reputations disappear, and the ethical or religious life seems just as precarious as the hedonist's. In his exploration of design and possible chaos in the universe, the poet will have to accept the ever present terrors as they are. His resolution is an act of faith, and it ends, not with a strident declaration, but with a searching question. The poet who grants that his central faith may be in error lives from a great depth of being; his admission is an impressive example of what Arnold calls "living by ideas" and of the critical spirit at work.

Even in "Prospice" (1861), which is Browning's strongest affirmation of immortality, his assurance that love for his wife will continue after death is won only with difficulty. As in Browning's other "testament" poem, "Confessions" (1859), it is only when time breaks apart, when the sick man hears the "buzzing" in his ears and discovers himself to be dying, that the instant of love becomes an eternal instant, a "perpetual now" that seems comparable to a simultaneous contemplation of all the moments in his life.

Just when Browning isolates himself most thoroughly, he is most completely united, like Childe Roland, with his "peers, / The heroes of old." The choice to confront death heroically is not just the cry of a hot-headed little gentleman bouncing out of his moral gymnasium into the silence of eternity. It is a personal decision to will courageously his own death, to make it an experience like Ulysses' last voyage, in Dante's and Tennyson's poems. What is lacking perhaps is repentance, the form that the battle with death traditionally takes. But Browning ennobles his death by choosing it, and in a rapid escalation of the three stages he passes from erotic love to the warrior's moral heroism and to a transformation of his love for Elizabeth into love of God at the end.

The abyss of the "black minute" when he is plunged into a void of raging elements and raving voices is the breach in which the ethical man becomes wholly nothing and continues to exist only through the grace of God, who renews his life from instant to instant. Browning formulates this dialectical advance through antithesis and paradox. The dark precedes the light and the pain the peace, as "sudden the worst turns the best to the brave," and the raving voices give place to his wife's "breast":

> And the elements' rage, the fiend-voices that rave,
>   Shall dwindle, shall blend,
> Shall change, shall become first a peace out of pain,
>   Then a light, then thy breast,
> Oh thou soul of my soul! I shall clasp thee again,
>   And with God be the rest!   [ll. 23–28].

Death becomes a dialectical term, implying its opposite, life. As the eternal instant unfolds majestically out of the black minute, the logical end of this progression is no longer dissolved in Platonic mist, as it is in Browning's early subjective poems. It is clearly beheld, in light instead of fog now, as his wife's redeeming person. Unlike Elizabeth's seductive caress in the Epilogue to *Ferishtah's Fancies*, her breast is no longer a reduction of divine love, but Browning's most assuring symbol of God's presence in the world.

Associated at the end with Christ, Elizabeth, in "Prospice," represents the attractions of religious mystery, "ordained" with the properties of a transcendent order of which she is now a part. But her power is still rhetorical, and she per-

suades her lover only because he must work to reach her.
The Victorian sage cannot allow a scaffold of ideas to replace the anguish of his own resolutions. His wife's "divinity" depends upon the thoroughness, even the rigor, of
Browning's dialectical enterprise. The lover's ascent of the
mountain, while involving physical dangers and exertions,
seems almost mystical, and is undertaken in answer to a call,
like the climbing of the mountain in Dante's *Il Purgatorio*,
which Browning may have had in mind. By combining erotic
meaning with the spiritual motivations of Dante's poem,
"Prospice" anticipates Browning's methods in *The Ring and
the Book*, which is one of the most exhaustive treatments of
such transcendence in English literature. In the lovers'
"dying" together, then ecstatically embracing, there would
be symbolically a consummation—an erotic union which
Browning converts into a metaphor of celestial union. Only
by using such imagery can the dialectician force us onto
levels of religious awareness that command our own assent.

5

" 'Childe Roland to the Dark Tower Came' " (January 2,
1852), which is Browning's most sustained use of the metaphor of a journey, will seem less enigmatic when approached,
like "Prospice," as a poem of transition and growth. But
whereas "Prospice" is on the plane of rational imagination,
"Childe Roland" enacts the very process of spiritual growth.
We have seen in the dramatic monologues how Browning's
intellectual sympathy enables him to criticize different points
of view from within. The only way he can enact a movement of transition and growth is by rehearsing a whole series
of roles. When the Victorian sage condenses this process into
a single poem like "Prospice," his willed understanding can
grasp the movement only from outside. "Childe Roland" is
Browning's attempt to combine the intellectual sympathy of

the dramatic poet with the economy of the sage. How can he place himself inside his subject, like the impersonator who writes dramatic monologues, and at the same time enact in a single poem a dialectical advance which only a whole succession of dramatic monologues can present?

Instead of merely exposing the limitations of a particular point of view, "Childe Roland" actually dramatizes the dialectical movement from one set of attitudes to another which such exposure makes possible. It perceives this transition from within by securing from dream experience a primary level of significance to which any reader may be expected to respond, without loss to any other level of significance. Browning told a stranger that the poem "came upon [him] as a kind of dream." To enact the process of transition, he appeals to the unconscious levels of our dream life, levels of response that enable him to reach the widest possible audience.

At the beginning of the poem Childe Roland abandons his hope of reaching the Tower: "just to fail as they, seemed best." But by renouncing hope he has unconsciously taken his first step. His willed death is a kind of birth in disguise, like the lovers' death in "Prospice." It is also an indication of incipient holiness, in Yeats's sense of sanctity as a "renunciation of personal salvation." Just as the relatives, who think the dying man is unconscious, cause him an anguish he cannot express, so Roland cannot articulate his suffering. Because he cannot dramatize the voids beneath his language or the terror in which he inwardly exists, the knight's attitude toward the world must be the ironical pose of the dying man who "may not shame such tender love." Forced back upon his inner resources, he can adopt no conventional attitudes. We glimpse his inner life only in certain obsessive images: the gesturing of the cripple or the terror of dying, which recalls the dark moment of "Prospice." Browning is a master of compressed insight and sudden illumination, witnessed in such recurrent images. His knight is passing beyond the aesthetic stage, even though in making the transition, he is "quiet as despair."

Despite his passivity, Roland is never in total bondage to his senses, if only because he can shift at will from one aspect of his situation to another. His imagination discloses so many possibilities that only by careful rereading can we distinguish actuality from make-believe. It may surprise the reader to recall that Roland never sees the water rats or the savage strife between "toads" in a "poisoned tank" and "cats" in a "cage." Even the supposed deception of the cripple is an imagined self-deception. At the sacrifice of vividness, Browning keeps inserting the words "like" and "so": "The fight must *so* have seemed," "*like* two bulls," "*like* giants at a hunting" (italics mine). This cautious use of simile is Browning's way of reminding us that, however accurately such fantasies may define Childe Roland's anguish, the terrors are only hypothetical ones and not externally real. Roland's speculations demonstrate that he can detach himself from the outer world and assume attitudes toward the "merely possible." We must not underestimate the power of rational imagination that continues to operate in "Childe Roland" even in the face of mystery. At the end of the poem, far from acquiring the exaggerated importance that we associate with Browning's early sensualists, the external impressions do not appear to register on the knight at all. The irony of Roland's not seeing the tower when daylight illuminates it and of not hearing the bells when they are tolling dramatizes, once again, the power of the rational imagination to detach itself from its environment.

The middle stanzas illustrate how Roland can escape the aesthetic man's bondage to his senses. Instead of passively receiving his sensations, he establishes the landscape as a focus for his inward nature. Like the Ancient Mariner, Childe Roland creates a supernatural world with a strange logic and coherence of its own. He conveys an impression of dream —of an abstracting poetry that will not confront his waking experience. Though his brilliant and absorbing visual impressions cling to the memory like a nightmare we remember, the eerie vista of the "grim / Red leer" and the "dying sunset" moving through a vibrant atmosphere, densely charged with bleeding color, runs directly counter to the "pathetic fallacy of the Romantic egoist. Instead of personifying the inanimate, Roland empathizes with the impersonal. By acts of sympathetic imagination he senses the intrinsic nature of inanimate objects. But unlike the sensualist, who becomes what he beholds, the knight can imaginatively re-create the quality of ghastly vibration in the spectral red which blazes forth in the "fire" of the Last Judgment, the "blades . . . kneaded with blood," the "red . . . neck," the "reddening face," the "rusty teeth" of the instruments of torture, and the final "sheet of flame."

The setting is not scrupulously externalized but becomes a kind of interior landscape, like the "Unreal City" of T. S. Eliot's "The Waste Land." The nightmare quality is evident in the way in which events merge without apparent logic or transition. The knight finds himself alone on a ghastly plain of weeds and stunted grass. A "blind horse" suddenly materializes out of nowhere, then just as mysteriously vanishes. Such passages imply that there are no precise limits to indicate where the subjective order ends and the natural world begins. As in the processional visions of a dream, the knight's lost comrades parade before him in misty and ethereal progression, then swim away again, dissolving like a baseless fabric into the darkening atmosphere around him. There are the sudden appearance and vanishing of "the little river," and the abruptness with which "the plain" merges into "moun-

tains" has all the indeterminacy of dream. This grotesque
interior landscape is not just a gratuitous indulgence in
Gothic horror. Simply by combining images like the palsied
oak, the great black bird, and the mountains, without speci-
fying their relations, Browning creates an awareness of meaning greater than what can actually be known. If he succeeds
in turning the landscape into a geography of Roland's soul, it
is not because he relies upon supernatural beliefs. It is because
he draws upon that other kind of actuality, the kind that is
bred in fitting images together. He enacts a sense of mystery
by combining symbols whose "connection is left for the
beholder to work out for himself," as Ruskin observes in his
analysis of Gothic taste, but which enable the supernatural
poet to express a truth "which it would have taken a long
time to express in any verbal way." [3]

It is necessary for Roland's salvation that he understand
the moral value of suffering and that he continue to suffer.
The one time he turns to the past for a "draught of . . .
happier sights," his reflection is directed back upon the
suffering, not *away* from it. The transition to more appalling
horrors turns the metaphor of the "wine," whose "draught"
of memories should relieve the wasteland drought, into an
ironic joke. When Chadwick asked Browning if his meaning
could be expressed in the statement, "He that endureth to the
end shall be saved," the poet replied, "Yes, just about that."
Of course, it is dangerous to invest such obiter dicta with
undue weight. There is little outside a poem like "Childe
Roland" to refer to for authority as to what the poet means.
When Browning tries to provide this authority, he is sometimes too dogmatic. But the critic has, presumably, an awak-
ened mind, and he must approach "Childe Roland" with
some conceptual framework. Though there is no available

[3] John Ruskin, *Modern Painters* (New York, 1907), III, 91.

edifice of meaning except the poem's own inner movement, it would appear, on the basis of this movement and from Browning's own testimony, that the knight makes his dialectical advance by consciously penetrating his suffering and refusing to turn aside from it. The ethical man understand so fully the universality and relevance of suffering that he finds every documentation of it superfluous. Though Roland has been training a whole lifetime for his last encounter, he is so accustomed to suffering that one further manifestation of it seems commonplace. He misses the Dark Tower, when it appears, simply because he understands its significance so well.

The use of pictorial details from Gerard de Lairesse's book on *The Art of Painting* is less random than at first appears. In "Childe Roland" they contain the germs of moral growth, and the poet's selecting presence may be felt behind the order in which he presents them. Roland's ethical responses range from empathy with animals and inanimate nature to sympathy for man himself. The knight's communion with the animals curiously qualifies our initial repugnance. Even the wounded "water rat" shrieks piteously like a babe. This recalls the "mad" Edgar's fantasy of swallowing "the old rat and the ditch-dog" (*King Lear*, III, iv, 137), as well as Lear's recognition of his community with the animals—"Man's life is cheap as beast's" (II, iv, 270)—and his revulsion from the betrayal of his dogs imagined as faithless daughters—"The little dogs and all, / Tray, Blanch, and Sweetheart—see, they bark at me" (III, vi, 65–66). As a victim of giants who stalk their game, Roland himself becomes a hunted animal. He overcomes his revulsion and achieves a sympathetic identification with subhuman forms of life. He also treats inanimate objects in nature as though they had human attributes. The "black eddy" spumes with "wrath," the "alder" kneels "down over it," and the "willows," like a "suicidal throng," fling themselves "headlong in a fit / Of mute despair." In the same way, Lear imparts his own attributes to the storm that "crack[s its] cheeks," "rumble[s its] bellyful," and utters "Such groans of roaring wind and rain" (III, ii, 1, 14, 47) that it seems to become an image of the tumult in Lear himself. Finally, in Roland's recollection of Giles and Cuthbert, comes the sympathy with human beings ("Dear fellow," "Poor traitor") and the sense that no one can afford to be indifferent to the fate of others. This is also Lear's discovery when he urges Kent and the fool to precede him into the hovel at the height of the storm and when his torment stimulates his powers of moral perception and sympathetic identification with all forms of suffering.

Childe Roland is a Lear upon the heath, and he responds to his companions as neither heroes nor traitors, but fully representative human beings. Friends testify that Browning was deeply moved by performances of *King Lear* and recall how "his face grew gradually paler, till at last tears, of which he seemed unconscious, ran down his cheeks." [4] The more that Roland, like King Lear, suffers, the more significant become the elementary things which all men possess in common. In the "pelting of [the] pitiless storm" Lear kneels down like a child at bedtime to pray, not for himself, but for all "Poor naked wretches, wheresoe'er you are" (III, iv, 28). In the same way, Childe Roland discovers "the moral equivalent" of salvation. To be saved one must become a "childe" again. Roland's awareness, like King Lear's, reveals the bonds of a common emotion, bringing all men together and approaching what in Yeats's view are the disinterested and inclusive qualities of tragic vision.

Of course, Browning enacts such truths by reproducing Roland's own responses, not by interpreting them from out-

[4] W. H. Griffin and H. C. Minchin, *The Life of Robert Browning* (New York, 1912), p. 286.

side. The achievement of "Childe Roland" is that it never substitutes a doctrinal interest for a represented one. It is about nothing but itself; it is its own dialectic, its own inner movement of transition and growth. Usually where such transitions occur in literature, they are recognized formally. But here, although the candidate is being hazed, first by the hoary cripple, then by the grinning animal and plant life he encounters, and finally by the trompe l'oeil that seems to conjure the Tower out of nowhere, neither he nor his "persecutors" recognize what is happening. Hence, nobody, including the reader, is quite sure what Childe Roland's "guilt" is, or what kind of transition he must make, or for what purpose. The knight's dialectical advance is worked out piecemeal, in ways that are unrecognized by him except for vague embarrassments, as when he seems to crush the water rat, then experiences pity for it. The suffering that purges in the enveloping "sheet of flame" appears first as a hideous "Red leer"; only the refining fire of the Last Judgment, though still far in the future, hints at the symbolic form the burning will take.

A speaker like the Duke of Ferrara rejects all the conventional categories that the reader or the envoy is tempted to apply to him. But the Duke's ability to create his identity from one moment to the next destroys his moral sense. The speaker in "A Toccata of Galuppi's" faces the opposite problem. Though he has the capacity to evaluate, his moral categories intrude between himself and his experience. They tend at first to narrow the range of his responses. Childe Roland overcomes both these limitations. Because he sees that the essence of moral energy is to survey all varieties of human experience, he can continue to create his identity from one moment to the next at the same time that he orders his responses into a moral progression, ranging from empathy with inanimate objects and animals to sympathy for man himself.

To create significance, Childe Roland must first compass great disorder. He begins with a mass of repugnant objects, but his imagination organizes these details to create an infernal world whose newness is not just another incoherence. The inanimate objects and animals take on a moral meaning which Roland himself cannot articulate but which Browning expects the reader to perceive.

The appearance of the Dark Tower is a turning point. It represents that shocked condition where an image like the destructive fire comes to include and express its opposite. The very language trembles between collapse on the one hand and supreme assertion on the other. It depends on what voice the reader hears in the questions "Not see?" and "Not hear?" and on the way he reads the final lines: "Dauntless the slug-horn to my lips I set, / And blew. *'Childe Roland to the Dark Tower came'* " (ll. 203–204). The blowing of the slug-horn allows, but does not itself release, a heroic gesture. The reader receives an impact from the speed of the words and the names that keep ringing in Childe Roland's ears. Though the sheet of flame and the final bugle call leave us in an ominous, terrified, and marveling frame of mind, they also leave us with a sense that the revelation we have been waiting for has either never taken place or is still to come. What we expect is a sudden insight at the end of a long converging train of partial revelations. Instead, Childe Roland simply tells us he has reached the Tower.

The knight has been near his goal without knowing it. When he thinks he is far removed from the Tower, his dread of being nothing and nowhere is also his discovery of himself and his goal. Childe Roland's cry is no longer that of a particular aesthetic man who suffers from the blindness of his own perspective. Indeed, the terror lies in his very recognition of what he is and what he seeks. This is the moment when Browning packs the most meaning into his language,

the "one moment" that "knell[s] the woe of years." Until
the end Childe Roland is both near and far from the Tower.
He is near the truth without being able to reach it; and this
paradox preserves the mystery. But because he has the intellectual sympathy finally to encompass every point of view,
Childe Roland becomes a being like King Lear, in whom all
human anguish resounds. By the end of the poem his feelings
overflow: he has achieved a dialectical advance that makes
him one with weeping trees, snakes, and poor traitors "spit
upon and curst." Though each man must overcome the limitation of his own point of view, Browning's doctrine of
imperfection requires that anyone who tries to grasp the
whole be destroyed. The greatest disasters are among those
men who are the best and matter the most. In reaching the
Tower, Childe Roland seems to illustrate the inevitability
with which life will destroy the man who tries to understand
it all.

⌘ 6 ⌘

The monologues on music and painting are less discussions
of artistic theory than attempts to reveal the limitations of
conflicting attitudes and beliefs. "A Toccata of Galuppi's"
(1847–1853) views the aesthetic bondage of the Venetians
from the ironic perspective of the ethical stage. But because
the speaker can see everything ironically, nothing, including
himself, can escape his criticism. The logic of his own
method forces him to participate at the end in the fate he has
established for the Venetians alone. For Master Hugues and
Andrea del Sarto aesthetic idolatry takes the form of mere
dexterity and technical mastery. To escape its contradictions,
each point of view must come to include its opposite. Dialectical logic requires that the technician become a humanist and
the craftsman a seer. Both transformations occur momentarily when Andrea assumes a communal role during his "kingly

days" at Fontainebleau. The opposites also unite in the "good minute" of "Abt Vogler" (1864), but once again their union is temporary. Only in "Fra Lippo Lippi" (1853) does Browning stage a complete ascent from the aesthetic to the religious stage.

The speaker in "A Toccata of Galuppi's" attempts a persuasive definition of the key word "music." He keeps constant the term's descriptive meaning as a synonym for the Venetians' aesthetic pleasures. But he alters the word's emotive meaning by showing how the "old music" becomes the "cold music": it must die, like the Venetians in the given instant. The speaker's method is first to portray the aesthetic responses he wants to criticize in the Venetians. By acts of intellectual sympathy he re-creates the eighteenth-century flavor of "grave and gay." He exercises poetic tact in using triplets to suggest the formality of the Augustan couplet without being confined by its tone and associated attitudes. But his sermonizing speech ("Oh, Galuppi, . . . this is very sad to find") fixes the speaker as a man of his generation, of the age that produced Thomas Arnold and his resolution to "abolish levity." His attempt to grasp his subject from within is part of his dialectical method. As a kind of Victorian Prufrock, he deftly diagnoses the aesthetic man's "rotation method" in the Venetians' feverish plans for new revelries after the all-night party.

The speaker first identifies with the Venetians' attitudes in order to expose their limitations. When his judgments find expression in the arresting symbol of "the dominant's persistence," and later, in stanza x, when there is a culmination of disaster, the plainness of his style cannot conceal his criticism. Despite the languorous cadences, which move him to accords so lulling and lascivious, the repetitions are as relentless as fate itself:

. . . till in due time, *one* by *one*,
Some with lives that came to nothing, *some* with deeds as well
undone [ll. 28-29—italics mine].

The dialectician gives short shrift to the hedonist's point of view. But at the same time that he criticizes the Venetians' attitudes from within, the intellectual sympathy that allows him to judge these attitudes becomes increasingly apparent. Toward the end of the poem this sympathetic identification is just as strong as the impulse to criticize. The verse has to move slowly, because the moralist's feelings overflow, and it is only with great reluctance that he is able to reveal at all the remorseless doom of the Venetian carnival.

The elegiac rhythms ("dead and done with," "Venice spent what Venice earned") operate with extraordinary force upon the intellectual framework—the hierarchy of souls rising "in their degree" from sensual bondage to intellectual and moral freedom and ranked with the rigor of a rationalist whose "pastime" is "Mathematics." The "secret wrung from nature," variously interpreted as evolutionary naturalism or the Victorian idea of progress, may simply be the moralist's complacent reflection that he has achieved a dialectical advance that places him securely beyond the Venetians' dissolution. But the opinion is no sooner formed than the "cold music" that "creep[s] thro' every nerve" restores the critic's more basic community with the sensualists, whom, in the first proud moment of ironic satisfaction, he has imagined he transcends. The piercing immediacy of the quivering "nerve" violates expectations and restores the irony at the speaker's own expense. It prepares for the final antithesis, not between the ethical and aesthetic man, but between the more fundamental opposites of life and death, which unite the Venetians and the moralist in a common fate.

The speaker tries to formulate a hypothetical syllogism

whose antecedent is that "Butterflies" like the Venetians never owned a soul, and whose consequent is that they must die. By denying the consequent, he is able to deny the antecedent and to infer that the man who is immortal is the man who possesses, like himself, the highest kind of soul; as a moralist with scientific interests, he therefore concludes that he will "not die": "it cannot be!" But the very task of relating the terms placed together makes us aware of unexpected reversals in the argument. Personal tones with their warmth of relation—the golden hair of the "Dear dead women," sensuously cascading over swelling "bosoms"—are brought up against images of remoteness and isolation—the creaking "where a house was burned." The speaker pities the women and would forgive them if he could. What begins as critical irony ends as immense charity, marked by grave pathos and extreme courtesy toward the dead. As his intellectual sympathy for the Venetians overpowers his impulse to criticize, the dialectician becomes increasingly the object of his own irony.

Irony at the speaker's expense is already implicit in the linking of "deaf and blind" with "heavy mind," where the rhymes lock his obtuseness into an inevitable pattern. Such preparations are what make the argument dramatic, and not melodramatic. Though the speaker's overt rhetorical aim is to convert the "old music" into the "cold music," he is a true ironist who can see himself involved in a pattern that is just as dialectical as his treatment of the Venetians. A subordinate but parallel shift in his view of his own situation leads him from a proud assurance that he "cannot die" to a recognition of his own mortality: "I feel chilly and grown old." The speaker is a Victorian Socrates, Kierkegaard's paradigm of the ethical man, who reveals the completeness of his ironic perspective only at the end, when he turns his indictment of the Venetians inside out by introducing a dialectic that subverts his own positions of privilege and pride. From disinterested listening to the toccata, he passes through moods of shock, irony, and pathos, and rises finally to a compassionate view of other people. Because nothing can escape his dialectical scourge, he emerges at the end with an awareness that is no longer aesthetic, moral, or even intellectual, but simply human in the fullest sense.

⁀⁀ 7 ⁀⁀

The organist in "Master Hugues of Saxe-Gotha" (*ca.* 1853) lacks the intellectual sympathy that characterizes the speaker in "A Toccata of Galuppi's." As a sage who is "zealous" for "man's effort," the organist is so eager to make the music rationally intelligible that he keeps limiting its meaning. His habit of putting questions to the music ("What do you mean by your mountainous fugues?") is Browning's way of discrediting the moralist who must abstract communicable public meaning from art. At the religious stage of "Abt Vogler," symbols like the "star" are too intrinsic to have their meaning extracted and interpreted in this way. In "Master Hugues of Saxe-Gotha" the organist's preoccupation with the complicated formal structure of the fugue may seem at first to qualify the sage's ethical emphasis: "Is it your moral of Life?" But both ways of interpreting the music make the identical error of failing to experience art in its own terms. The technician and the moralist both forget that art must overcome and absorb the formal and intellectual devices by which it undertakes its greatest quests. Instead of allowing the music to expand its significance, the organist's obsession with technique so limits the meaning that he can evoke the composer only in terms of his musical notation. When he tries to interpret the music conceptually, the organist's moral ideas limit his experience and become a substitute for what they cannot enclose.

If aesthetes like the Venetians suffer from a warped perspective, moralists like the organist are equally ridiculous. Though the aesthete can achieve immediacy, whatever is immediate is usually ineffable. And since the ineffable can seldom be communicated, the aesthete's experience generally collapses into an instant without duration. Not content with this limitation, the aesthete must become his opposite, a moralist like the organist. But the discursive language of the sage is incompatible with immediacy. Must the organist become an aesthete again, or can he advance to some higher stage? Browning shows how every point of view must come to include and express its opposite. The union the sage is seeking comes only at the religious stage. An aesthete may achieve immediacy, but he can seldom express or prolong it. A moralist can communicate his ideas, but his truths remain universal and abstract. Only a seer like Abt Vogler can communicate to others all that is most immediate in his own experience.

ꟾꟷ 8 ꟷꟾ

"Abt Vogler" (1864), like "Saul," is one of Browning's rare experiments in a visionary, or (as the poet himself would say) "lyric," mode. By speaking through Abt Vogler in his own voice, as his wife had urged, Browning is able to pass from a merely subjective point of view, in the second and third stanzas, to a sympathetic identification with the living, "the wonderful Dead," and "ages" still "to come," and to a new use of nature at the religious stage. In stanzas IV to VII, wandering stars and other celestial phenomena become the containing forms of nature, and heaven seems responsive to man's imaginative control. Browning's cosmic geography translates the intuitions of the subjective poet into a universal language. Freed from the tyranny of the merely self-expressed, the visionary poet can now communicate his intuitions to others by framing "out of three sounds . . . not a fourth sound, but a star." But as Browning had complained in a letter to Miss Barrett dated February 11, 1845, the visionary light which should sustain the lyric poet leaps out for him only "for a moment, from the one narrow chink, and then [interposes] the blind wall between it and [himself]." The action of the last five stanzas of the poem takes place at the ethical stage, where the moral reflection of the sage reminds us that no revelation in human terms is complete. The ethical man can confront the mystery only on the plane of rational imagination. Since no human subject can grasp the total truth, the seer's revelation can be only momentary.

Up to the fourth stanza, the natural descriptions are all pictorial and carefully externalized through the use of simile: "gold as transparent as glass"; the elaborate comparison of spiritual illumination to the progressive lighting of torches during a Roman festival. The use of "Meteor-moons" and "balls of blaze" may seem at first to be quite similar to the simile of the runner's lighting of torches, where nature is viewed as an external order. But the picture of heaven touching earth and earth scaling heaven does not confirm the impression. Abt Vogler is shifting his scene to a surrealistic vision of constant meteors and wandering stars that no longer "pale nor pine." Though the musician's vision does not arise from phenomena "out of nature" (to use Yeats's phrase), his cosmic landscape is a sacramental one. He is not giving a lesson in astronomy; this is a geography of the soul, and his spiritual meaning precedes any discoveries he can make in an actual observatory. Visions of primeval protoplasm supervene, and the "kindlier wind" is no longer a tempest sweeping across an ordinary plain. The breeze enables the "Dead" to breathe again. It infuses the whole scene with a creative power, and like the presence of the Holy Spirit, it can be expressed only by a series of metaphors.

In this power that sustains the eternal instant there is no past or future. For temporal succession Abt Vogler substitutes the coordinate syntax of a continuous present. He renders the miracle of musical creation through a daring use of synesthesia, in which the aural becomes visual and the soul flows "visibly forth" through sound. There is no uncontrolled multiplication of metaphor, as there is in the early subjective poetry, because far from celebrating his own powers, the visionary poet is now inside a world which is of divine, rather than merely human, construction. Of course, Abt Vogler must assist at this construction, and his spiritual doctrines are redeemed and illuminated only by the human analogies to which they cling. Just as David builds from human to divine love in "Saul," so the musician must project from man the creator (as artist) to God the Creator: "But here is the finger of God, a flash of the will that can." Browning treats musical creation, not simply as a metaphor for God's creative acts, but as an analogue, which affirms the operation of a single principle in two different forms. As Holloway observes in his analysis of Newman's rhetoric, "The philosopher or sage . . . can use [such analogues] either to suggest that two things result from a single power or principle when he could not prove that they do; or to suggest that they are wholly the result of a single power or principle when he could only prove that they are in part." [5] By combining sounds that in themselves are "naught," Abt Vogler can use the parts to represent a "star"—a whole that is qualitatively distinct, just as God can make what "is naught" into part of the divine nature by breathing his spirit into human flesh.

The passing of his vision plunges Abt Vogler into the abyss he described at the beginning as "a blind plunge down to hell." Only through desperate self-persuasion can he reason his way back to faith in a beneficent God. To convince

⁵ John Holloway, *The Victorian Sage* (New York, 1953), p. 182.

himself that the "good minute" will return, he tries to establish that he is saved because he is physically the same person to whom God's grace was granted. But he is spiritually the same person only if he is saved, and this is the very proposition he is trying to prove. Half sensing the fallacy, Abt Vogler negates his own conclusion:

> because I cling with my mind
> To the same, same self, same love, same God: ay, what was,
> shall be   [ll. 63–64].

Here are, not Pope's ten "low words" creeping in one "dull line," but fourteen painful, grinding monosyllables. The repetition of the fourfold "same" drains all energy out of the verse as it seems to drain all conviction out of Abt Vogler.

The sage must renew his effort to gain assurance, this time through a rhetoric of naming. In calling God "thee who art ever the same" Abt Vogler is not simply using a neutral definition of deity. Since he wants assurance that God will not permanently withdraw his grace, it is important to him that God is "ever the same." Abt Vogler can give "the ineffable Name" whatever epithets he wants, and then assume that, since God *is* His attributes, He must act the role his titles imply. This logic of naming, which looks at first like religious adoration, is in fact a form of persuasive definition. It makes it easier for the sage to believe that the ineffable God will honor His guarantee of that permanence which has been ascribed to Him as a proper attribute.

In developing Augustine's thesis that evil is only privation, Abt Vogler is not saying that we live in the best of all possible worlds. Though we have been accustomed to regard evil as something real and painful, Abt Vogler insists that it is not a "fact" of nature, any more than is silence, but a linguistic invention, a function of a symbol system. The narrower and more precise meaning of "being," which enables the sage to define evil as nonbeing, has a certain shock value, like his later declaration that failure is the evidence of triumph. But the dialectician is reserving his prize word, "being," for the special instant of divine grace. By comparison with this moment the rest of his life seems indistinct and unreal. He is not saying that there is no suffering in the world, but that pain can never be as overpowering as the grace which invades him at these special moments. This redefinition of "evil" is not facile theodicy, but an affirmation of orthodox Christianity against a Gnostic dualism. Abt Vogler's life on earth becomes a series of "broken arcs." The "arcs" are the eternal instants, and the breaks the "evil," the merely temporary withdrawals of grace. "When eternity affirms the conception of an hour," the "beauty," "good," and "power" will become continuous. Heaven is the goal of the dialectical process, a closing of the gaps between the "broken arcs" and the "perfect round." But on earth man can never reach "the perfect round." If he could, his dialectical pilgrimage would be at an end; he would no longer be capable of moral or religious growth. Though these reflections of the sage bear only a slight relation to the seer's opening vision, the slighter the relation, the more genuine the feeling conveyed by the poetry. The "failure" is illustrative: the less connected the rhetoric seems to the preceding vision, the more it dramatizes the sage's own despair. The moral reflections perform the same function as the events in a narrative poem; they produce a rhetorical medium in which the poem's real substance may be borne.

Abt Vogler's sheer delight in creation matches David's fervor in persuading Saul. In both poems there is a purely formal appeal—to discover the meaning of height and depth experienced by one to whom spiritual climbing is both an effort and an exaltation. But while Abt Vogler's "climbing" is in answer to a call, it is an unspecified call, unlike David's, which is unexpectedly specific: "See the Christ stand!" Abt Vogler's soaring rhapsody never confuses the grace of God with artistic "grace." But because the sage builds his religious vision on a musical analogy, his stress on virtuosity prepares for his precipitate descent. By invoking a principle of "weakness in strength" in his analogical argument, David builds a ladder that enables him to remain at the religious stage and that, unlike Abt Vogler's ladder, does not collapse from an excess of grace the moment he has climbed to the top.

9

If Abt Vogler mounts to the "perfect round" only to fall into the "broken arcs" of his moralizing, Andrea del Sarto is a victim of the aesthetic life who has mounted to the ethical stage only briefly, during his "kingly days" at Fontainebleau, and who now merely apes the postures of the ethical and religious man. He is the perfect example of Kierkegaard's aesthetic man who "seeks as far as possible to be absorbed in mood." Robert Langbaum has shown how Andrea "washes away with an enchanting vagueness all [the] moral issues." [6] The more completely he disappears into his twilight of mood, the more completely he can take refuge in the aesthetic life, till nothing remains which cannot be inflected into it. The speaker in "A Toccata of Galuppi's," who also responds to atmosphere, senses the pathos of those Venetians who live *in* the mood. Because he is always a master *over* atmosphere, he sees the carnival mood beneath him, as it were. When Andrea recalls his "kingly days," he is also surmounting the aesthetic stage, and this is why I must consider the poem with the other ethical monologues. Kierkegaard says that the man who lives aesthetically has no memory of his life, and this is obviously untrue of Andrea. But unlike the moralist in "A Toccata of Galuppi's," whose intellectual

[6] *The Poetry of Experience* (London, 1957), p. 150.

sympathy enables him to expose the limitation of the attitude he shares, Andrea is overwhelmed by mood. He is incapable of using his sympathies to grow in stature. Instead of his having a controlling aim, his moods, always eccentric and erratic, seem to control *him*.

Andrea's most important auditor, the person he most wants to persuade, is not Lucrezia but himself. He is only ostensibly trying to defend his art or persuade Lucrezia to remain at home with him. The rhetoric is designed to fail in its apparent aims, so that Andrea may discover new connections between his failures and his marriage. If he can appear mistreated in his own eyes, then he can blame Lucrezia, not simply for abandoning him that evening, but for all his failures, particularly the moral crimes against King Francis and his parents.

Andrea's painting suffers from its visual perfection, which is never powerful enough to transform the subjects that it treats. He has betrayed his obligations to his parents and King Francis because of his bondage to a special visual segment of experience—his "moon" Lucrezia. Andrea receives sexual gratification merely by gazing at

> My face, my moon, my everybody's moon,
> Which everybody looks on and calls his,
> And, I suppose, is looked on by in turn,
> While she looks—no one's   [ll. 29–32].

The change from active to passive voice registers Lucrezia's inertia. Her qualities are those of a well-managed visual surface and enact the promiscuity of her undiscriminating mind. Though such traits may enrich if they transform, Lucrezia's qualities simply impoverish what they adorn. Because everything is on the outside, as in one of Andrea's paintings, there can never be any problem of intellectual interpretation. Andrea joins double meanings in the final "looks" ("gazes" and "appears"), and his lively play of wit continues to center in punning metaphor ("very dear, no less"). The pivotal term "dear" creates meaning just as conscience creates judgment. It makes us feel the inner bite of affective and economic values forced together. As Andrea composes the scene into a painter's "twilight-piece," his details fall into catalogues as neatly as the objects of the landscape fill his canvases. The phrase "Autumn in everything" deftly caps the diffuse and gentle pathos emanating from the vibration of light and air in the darkening landscape, from the departure of the "last monk," reminiscent of the weary "plowman" in Gray's "Elegy," and the clinking of the chapel bell—all so finely and movingly recorded.

A philosophic voice, less sweetly languorous, emerges in the pseudopious apostrophe: "Love, we are in God's hand" (1: 49). Such sententious reflections abound in Andrea's speech. Aristotle recommends them because they seem to represent the testimony of many men. Such maxims sometimes give Andrea dignity, but they contribute to the impression of his futility by revealing him as a man, not of action, but of platitudes. Moreover, when he says he is "in God's hand," he is really thinking of himself as in Lucrezia's hand. Though he does not possess the religious man's understanding of God, he has the sensualist's knowledge of his wife. As a philosopher of determinism, he wishes to indicate that he is not responsible for his personal disasters. But the grand imperative "let it lie!" ironically contradicts the determinism, for if "All is as God over-rules," then it is not in Andrea's power to will anything.

What seems to be philosophic self-refutation is not a contradiction if for "God" we read Andrea's own uxorious attachment to Lucrezia. "Let it lie," far from reasserting his ethical freedom, then becomes an abdication of it in sensual enslavement. By masking his idolatry under religious cate-

gories, Andrea is trying to win God's approval of his sensuality. The irrationality of "I feel he laid the fetter" is less
apparent when assimilated into the alliterative pattern. But
Browning is submitting to comic analysis aesthetic attitudes
more subtle than any he has yet dramatized. He is inviting
the reader to resolve the contradictions at the philosophic
level by substituting psychological equivalents that preserve
their own logic, even though they are quite subversive of
Andrea's professed piety.

Our suspicions are confirmed when in his next breath
Andrea accuses Lucrezia directly, first of terminating their
love, and then of being indifferent to his art. His praise of his
own paintings is designed to make his wife more appreciative.
But Andrea cannot resist making jabs at Lucrezia. He accuses
her of smearing his paintings (ll. 74–75), even though the
accusation defeats the strategy he is pursuing at the moment.
Such indiscretions keep suggesting that love-making and art
are not the real purpose of his rhetoric.

Since Lucrezia is no longer listening, Andrea is now his own
auditor. But he is still just as rhetorical as when he was using
arguments to influence Lucrezia rather than an audience that
is within himself. The artists who were first introduced to
persuade Lucrezia of Andrea's superiority are now used to
develop the contrary thesis. The reversal is apparent from
single words: "Well, less is more, Lucrezia: I am judged."
Andrea turns over "less" and "more" to give them new
force, playing on contradiction and paradox. Characteristic
of this strain of "talking poetry" is the caustic irony of anticlimax and antithesis, often joined with severe rhythmic
jolts: "Reach many a time a heaven that's shut to me" (l.
84); "My works are nearer heaven, but I sit here" (l. 87).

Andrea is playing a conversational game in which the
shocks, though never as complete as the reversals in "My
Last Duchess," are much more frequent, discontinuous, and
sporadic. He can recall his "kingly days" when the Creator

breathed on him through his "humane great monarch," just as "the finger of God" touched Abt Vogler. But now he finds it hard to describe the moral and spiritual power he lacks, and is forced back upon reductive metonyms—corporeal equivalents like the "sudden blood" that "boils," or references to physical organs like the "brain" and "Heart." Whereas technically inferior artists address society and are moved by men's reactions to their work, Andrea is indifferent to all praise or blame, "painting from [himself] and to [himself]" (l. 90). He is like the young Browning who, after aspiring too high as a subjective poet, has to portray many points of view in the objective world. It takes Browning a long time to realize that his experiments with many phases of life in his dramatic monologues enable him to develop his powers far more effectively than he did as a merely subjective poet. He continues to feel that there are heights of spiritual experience which he, as the "Sun-treader's" disciple, must still reach. But outside his few successes as a subjective poet—in the coda of "Saul," parts of "Abt Vogler," and *The Ring and the Book*—Browning cannot ascend to the "pure white light" directly. Andrea's self-criticism is especially moving, because massed behind it there is evident an awareness of a similar limitation on Browning's part. Even if we question the domestic parallel and reject Mrs. Miller's hypothesis that Browning was uxorious in his attachment to Elizabeth, the artistic parallels are clear. Like the mature Browning, Andrea is no subjective artist. It is not that he "comes back and cannot tell the world." His problem is that only at Fontainebleau has he been beyond the aesthetic stage at all. Just as Michelangelo's transcendent visions are closed to Andrea, so the "heaven" of the Shelleyan Raphael is a domain Browning cannot take by storm. He can reach it only at the end of a long dialectical pilgrimage through the objective world of his dramatic monologues.

    Though Andrea knows what he must attempt to do, he

cannot make the effort. Instead of confronting his despair directly and allowing it to carry him through to ethical awareness, he rotates his empty aesthetic pleasures. Yielding to the suggestions of the painting, Andrea wants to correct Raphael's draftsmanship, then concedes his own inferiority and tries to blame Lucrezia. He believes that if his wife had "brought a mind," he might have succeeded. Lucrezia can deny for herself the antecedent, and when she negates the consequent, the cause of Andrea's failure seems to follow. But the hypothetical syllogism takes the form *if* p, *then* q; *but not*-p; *therefore not*-q, which is invalid. The formal fallacy overlooks the possibility that there may be other causes of Andrea's failure. When he blames Lucrezia, she protests, and Andrea appears to withdraw the charge, only to introduce it in disguised form.

The premise that he wants to establish is: "All is, not as God, but as Lucrezia over-rules." But at this stage he dare not admit this, even to himself. Instead, he shifts responsibility to God, and then, to escape the charge of blasphemy, tries to re-establish God's beneficence by asserting that "incentives come from the soul's self." But a doctrine of free will flatly contradicts his opening proposition, "All is as God over-rules." When Andrea's rhetoric violates logic, it usually justifies this violation psychologically. Under the mask of piety Andrea is once again trying to insinuate his charge against Lucrezia. But in clearing himself of blasphemy, he has also freed Lucrezia of blame, as he realizes in his rhetorical question: "Why do I need you?" To escape responsibility, he generalizes from his own experience:

> In this world, who can do a thing, will not;
> And who would do it, cannot, I perceive   [ll. 137–138].

Andrea can turn a neat epigram, and performs a logical conversion, this time in a valid mood: *if* p, *then* q; *but not*-q;

therefore not-p. But he demonstrates merely the logical consistency of an irrational premise. In saying that good artists are morally weak, he is too much influenced by his own case and reaches a conclusion that is not typical. There are artists who are just as skilled as Andrea and who have the will to succeed as well as the technical ability. To conclude that morally good men are bad artists is to commit a peculiarly aesthetic fallacy. It is to make virtuosity more interesting than virtue. Andrea half senses his error and combines the rigor of his logical conversion with the protean disordering of the syllogistic argument: "Yet the will's somewhat—somewhat, too, the power— / And thus we half-men struggle." The dislocation that such fragments undergo is Browning's calculated means of reordering our judgment with sudden insight. Enthymemes are the prime figures of a play of mind and capture the equivocating quality of the argument. Its meanings are unstable and keep shifting till Andrea reaches a damaging conclusion that suddenly radiates in all directions: "Who can do a thing, will not"; "I can do a thing" ("incentives come from the soul's self"); "Therefore I must be deficient in moral will, and personally responsible."

He would like to see himself as one of the "half-men." He has "the will" but not "the power" (l. 139), he believes. But if "incentives come from the soul's self," the lack of power cannot be absolute, and therefore not absolving. There is accordingly an unconscious irony in his complacent reflection that "God . . . compensates, punishes." In conceding his own disgrace, Andrea, like an accomplished dialectician, hopes to spring a daring coup. By showing how their taunts and abuse assure his reward in the afterlife, he is trying to turn back on his detractors their own objections. But the God who compensates Andrea will have to be a strangely aesthetic God, who values the morally weak artist more than the spiritually strong man. As with Johannes Agricola, "The award" (l. 142) is bound to prove "stricter" than Andrea thinks.

Andrea comes closest to recognizing his present limitations when he recalls his "long festal year at Fontainebleau" (l. 150). As the cynosure of the French court, Andrea was able to "leave the ground" of the aesthetic stage and "Put on the glory, Rafael's daily wear." In the praise of King Francis, Browning's tribute to his wife's inspiration in his own life can insinuate its meaning unobtrusively. The poet seems to speak simultaneously for himself and Andrea, and puts his message at that precise point in the poem where both protégé and lover may speak in agreement.

But the "jingle" of the "gold chain" prepares for Andrea's debasement of the monarch's "golden look." "Gold" undergoes a fragmented version of the kind of dialectical transformation that "body" does in "Fra Lippo Lippi." Unable to sustain the stress of his "kingly days," Andrea turns their spiritual gold to hard, economic gold, which he steals for Lucrezia, whose golden hair ensnares him. In his use of Lucrezia as the climax to cap all the glories of Fontainebleau we enjoy the momentary deception of a culmination happily contradicted by the word "face," which reverses the moral and spiritual values. The "face" which should climax the alliterative progression "frank," "French," "fire" (l. 160) deftly undermines it. Andrea has been presenting Lucrezia as another Virgin, who carries him to Paradise after the secular inspiration of King Francis and his court has done its utmost to elevate him. But his highest expression is in the vacantly sweet and tenderly amorous strain: "You beautiful Lucrezia that are mine!" Even Andrea's faintly sensual framing of Lucrezia's golden hair serves only to emphasize the lack of urgent passion. Like the Duke of Ferrara, he has cast his wife in a role for which she was never fitted. "The Cousin" has moved into his theatre and shown him how grossly deceived he was in mistaking Eve for the Virgin. With himself as his own auditor, he must now score a triumph which he has never had the skill to achieve in open debate. He can win a nominal victory by seeming to blame Lucrezia for his failure. In point of fact, however, his wife is not even attending to the arguments and interrupts only when Andrea, who prides himself on his rhetorical skill, becomes openly insulting.

His tender appeal, "Come from the window, love," concentrates emotion with utmost poignancy. In the gentle anguish of "the melancholy little house / We built to be so gay with," the reader experiences the fullest possible sympathy with him. But from the deepest seriousness, Andrea, carried on tides of emotion and regret, fretfully recedes into other moods. Because he experiences a continual weakening of his sensations, of the very impressions on which his fancied happiness depends, the sensualist is filled with terror at the prospect of facing the evening all alone. Thrown into an involuntary anxiety of vague desires, stirred by the never relenting memories of his "kingly days" and his betrayal of King Francis, Andrea masochistically reveals all the painful truths about Lucrezia and "the Cousin." His climactic argument to persuade Lucrezia to remain at home combines elements of all his previous approaches. But because he wants to dramatize her infidelity and make credible the blame he is about to attach to her, his rhetoric is carefully designed to "fail." Andrea is trying to invent situations in which he can repair imaginary injustices with imaginary sacrifices. He knows his wife will refuse to stay at home, and to ensure this refusal, he deliberately insults her by coarsely joking that Lucrezia is intimate with too many "Cousins" to pose as the Virgin (l. 231).

Andrea tries to excuse his betrayal of his parents by arguing that he himself was poor. Instead of lying outright about his wealth, he can practice the same deception indirectly by denying an exaggerated version of the truth: "And I have labored somewhat in my time / And not been paid profusely" (ll. 254–255). But because he has just given Lucrezia money for much less reason than he has denied it to his parents, the understatement cannot disguise the weakness of his argument. He therefore says, "there's something strikes a balance." If he is a moral failure, his technical skill as a craftsman redeems him. Yet, as Langbaum observes, the "something" that redeems is also Lucrezia, not because she was the Virgin Andrea supposed, but precisely because she was his Eve, and hence the agent responsible for his moral and artistic "fall."

This final unmasking of Andrea's piety should alert us to all his earlier deceptions and confirm our worst suspicions. Whenever the nominal themes of defending his art or trying to persuade Lucrezia supervene, irony intrudes. The only activity that Andrea is wholly unironical about is self-justification. His real audience is himself, his final argument an attempt to excuse himself in his own eyes. Lines like "there's something strikes a balance" make emphatic the meaning Browning has been implying throughout. A transfer of blame, too subtle for the person blamed to detect, hence innocuous and unchallengeable, is the only rhetorical refinement which Browning can allow the aesthetic life to yield.

In his vision of the New Jerusalem, Andrea seems to be addressing the cosmos, but because he always has Lucrezia, the apocalyptic drift is still toward irony. The use of "still" to signify both "nevertheless" and "perpetually" is a final reminder of Andrea's capacity for compressing multiple, sometimes opposite, kinds of meaning into single words. Though he rejects the aspirations of the ethical and religious life, he continues to ape the ethical man by using, quite illegitimately, the moral word "choose." Since his decision to remain at the aesthetic stage involves an abdication of all volition, it cannot be dignified by his use of a moral term. Andrea has renounced all choice, only to "choose" never to choose again.

Browning seeks to do justice to the contradictions of the aesthetic stage, and he sacrifices most of our sympathy for Andrea to the full "ironic truth." But because Andrea can never overcome his limitations, the irony is mainly at his own expense. According to Kierkegaard, all ethical men are ironists, but not all ironists have ethical awareness. Andrea's "irony" comes from a deluded sense of his own superiority. When a genius like Raphael's appears that is higher than his own, he assumes an attitude of subjection and becomes servile. Fra Lippo's irony, on the other hand, is always under his control. He uses irony as a means of establishing an incognito, for he grasps the contradiction between the manner in which he exists inwardly—spiritually and religiously—and the apparent sensuality which cannot outwardly express his interior conviction. Only a dialectician who functions at an ethical or religious level is capable of the kind of irony that allows for self-development and growth. In "Andrea del Sarto" there is no careful redefinition of terms like "flesh" and "body," such as we find in "Fra Lippo Lippi." There is only accidental and sporadic development in the use of terms like "God" and "gold." Andrea is a more inventive rhetorician, more agile and witty than Fra Lippo; indeed, in no other poem does Browning submit to comic analysis attitudes that are so subtle and complex. But this very complexity makes it easy for Andrea to deceive himself. Incapable of growth, he lacks the capacity for self-criticism that distinguishes Fra Lippo's genuinely Socratic speech.

10

At first Fra Lippo seems to live in bondage to his senses, like a more robust Andrea del Sarto. But as we read further in his monologue, we begin to sense that he is a comic philosopher who mimics the self-delusion of spiritual experts like the Prior in order to expose their contradictions. His dialectical method is the logic of comedy par excellence. By kindling our laughter at the sight of folly so everlastingly rampant, Fra Lippo turns his comic impersonations into an instrument of transition and growth. His dialectical advance beyond the "beast" and "flesh" that he celebrates at the beginning is re-enacted in the very structure of his monologue. His discourse is formed in such a way that the addition of soul to flesh, in the middle of his monologue, matures his original confession of bestiality, and his final resolve to interpret God to all men transcends his earlier kissing of the girls. The monologue takes the form of a Socratic discourse, which is a process of changing the position at the start so that it can then be viewed in terms of the new motivations encountered en route. But the position at the end is already implicit in the position at the beginning. When he says that to "find [life's] meaning is [his] meat and drink," we are able to see back, as it were, to the place where he had started with his "mouthful of bread."

Fra Lippo's "hunger-pinch," which is on the level of bodily wants, develops into a voracious appetite for new experience. His monologue with the officers is itself a "feast of discourse" that betrays his social instinct and desire for fellowship. From being merely the contents of "the good belly-ful," food becomes the loaf dropped in the box at the poor girl's religious offering and the cup of wine that runs over in a spirited affirmation of the joy inseparable from merely being alive. Closely connected with the transformation of food, drink, and hunger is the imagery of flesh and intercourse. Once again, we pass from the sheer bodily appetites of the skipping rabbits or highly sexed rats, nipping "each softling of a wee white mouse," to the gregarious sensualist who desires the company of women as much for their songs as for their flesh. Then Fra Lippo passes to the purely intellectual satisfactions of his Socratic intercourse with the officers. Sitting down "hip to haunch," he finds that in his spoken words with the officers he can find the completest form of love, just as Socrates found it in his dialectical intercourse with young men. And just as Socrates' dialectic, especially in the *Phaedrus*, had the "ambivalence" of its "homosexual potential," as Kenneth Burke observes,[7] so Fra Lippo's discourse has the ambivalence of its erotic potential in the "sportive ladies" who "left their doors ajar" at night. But though his discourse begins at the erotic level, and even returns to the erotic level, the new terms discovered on the way make it improper for the ascetic Prior to reduce Fra Lippo's dialectic to its simplest and most guilty biological terms.

There is rhetorical cunning in the monk's casting so much of his discourse as a "confession." He is confessing what are faults only to anemic priors. And by carefully aligning the officers with himself as unlearned opponents of the Prior —"You speak no Latin more than I, belike" (l. 281)—he converts his argument against the ascetic life into a partly *ad hominem* argument against its unprepossessing advocate. "Latin" is like one of Matthew Arnold's "hangdog terms," a distinctive label which Fra Lippo keeps using to "represent [a] temper of mind."[8] The monk's refusal to speak Latin is also a counterpart of Browning's own stylistic strategy. The poet has a philosophic proposition to communicate, but he cannot deliver it "in Latin." Latin is a metaphor for the Prior's pretentious vocabulary of "spiritual" motivation: "Give us no more of body than shows soul!" Like purely conceptual language, it is devoid of the rich tonalities which

---

[7] "The Socratic Transcendence," *A Grammar of Motives* (New York, 1945), p. 427.

[8] Holloway, *The Victorian Sage*, p. 225.

contribute to the full, complex appeal of Fra Lippo's speech. By itself, Browning's Christian dialectic, like the Prior's "Latin," will convince no one. But just as Fra Lippo's frank confidences and wordly tone enable him to procure the good will of the officers, so his subtle ingratiation of himself manifests Browning's own persuasive powers over the reader and enables the poet to include all the intellectual development the irony will sustain.

When establishing the relation between spirit and substance, Fra Lippo uses dramatic analogies to make his meaning clear. To march in step like soldiers is to assist at the evolution of an equal relation, a union of substance and spirit, as it appears both in the classical style of Italian painting and in the medieval doctrines of philosophic "realism," which creates an analogy of the problem in its own sphere. Only perverse nominalists like the Prior insist on walking on one leg. Granting that there may be a soulless beauty like Andrea del Sarto's, though he denies he has ever seen it, Fra Lippo argues that such beauty would still be "about the best thing God invents" (l. 218). If a work of art has no soul, it is because observers like the Prior have no soul to bring to it. This recalls *Sordello*'s doctrine of the "Maker-see," the poet who invites his audience to bring their "soul" with them, to help make out his meaning for themselves.

But because Fra Lippo is now in danger of losing his audience, Browning must implement the rhetorical theories the monk has just formulated by engaging the reader (and his surrogate, the officer) in further dialectical ascents. To this end Browning first has Fra Lippo return with a rude jolt to the most sensual level. In speaking of kissing the girls and sliding down the great rings in front of Cosimo's house, Fra Lippo is trying to sound as salacious as possible. One suspects that his "Freudian slip" is deliberate and calculated to amuse the officers: *"You keep your mistr . . . manners, and I'll stick to mine!*" (l. 239). From such a sensual base Fra Lippo can rapidly remount to a new climax of spiritual intensity: "And my whole soul revolves, the cup runs over" (l. 250). His religious feeling rests in the belief that he can see the Creator directly in everything. The vision of God creating Eve rises instinctively and releases an incorruptible impulse to glorify God and His creation. But once again he is becoming too solemn, and for the second time he must return abruptly to his sensual base: "I'm a beast, I know" (l. 270).

Fra Lippo wants to celebrate the power of art and can praise in "Hulking Tom," his apprentice, what he cannot modestly celebrate in himself. He steps aside for a moment to marvel at "The shapes of things, their colors, lights and shades," then speculatively prods his auditors: "What's it all about? / To be passed over, despised? or dwelt upon, / Wondered at?" (ll. 290–292). The artist's moral function, as a mediator between God and man, is to teach others how to see creation. This is exactly the function of the poet in "How It Strikes a Contemporary," who is the king's counselor and God's chief agent. It is what enables Fra Lippo to serve as the principal exchange center between God and man and to announce that he will "Interpret God to all of you." After defining what art "was given for" (l. 304), he proceeds to distinguish the Prior's conception of art from his own. Fra Lippo classifies the devotees of spirit by associating their use of the term "art" with their use of phrases like "skull and bones" and "pious rage." Their morbid religious iconography makes the artist a scapegoat and the congregation a mob.

Near the beginning of the poem there is a reference to Fra Lippo as a "beast" (l. 80). But as the monk lifts the discourse to a philosophic plane by celebrating man's physical nature—"Being simple bodies" (l. 168)—we see that the "beast" is not merely a sensualist. His spontaneous appreciation of the physical world is a form of gratitude, of appetite for new experience (almost as pronounced in Browning as in Henry James), and the closest secular equivalent in the monk (as in his creator) to the traditional religious motive of glorification. Like every primitive sensibility, Fra Lippo is instinctively a "realist," in the medieval sense. He posits a *universalia ante rem*, a "meaning" behind the "world" ("To find its meaning is my meat and drink"), and in proclaiming the value of all created things, he projects every object as "an entity . . . [upon] the heavens": [9] "God made it all!" Whereas the sensual monk is orthodox in his theology, the ascetic Prior stands convicted, if not of heretical nominalism, at least of a radical perversion of the realist philosophy. In condemning Fra Lippo, the Prior is indicting the artist's reenactment of the central Christian mystery: his "incarnation" of a truth greater than mere reason can attain. The Prior is resolved to refine this mystery into "vapor"—or "soul," as he prefers to call it. Fra Lippo's orthodox Christianity transcends the senses, but this transcendence transcended produces the Prior's heresy of Gnosticism. In order to discharge their pious "rage," the Prior and his disciples have "scratched and prodded" Fra Lippo's picture of the pagan "slaves." Their holy concepts, like the Spanish monk's idea of the Trinity, have degenerated into mere superstitions. Like nominalists who reject the universals, these pious "fools" have failed to fathom the surface meanings. The more "spiritual" have never penetrated to the spirit in themselves. Because their "simplistic" theology is rooted in a defective formalism,

[9] J. Huizinga, *The Waning of the Middle Ages* (London, 1924), p. 186: "Every primitive mind is realist, in the medieval sense, independently of all philosophic influence. To such a mentality everything that receives a name becomes an entity and takes a shape which projects itself on the heavens." For an excellent discussion of this whole question, see chapter xv, "Symbolism in Its Decline," pp. 182–194.

Browning shows that it is not the ascetic Prior or his "spiritual" followers, but the high-spirited "realist," Fra Lippo, who discerns, in analogy to the Christian Incarnation, the immanence of a spiritual power in nature.

Fra Lippo steadily prepares for his three climaxes: "You get about the best thing God invents" (l. 218); "I always see the garden and God there / A-making man's wife" (ll. 266–267); and "Interpret God to all of you" (l. 311). The severest jolts come when, after disclosing their full symbolic power, he reduces these climaxes to the physical level. This dialectical movement extends to the characterization of Fra Lippo himself, who expands from a sensualist into an ethical and religious philosopher. He becomes "round," then collapses into sensual "flatness" again, and builds three times toward a religious climax. The conflict between flesh and spirit has thus its intriguing parallel in Browning's own rhetorical art—in the interaction between the concrete elements of dramatic personality, which are the "flesh" of Browning's poem, and the ideas they support. The presentation of Fra Lippo's philosophy is also a reflection of Browning's method —a dialectical play of opposites, brought together at their climaxes, like body and soul, in a synthetic union of personality and ideas. But if the "philosophy" solves the problem that the speaker raises (if, in this case, the dialectic of flesh and spirit is resolved, as it almost is), then the poem will cease to be a dramatic monologue—an attempt by Fra Lippo to secure some personal advantage from the officers—and become instead a mere lecture by the poet himself.

Fra Lippo's picture of himself as a blushing sensualist, hiding for very shame among the "company" of the blest, puts his case on the lowest possible level. The painting enacts earlier relations and appropriately fixes them in a dramatic analogy. The Prior and his disciples continue to patronize Fra Lippo in Latin: *"Iste perfecit opus"* (l. 377). But when he decides to populate their heaven with a "bowery flowery angel-brood," Fra Lippo's inane use of like endings appropriately mocks their pretensions. Fra Lippo's abrupt intrusion into his own painting also repeats the reversal of perspective established in the opening, when he turned to involve the reader directly in his own poetic world—"I am poor brother Lippo, by your leave!" (l. 1)—and so affirms the pattern. The monk in the painting engages his audience in a round of sensual activity that is as totally opposed to his sacramental doctrines of nature as is the nonartistic world the audience inhabits to the aesthetic realm of his painting. The genius of this "violation" is that it is also a way of being consistent. For it preserves the dialectical condition and prevents the poem from becoming a philosophic disquisition. Once a character discovers the "truth," his dialectical pilgrimage is over. Because we can predict what such an oracle will say, he is seldom entertaining as a person. This paradox helps explain why Browning's increasing preoccupation with the "truth" could prepare for the tedious exposition characteristic of his later period. The coda is the poet's unobtrusive way of reminding us, especially after Fra Lippo's lofty discourse, that the interaction between flesh and spirit, personality and ideas, which is the very condition of Browning's rhetorical art, must not be suspended. Whereas the limitation of many of the aesthetic masks is that they make everything over in their own image, the danger with a subjective poem is that it may project no image at all. The achievement of "Fra Lippo Lippi," as of most of Browning's successful monologues, is that just as the monk cannot separate flesh from spirit, so we, as readers, cannot isolate the characters from their ideas. In contrast to the early subjective poetry and the later didactic verse, most of the ethical and religious monologues evolve a synthetic image, an indissoluble fusion, of character and philosophy conjoined.

Whereas the three-part structure of "Fra Lippo Lippi" is incremental, "Andrea del Sarto's" form is random and non-progressive, as sporadic and meandering as its speaker. Its structural principle is not dialectical but repetitive. The key to its form is Andrea's self-exculpation under a bewildering variety of masochistic guises. At first Fra Lippo, in revealing his many misdemeanors to the officers, seems to be swayed by a similar motive of self-punishment. He appears to be moved, like Andrea, by the rhetorical motive per se, by the desire to bear witness, to address an audience, so his transgressions as a monk, like his transgressions as a painter, are a kind of continuing "martyrdom." But whereas Andrea's false wit and ingenuity are a complexity which is really a simplicity, Fra Lippo's dialectic is a simplicity which is finally a complexity. It enacts three times a complete movement from the aesthetic, through the ethical, to the religious stage. Andrea's irony begins in complacency and ends in personal disaster; Fra Lippo's humor begins in personal embarrassments and ends as a form of secular prayer.

7

Rhetoric at the
Religious Stage

If boredom is the final contradiction of the aesthetic stage, Browning's ethical man is the victim of a merely rational awareness whose furthest reach is a sense of futility or despair. Speakers like Karshish and Cleon are endowed with intellectual distinction, but only when they ramble in imagination beyond the domain of strict reason do they begin to think imperially. At other times they are no more capable of comprehending the mysteries of religion than is a creature living in two dimensions of understanding a third. To be translated from the aesthetic or the ethical to the religious sphere is like being annihilated by the invasion of some higher force. For this reason, the religious monologues present the greatest challenge to Browning's dialectical art of forcing his personae and the reader from the lower aesthetic and ethical stages onto a level of spiritual awareness that commands their own assent.

Of the major Victorian writers, Browning is among the most imaginative religious thinkers. Always excitingly suggestive, he is often profound in the depth and range of his religious speculations. Certain drifts of his thinking are roughly classifiable, and have, perhaps, been too readily catalogued as indicative of unreflective optimism, fideism, or

164

"emotional gnosticism," even by such outstanding Browning scholars as W. O. Raymond [1] and Sir Henry Jones. But Browning is not a systematic theologian, and even in treating the poet as a philosophic and religious teacher, Sir Henry concedes that Browning's art "resists the violence of the critical methods of philosophy." [2] Browning's best religious monologues give the experience of what he goes through in the progressive act of thinking. When he tries to convert that thought directly into poetry, it is usually at the expense of both the poetry and the thought.

Despite the attempts of such dissimilar critics as F. R. Leavis and Dean Inge to dismiss Browning as a mystagogue without a mind, the poet's religious speculations appear to have been nourished by an energetic intellect. His rational imagination keeps debating a few great problems, such as the likelihood of immortality and the mystery of evil. These are problems which, though never more disregarded than in the twentieth century, have never been permanently solved and still remain a matter of universal interest.

As a religious poet Browning is caught in a cross-fire of conflicting charges. Victorian religion, we are told, was a series of tea meetings and sermons carried on to the sound of trumpets. As its chief spokesman, Browning is too often treated as a superficial optimist. Scholars like F. R. G. Duckworth have accurately characterized the undisciplined raptures of the early Browning societies as an apparently "subtle plot to ruin the poet's reputation." [3] But the deliberately "unscientific" temper of the societies' moral and religious earnestness has been revived (evidently in reaction to the

[1] "Browning's Casuists," *The Infinite Moment and Other Essays in Robert Browning* (Toronto, 1950), p. 131.
[2] *Browning as a Philosophical and Religious Teacher* (Glasgow, 1892), p. 3.
[3] *Browning Background and Conflict* (New York, 1931), p. 69.

Victorian idolaters, though in point of fact with equally
strong emotion) by such distinguished detractors as George
Santayana [4] and F. R. Leavis.[5] In default of any poetic
analysis, their moral outrage is a kind of rhapsody in reverse.
Like the raptures of the early Browning Society, their sple-
netic ardor replaces all intelligent concern for literary value.
In a somewhat similar vein, neohumanists like Irving Babbitt
accuse Browning of forswearing "right reason," and Dean
Inge calls him a misologist. Other readers make the opposite
charge and object that in religious poems like *La Saisiaz*, the
search for truth begins to divorce itself from the search for
form till, as W. C. DeVane observes, "character and melody
[are] all but stifled in 'mere grey argument.' " [6]

If the Victorian conception of Browning as the "poet of
the soul" is an antiquated fetish, the tendency of other critics
to value Browning's poetic "form" and discount his religious
"thought" is just as idolatrous. From the contradictory
charges that Browning is too philosophical or not philosophical enough, that he is not sufficiently versed in theology or is
so thoroughly grounded in it that he is ruined forever as a
poet, we can conclude only that critics are being neither fair
nor imaginative when they classify Browning quickly at a
surface glance. Browning is a Christian poet with an interest
in philosophic speculation, but he is not a self-righteous sec-
tarian, and he scrupulously avoids polemical stridency and
the niceties of dogma. His arguments push far beyond that
theology which is merely idolized as social convention or a
dull set of moral precepts. Many times, familiar ideas are expressed in a compellingly dramatic form, in a memorable
phrase or fresh context. At such moments they seem to

---

[4] "The Poetry of Barbarism," *Interpretations of Poetry and Religion* (New York, 1900).
[5] *New Bearings in English Poetry* (London, 1932).
[6] *A Browning Handbook* (New York, 1955), p. 29.

penetrate the very mystery of existence and raise the central religious questions in all their complexity and power. Monologues like "Cleon" and "Caliban upon Setebos" will live, by the perpetual relevance of their philosophic thought, in that middle ground between drama and debate where Browning's poetic and intellectual supremacy, like that of Plato and Shaw in similar genres, is unsurpassed.

1

We can usually plot Browning's development chronologically, for his most dramatic masks belong to the early aesthetic stage and his most dialectical monologues to his later period. One of the striking exceptions to this rule is the religious monologue " 'Imperante Augusto Natus Est——,' " written in the last years of the poet's life, probably in 1888. In this poem, as in "Cleon," Browning balances different views of Christianity and the Graeco-Roman world. But so far is he from being polemical that he neither argues nor asserts; he simply presents. As in the early aesthetic monologues, he compresses debate into metaphors of dramatic situation with double, sometimes opposite, kinds of meaning.

The speaker of the monologue is a Roman senator, and his references to the thirteenth consulship of Augustus set the poem in the year 2 B.C. His language of deification is impressive and commanding. Its heroic elevation ("Be Caesar God!") and Latinate grandeur ("Where was escape from his prepotency?") violate the colloquial tone that Browning has already established in the speaker's use of the secret exhortation and the parenthetical aside, and in giving the reader the constant sense that someone is speaking confidentially and familiarly to someone else. Varius' reported panegyric brings home to both reader and speaker the heightened dignity of the Emperor Augustus as man and god. This vision of imperial grandeur stimulates the senator's imagination and causes him to see himself as a patronizing Caesar playing god to the outcast beggar whom he fancifully types as a debased "Anti-Caesar," a "monarch in the mud." Browning demonstrates how closely social and religious hierarchies are linked. He plays upon the paradoxical inversion of election to lowly social status and imperial "nobility."

The "glory's summit" of Augustus' reign, during which Christ was born, is both a moment of high triumph (" 'He's God!' shouts Lucius Varius") and of imminent disaster ("Crown, now—Cross, when?"). The "monarch in the mud" is at once Caesar and Christ. He is literally the Emperor Augustus who, as a kind of Roman Caliban, has chosen to abase himself, even at the height of his glory, to appease "Some [greater] Power, admonishing the mortal-born." But the man-god who "stoops . . . to rise," according to St. John's description in "A Death in the Desert," [7] also prefigures the Son of Man. The success of the poem depends on the reader's receiving both the surprise of the Emperor's prefiguring Christ and the speaker's surprise at penetrating the beggar's disguise. Browning carefully subordinates the local historical ironies—such as the relative obscurity of Virgil and Horace and the current prestige of the poet Varius—to the controlling irony of the speaker's complacent assumption of superiority to the beggar: "As to me Caesar, so to thee am I." This analogy sets up the hierarchical background against which the surprise is to stand out. The fumbling apology ("My gesture was a trifle—well, abrupt") marks the breakdown of the speaker's composure. The marveling exclamations, culminating in a kind of dumb terror, confront the senator with the shocking energy of his own abruptness with the Emperor. The stumbling dashes ("Whose—whose might be the face?") both imitate and rebuke his energy by setting it in implicit contrast to the

[7] L. 134: " 'Such ever was love's way: to rise, it stoops. . . .' "

stern gaze of the motionless Augustus and, later, to his own mute wonder.

These halting rhythms expand into visionary utterance and, as they move, give fitful glimpses of revelation. Like Yeats's "rough beast" that "Slouches towards Bethlehem to be born," "the petted lioness" that "Strikes with . . . sudden paw" is the Roman's intuition that a new revelation is at hand, but that the revelation will be a terrifying one, or an ambiguous one at best. Irony permeates the frightening image of the Roman attendant who supports the Emperor's crown with one hand and points to "the instruments of shame" with the other. The metaphor of the cycle dominates the conqueror's rise to "glory's summit" and his subsequent fall into oblivion, and suggests that civilized order depends on barbarism, violence, and the horror of "The malefactor's due."

"Crown, now—Cross, when?" is probably the poem's most brilliant link, for "crown" takes us back to the conqueror's military triumph but also anticipates Christ's crown of thorns, for which the satiric mockery of "anti-Caesar, monarch in the mud," has partly prepared us. The "Cross," of course, prefigures the central Christian mystery, and is therefore a source of both creation and destruction. As a result of the Sibylline prophecy that a king from "blind Judea" will master Caesar and rule the world, the Roman senator, like Yeats's persona in "The Second Coming," fears the rise of a new cult of violence. The Roman construes the oracle as a prophecy that a latent barbarism will triumph in the future, and he can regain his equilibrium only by dismissing the story as an "old-wife's tale." But the final irony is one to which the speaker is naturally "blind." Only the reader knows that the king from "blind Judea" was destined to find his largest Roman following among the slaves—menials like the "Bath-drudge" whom the snarling patrician threatens to lash, in his most revealing disclosure of pagan pride, in the last lines of the poem.

↗ 2 ↖

The weakness of " 'Imperante Augusto Natus Est——' " is the absence of rhetorical preparation, which makes its climactic reversal melodramatic rather than dramatic. Though Browning carefully avoids all explicit argument by balancing different views of the pagan and Christian worlds through a series of allusive symbols, most of the poem is still disguised "rhetoric." Instead of presenting its doctrine as emotion, it generates emotion out of its contrived situation. Browning turns a character sketch into a lecture and consciously addresses the reader rather than the auditor in the Roman bath, whom we soon forget. By only pretending to avoid polemics, he tricks us into figuratively going to church and makes us captive auditors of a doctrinal exhortation.

Like " 'Imperante Augusto Natus Est——,' " "An Epistle containing the Strange Medical Experience of Karshish, the Arab Physician" (1853–1854) makes evident its opposing forces, not through a play of ideas, but through a psychological conflict between science and religion in the soul of a skeptical physician. But unlike the later poem it carefully prepares a symbolic matrix that enables the religiously elevated coda to tower grandly above the rest of the monologue without producing the kind of melodramatic shock we might receive if we were looking at a painting in which a cherub suddenly materialized from a thunder cloud to deliver us a sermon.

Browning tries to overcome the reader's own resistance by having the Arab physician Karshish approach his subject from the point of view of his skeptical teacher Abib, who functions as the reader's surrogate. By creating a curiosity in his master Abib, who embodies the impulse to disbelieve,

Karshish creates it in the mind of the reader, too. The satisfaction of this curiosity temporarily involves a set of frustrations, but in the end these frustrations prove to be simply a
more involved kind of satisfaction that makes the fulfillment
more intense. Karshish could have recounted in ten lines his
story of the baffling *idée fixe* that has taken possession of a
certain Lazarus, a Jew, who insists that after being dead for
three days, he has been restored to life by a Nazarene sage.
To defend Browning's ampler narrative we must refer, not
to the inherent complexity of his doctrine of imperfection or
his belief in a God of love, but to the needs of the skeptical
Abib and, even more, to those of the neutral reader. Many
twentieth-century readers are more embarrassed by references
to moral and religious elevation than were the Victorians,
and less embarrassed by other subjects, such as sex. But they
are seldom disturbed by the religious elevation of Dante or
Milton, which still retains its formal and psychological appeal. Religious persuasion that may have moved the Victorians, because the subject of religion was intrinsically appealing to them, can still interest modern readers by its formal
merits, after the appeal of the rhetoric as "doctrine" or
"truth" has faded. "An Epistle . . . of Karshish" is calculated to command the assent of such readers by subordinat-
ing its "psychology of information" to its "psychology of
form." Its most interesting parts are those passages in which
the religious "matter" leaves off and the rhetorical "manner"
begins.

Karshish is a skeptical scientist with a mixture of true
knowledge, partial apprehension, and the immense curiosity
of an Arabian Fra Lippo: "An itch I had, a sting to write, a
tang!" At first he produces a distracted, scatterbrained effect
by using catalogues and lists, often syntactically unconnected
and separated only by dashes. Browning reinforces this impression by using a "language of gesture"—what R. P.

Blackmur calls "the language beneath or beyond or alongside of the language of words." [8] Though the jumbled minutiae of his medical lore achieve an effect of mental clutter, Karshish creates the impression of functioning at a higher level of awareness and of obtruding his litter of details to hide his real concerns. He is the ethical man, confronted with the mystery of a whole new dimension, whose speech at first records protective trivia like a strip of tape that keeps unrolling. But unlike the early sensualists, who are passive and distracted, Karshish calculates all his effects. By anticipating Abib's ojections ("Thou laughest here!"), he robs them of half their force. To whet Abib's interest, he feigns a reluctance to tell his story, a hesitancy of which Shakespeare's Antony and Iago are less scrupulous masters: "I half resolve to tell thee, yet I blush (l. 65)." His penchant for understatement takes the form of professional detachment: " 'Tis but a case of mania—subinduced / By epilepsy" (ll. 79–80). In case he may be suspected of being a prejudiced narrator, Karshish supplies his rational solution to the mystery even before he relates his story.

In recounting the case history of Lazarus, Karshish deftly controls his analogies. Just as the fortune that the beggar acquires through no effort of his own unfits him for living, so Lazarus' passive reception of spiritual truth during his three days' trance leaves him dazed and stupefied. His mind has become a *tabula rasa:* "The man is witless," Karshish says. The doctrine of imperfection is important to Browning, because to know everything is to be denied freedom. Faith is chosen from necessity; but it is also the freedom to choose that is beyond necessity. The link between his doctrine of imperfection and his belief in a God of love is not simply the mechanical link Lazarus. It is the freedom essential to the transformation of religion into an internal dialectic—a prin-

[8] *Language as Gesture* (New York, 1952), p. 3.

ciple which both the Romantic aspiration for perfection and the voluntarist God of power repudiate. The religious man at the highest stage can remain in his freedom only by constantly realizing it, like David in "Saul" or like Pompilia in *The Ring and the Book*. Because Lazarus, on the other hand, has never chosen to be free, he can interpret God only abstractly, as an external power that has at one time invaded his life without transforming it.

To win assent to Lazarus' story, Karshish first compares him to the old lord known to Abib and himself, the sage whose "magic" was an accredited part of occult learning (ll. 167–177). In disbelieving Lazarus, Abib and the reader are like those youthful skeptics whom the old sage used to chide for their scientific dogmatism. Karshish implies that if the suprarational fire can derange Lazarus by merely touching him, it can completely consume such scoffers. The second time Karshish mentions the sage (ll. 253–255) is when he is trying to transfer the sanction of the suprarational, which both he and Abib have recognized in their avowed "lord," to the Nazarene physician, who is also called a "sage" (l. 244). The earthquake which prefigured the death of their "lord" took place at the time of the Nazarene's death. Though prepared to grant Christ the powers of wizardry, Karshish can still not discard his own rational postulates. He assumes that the skeptics murdered Christ when his art failed and asks them how the Nazarene's magic could have stopped the earthquake. The irony is multiple; in the first place, Karshish has his chronology wrong. He thinks that the earthquake, which followed or closely accompanied Christ's death, came earlier. As usual, Browning is treating "fact" and "fancy" ironically, as F. E. L. Priestley has shown in his study of *La Saisiaz*.[9] Half of Karshish's "facts" are wrong or wrongly

[9] "A Reading of 'La Saisiaz,'" *University of Toronto Quarterly*, XXV (1955), 47–59.

interpreted; what he rejects as "fancy" is truth. Moreover, what Karshish intends as a rhetorical question the poet takes as a straight interrogation. Because Browning expects us to share the view that Christ could have stopped the earthquake if he chose, Karshish is being ironical at the skeptics' expense while Browning is being ironical at his.

The great prophetic evocation of "So, through the thunder comes a human voice" and the religious elevation of "O heart I made, a heart beats here!" (ll. 306–307) loom grandly above the rest of the poem. The mystery of a God who "dwelt in flesh" on earth "awhile" violates the Arab's monotheism only to justify this violation by an implicit deeper logic. The human voice that speaks through the thunder, and mirrors the Arab's face in its own, seems to reverse the physician's use of language which can proceed only from the higher to the lower term.

> The very God! think Abib; dost thou think?
> So, the All-Great, were the All-Loving too—
> So, through the thunder comes a human voice
> Saying, "O heart I made, a heart beats here!
> Face, my hands fashioned, see it in myself!
> Thou hast no power nor mayst conceive of mine,
> But love I gave thee, with myself to love,
> And thou must love me who have died for thee!"
>
> [ll. 304–311].

The voice's disrespect for nature is a signal to the reader that this new method of using words overcomes both the empiricism of Karshish, who fails to see that the mystery of the nitrous plant also affirms the mystery of God (ll. 280–282), and the madness of Lazarus, whose view of things *sub specie aeternitatis* unfits him for life in this world. Because the Incarnation makes God immanent in the world, the believer who sees a whole universe riding in a grain of sand is no longer undergoing, like Lazarus, a kind of spiritual rape.

But since the Christian God is also more than this world, Karshish's nature is now part of a transformed whole. When "the All-Great" becomes "the All-Loving" (l. 305), and the God of power becomes a God of love, the substitution of freedom for necessity enables Karshish to possess himself in Christ, just as the lover in "The Last Ride Together" had tried to possess himself in the woman and had failed. In Karshish's life this moment represents what the Incarnation does in the history of all mankind. As a physician, Karshish inhabits a world of mechanical causes. But in confronting the Nazarene sage, he is suddenly no longer joined to a determining past. This transcendence of time makes apparent the irrelevance of all objections to Browning's anachronistic ascribing of a strict monotheism to a first-century Arab: "God forgive me! who but God himself?" (l. 268). For into the midst of Karshish's life there now intrudes the nonhistorical, transcendent moment in which the Arab has the opportunity to assert his faith and complete himself. But because some readers will be too easily attracted and others too easily repelled by the religious language, Browning has to restore the experience of unbelief together with the experience of belief. He must once again incorporate those wavering attitudes—skeptical and credulous, curious and disengaged—in whose dramatic clash his whole "psychology of form" consists. To this end he has Karshish conclude with an adaptation of the argument *ad hominem* that tries to discredit the doctrine by rejecting Lazarus as a simple "madman."

Karshish first uses "mad" as a medical term to diagnose the Jew's fixation (l. 79). But from this descriptive use it is only a short step to the skeptic's use of "mad" to justify a scientific rejection of the Jew's mysticism. "Mad" is transferred from the patient to his story, and Karshish speaks of his "crazy tale" (l. 224). The Arab uses "mad" in a third sense, as a form of name-calling. When he says "our patient

Lazarus / Is stark mad" (ll. 263–264), he is not diagnosing the Jew's condition but using "mad" to discredit what Lazarus says. Most uses of "mad" in the poem hover somewhere between the two extremes of the medical term and the opprobrious epithet. "Thy crazy tale" and "The madman saith He said so" are not simply attempts to discount the Jew's story. Since the reader is not in the habit of dismissing the Christian story as "crazy," the definition forces him to break through rigid distinctions between madness and rationality. Such uses of "crazy" and "mad" have the effect of giving insanity a broader meaning. They affirm the sanity of religious genius and the madness of the merely rational mind. If the marvelous solution of the coda is "crazy," then how sane is the rationalist who rejects it? The "madman's" religion is a source, not, to be sure, of scientific "truth," but of human meaning, which, as C. S. Lewis finely says, is "the antecedent condition both of truth and falsehood, [and] whose antithesis is not error but nonsense." [10] If this is madness, it is the lunacy in which the meaning of life consists, in which man's dignity and worth reside.

But "mad" can never be a neutral term. In calling Lazarus a "madman," Karshish is also drawing attention to the difference between his own constant activity and the apathy that leaves Lazarus deranged. Karshish's profound skepticism, which is always waging war with his impulse to believe, is the way of the truly religious man who must struggle for his faith and continually realize it from moment to moment. In a paradoxical way the scientist's attitude of active skepticism, of faith that the world is rational and of disbelief in our present understanding of it, is Browning's own attitude of undogmatic and corrigible faith. It is the very condition of his dialectical art, which portrays many points of view in order to overcome their limitations. In his attitude to religion, as in

[10] "Bluspels and Flalansferes," *The Importance of Language*, ed. Max Black (Englewood Cliffs, N.J., 1962), p. 49.

his attitude to the very principles of his medical investigation, Karshish has a robust faith and yet does not believe. If Lazarus is the lowest product of the religious life, Karshish is the highest product of the ethical. His active faith without belief (though it finally consigns him to a lower stage) is preferable to the passivity of the Jew's belief without faith.

The Arab's opening "confessions" to Abib gradually cast off his guilt. As they become more and more like "professions," they expand in the coda into a grand statement of faith. As "profession" overpowers "confession," Karshish shifts from persuasion of Abib to a form of visionary utterance. This is another way of saying that his audience changes. Karshish begins by confessing his own folly to Abib. But he is also confessing, and finally professing, in the presence of God alone. As the method of the monologue undergoes "conversion," the second auditor becomes more important than the first. Because he is always making room for another idea, Karshish can keep his mind flexible. Between a science which is forever becoming more exact in measuring how much its formulas diverge from the facts they are supposed to express and a faith that rejects finality as a matter of principle there is a spontaneous convergence. The Arab's imaginative skepticism transcends itself, not by a *non sequitur*, but by tautology. His intense enthusiasm as a medical researcher is already a form of that imagination which succeeds, that intuition which guesses the principle of experience. Like Fra Lippo's curiosity, his hunger for the truth is a secular form of grace. The scientist is a realist and unbeliever, in his understanding both of this world and the other; and his life of skepticism is rooted in God.

〰 3 〰

In "Cleon" (1854), as in "An Epistle . . . of Karshish," a character apparently immune to disruptive impulses, who is sustained by Greek philosophy and art, as the Arab was by medical research, confronts an event which calls into question the validity of his experience—which threatens to dissolve and then reshape his whole way of living. The poem is closest in structure to "Fra Lippo Lippi." It stages a three-part dialectic in which Cleon rises from the aesthetic and ethical stages to a series of dim adumbrations of the religious life. But the oppositions that grow out of these perspectives prepare for the reversals at the end of each section: "I pass too surely: let at least truth stay" (l. 157); "Most progress is most failure" (l. 272); "Zeus has not yet revealed it" (l. 334). In each case Cleon turns his philosophy inside out, arguing for a position that subverts his argument. There is a disparity between terms like "philosophy" or "culture" and the proud pagan values served by their use. By abstracting Cleon's pride as a single element, first in Greek culture, then in man, and finally in his individual achievements, Browning prepares for the toppling such dignities are to suffer. The results of the whole process are stated in the bold conclusion, where Cleon's pride emerges most contemptuously as the pagan "rationality" which, in forbidding Protus to think imperially, is really a form of madness in disguise.

Browning's choice of an epigraph from the Acts of the Apostles implies a relational argument. If pagan Greeks believe in God, as St. Paul suggests, even though they give their beliefs a different name, then Christians must believe a fortiori. The religious monologues embody a form of the a fortiori argument whenever they reason from the "impossible" case and bring a character like Cleon, Caliban, or Karshish to the threshold of Christian belief.

The opening movement (ll. 43–157) is a defense of Greek philosophy and art. Cleon compares the rarefied thoughts of himself and his contemporaries, the outcome of the labors of past generations, to the "subtler element of air" within a hollow sphere, which "the vulgar" call empty be-

cause they are ignorant of "air's . . . hidden properties."
But in presuming to apprehend the "vulgar" as comical,
Cleon's attempt to establish his own superiority over the
ancients becomes itself an object of irony. In a world where
all progress is failure, the proud boasting of the culture hero
is inevitably a comic butt. His philosophic voice, ludicrously
expansive and pedantic, sounds less like Aristotle than like
Chaucer's eagle. Cleon seems to have more of Polonius in his
veins than of Plato. He finally sees that there is only one way
he can be at home in the world. He can escape his isolation
only if the world itself becomes a personality and he can
"prove Zeus' self, the latent everywhere!"

The need to find his own personality mirrored in the
world is a philosophic exigency so compelling to Cleon that
even if the Incarnation never existed, it seems for a moment
necessary to invent it. An all-encompassing thought, rousing
him out of his comfortable pedantries, solemnly presents the
spectacle of life passing before him. It leads him to consecrate
the terrors as well as the sanctities of history as a form of
religious emotion. But Cleon's "dream" of rendering clear to
the popular imagination "some eternal greatness incarnate in
the passage of [natural and] temporal fact," which is A. N.
Whitehead's prophecy of the kind of religion that will
triumph,[11] immediately undergoes a shift in meaning. Cleon's
first use of "dream" is a detached definition of religious myth,
but then he changes its emotive meaning to signify the
"illusory" or "self-deceiving." When his faltering ascent toward religious truth collapses, Cleon's distinction between the
ethical and aesthetic stages also breaks down. Instead of dem-
onstrating that he is the final product of a great order, his
reasoning forces him to recognize that he is only a small part
of that order: "I am not great as they are, point by point."

[11] *Adventures of Ideas* (New York, 1933), p. 41.

What should be the climax of Cleon's argument is, in fact, the turning point. His pride in embracing the whole is ironically dwarfed and finally drowned in the appalling prospect of "running" everything (including Cleon himself) "into one soul." The "truth" that "stay[s]" is something outside himself in which he cannot participate. His lonely voice rejects the world even as he proclaims his faith in the permanence of a different order: "I pass too surely: let at least truth stay!"

The second movement (ll. 158-272) is Cleon's reply to Protus' inquiry about how he should confront death. If the first section tries to prove that Cleon, as a culture hero in the great tradition, is more privileged than the ancients, the second movement celebrates the privileges which all men enjoy over the rest of the created world. But unless he has reached the higher religious stage, man's ethical life proves even more contradictory than the life of fish and snakes. Since the magnificent absurdity of such a world is something man transcends, Cleon can begin by mocking the life he shares with the animal kingdom. Though this life proceeds in one direction only, from consciousness to matter—"It has them, not they it"—such limitations are painless to Cleon, for his rationality and "sense of sense" resolve these contradictions.

But when Cleon discovers even greater incongruities at the ethical stage, his apprehension ceases to be comic, for this time he despairs of a solution. Man's mortality, which is the aesthete's delight when he luxuriates in it or defies it, is the moralist's deepest anguish. Because his soul is "fastened to a dying animal," Cleon climbs higher than the animals "just to perish there." Man at the ethical stage is like a naiad sending water through its tube. But whereas the naiad is unaware of larger reservoirs on the hill, which would allow her to "spout oceans if she could," man knows he is limited in ways that

are past his "power to widen or exchange" (l. 258). The
more Cleon relishes his life, the greater his resultant melancholy. Without the assurance of a sphere beyond the ethical,
there exists a contradiction that enables the "paragon of
animals" to see that he is also "the quintessence of dust"—a
disparity which obsessed Tennyson and Hardy as well as
Hamlet. To create in man longings for knowledge he never
can attain seems either a refinement of malicious irony,
worthy of the God of Caliban, or else a promise of fulfillment. But if of fulfillment, "where is the sign?" Man succeeds that he may "use but a man's joy / While he sees
God's." God puts man on the ethical rack to anguish his
spirit, and by suspending him there over the "surrounding
flats of natural life," He creates an abyss that is deeper for
man than for the animals. The oxymorons of despair—breadth
of vision is desolation, and "Most progress is most failure"—
are blunter versions of the paradoxes already formulated,
which Cleon can resolve only by using some higher term.

The third movement (ll. 273–335) begins as a refutation
of Protus' attempt to ascribe value to the aesthetic life. By
expanding into syllogistic form Protus' causal enthymeme
that the poet leaves "behind [him] living works," Cleon attacks the fallacy of the major proposition: "All who create
living works live." A principal argument of Collard's treatise
on logic, which was one of the books in Browning's library,
is that most errors in reasoning occur when thinkers conceal
their hypotheses in suppressed propositions.[12] The fallacy of
Protus' hypothesis is that, in transferring the quality of "life"
from the art to the artist, he shifts from a qualified to an absolute use of the word "life." Cleon perceives that he and his
art appear to transcend time only by abstracting from the
sensuous immediacy they can depict but never share:

[12] J. Collard, *The Essentials of Logic, Being a Second Edition of
Collard's "Epitome" Improved* (London, 1796), p. 236.

Because in my great epos I display
How divers men young, strong, fair, wise, can act—
Is this as though I acted? if I paint,
Carve the young Phoebus, am I therefore young?
[ll. 285–288].

The discovery that the celebration of the "rower . . . with
the molded muscles . . . all a-ripple on his back" must be an
elegy on Cleon's own failing powers produces a faltering of
the voice. Cleon can write about love but not make it; he can
pontificate about kingship but never rule. The immortality
that rewards the artist is figurative immortality—fame—
rather than literal. If Sappho and Aeschylus "survive" absolutely, and not merely in this qualified sense, then "let them
come and take / Thy slave in my despite, drink from thy
cup, / Speak in my place" (ll. 306–308). By leaving Protus
to deny the consequent of this hypothetical syllogism, Cleon
also negates the antecedent. Cleon's dilemma is really logical
in form: when young, man is ignorant; when old, he cannot
experience. Since man is either young or old, he either cannot
experience or cannot know. The crucial moments in life are
over just as he begins to understand them.

In a brilliant use of the rhetorical technique that Holloway
has analyzed in illustrating how Cardinal Newman enlists
negative evidence,[13] Cleon demonstrates that the very qualities which in Protus' view make the intellectual's life a privileged one make it most intolerable. As the philosopher's soul
grows more acute, "intensified / By power and insight," the
"heavy years increase— / The horror quickening still from
year to year." Like William James, who felt that in old age
he was just becoming fit to live, Cleon fears the "consummation," when he "shall know most, . . . yet least enjoy."
From an "old man's frenzy" ("I, I the feeling, thinking, act-

13 *The Victorian Sage*, pp. 168–171.

ing man") he passes to an ineffably pathetic contemplation of the "man who loved his life so over-much," asleep now in his urn. The thought is so "horrible" that he must completely break with the pagan consolations and turn for aid in a new direction.

Separated from the state of nature through his capacities as a symbol-making animal, Cleon's response to hierarchy and order provides an analogy for his idea of heaven. His grand vision of "Some future state revealed to us by Zeus, / Unlimited in capability / For joy, as this is in desire for joy" communicates the deepest yearning, somehow impersonal in the very depth of its commitment. Its religious solution is a sheerly dialectical ascent forced on Cleon by the logic of his system. But it is so universal and comes so close to visionary utterance that we seem to hear a more all-pervading voice than that of either Cleon or Browning. It is almost as though the monologue were to become a dialogue—an awestruck conversation between God and man. Cleon is momentarily compelled to stand outside himself, "ecstatic" in the original sense of that word, and to peek in wonder beyond the fact of death. The evolution of worm into fly adumbrates man's own destiny. It substitutes for the empiricist's reduction of the whole to the part the soul's reverse passage from the material part to the spiritual whole. This process gives symmetry to creation and provides a correlative in nature that makes man's religious vision more than a "dream."

But the "truth," especially when revealed in a "dialogue" with God, is not the "destiny" of a dramatic monologue. To preserve the dialectical condition, Browning must bring into play the other elements of Cleon's character. As a philosopher who has also proved "absurd all written hitherto" upon the soul, Cleon represents just those elements of Greek rationalism which thwart the development of his religious nature: "But no! / Zeus has not yet revealed it; and alas, / He must have done so, were it possible!" Cleon's attitudes are composed partly of pagan rationalism, partly of instinctive aestheticism, and partly of a human sensibility bred by experience to the point of insight. But while there is an important sense in which the very method of his dialectic undergoes "conversion," Cleon himself is never transformed. His intellectual superiority rejects every disclosure of his own limitations; it negates the very ascent that could have saved him. Because his climaxes are never accepted as such, his downward movements, unlike Fra Lippo's, never infuse his terms with the spiritual power he encounters en route. His Epicurean blessing is a parody of Christian benediction and ends as a kind of curse: "Live long and happy, and in that thought die." The rejection of St. Paul marks Cleon's final return from the intensity of his private vision to pride in his professed ideals. The pagan philosopher is too much his superior to hear the "barbarian Jew" in person and indicts him on hearsay from a bystander. Browning is mocking the rationalist who uses an irrational method of proving that his rival is irrational.

Cleon keeps using his disenchantment to turn a melancholy period, and he toys with the grandeurs of irony while himself remaining a Philistine. To be sure, an impressive list of his intellectual interests could be drawn up, ranging from pre-Darwinian theories of evolution and tragic speculations on man as the cosmic accident to the Christian view of human dignity. But because Cleon's despair and disillusion are species of inverted pride, he remains a puzzled and human questioner, who can never share as actively in Protus' "profound discouragement" as David does in Saul's. His ironic apprehension is partly illegitimate, and intellectual presumption is the only residue that Browning can allow proud irony to yield.

༺ 4 ༻

Browning's religious monologues reject ideas only when they are held as rigid frames to limit experience and to take the place of a mystery they cannot explain. Even in rejecting such ideas, Browning nourishes his religious poems with more rational imagination than most critics of his "emotional gnosticism" seem ready to admit. As we have seen, Cleon's sheer power of mind forces a religious solution which his pride in reason paradoxically negates. And in "A Death in the Desert" Browning celebrates St. John's discovery of the great wealth of logic behind the mythical thinking of Christianity. Under the impact of the higher criticism the historical Christ had vanished altogether, and St. John was resolved into Plato. Browning's St. John is a rationalist, who tries to establish the transcendent logic of a "love" behind "the will and might." Browning wants to show that, regardless of its historicity, this logic requires, for reasons of inherent persuasiveness and on grounds of sheer dialectical symmetry alone, the authenticity of the Christian narrative.

The argument takes place in the "black minute" of "Prospice," that abysmal instant in which St. John, suspended between life and death, experiences the miracle of his continued existence as an act of grace renewed from instant to instant. If it were necessary for his defense of Christianity to future generations, he trusts that God would continue to confer this grace for "a new hundred years." John moves from psychology to personal biography to universal history, and at all times his progression has its own theological correlatives. His dialectic is ingeniously repetitive—a consistent maintaining of the aesthetic, ethical, and religious stages under a variety of guises. His doctrine of the three souls is the psychological equivalent of these three stages—"what Does," "what Knows," "what Is"—and they find their theological counterpart in the Father, the Holy Spirit, and the Son, respectively—St. John's "the Way, the Truth, and the Life." The three stages mark the different phases of John's own ministry.[14] At first he preaches the "very superficial truth" of what he has seen and heard. Then he begins to reason from his "knowledge" and to write epistles. Finally, at the third stage he receives, on Patmos, God's direct revelation of "what Is." At the aesthetic level of "what Does," John is like those poets in *Sordello* who merely say that they have seen; in trying to interpret Christ at the second stage, he resembles those artists who explain what it is they have seen; only in his state of physical decay, when he finds himself at the level of "what Is," can John impart his gift of spiritual vision to others. His attempt to predict from his own experience the difficulties of future generations marks his transition from personal to universal history.

Since John is the last disciple alive with a direct memory of the historical events, he has to address men denied the "very superficial truth" of his direct witnessing. When addressing such men, he tries to express the Christian story in its logical form. Its narrative events are mere "points" at the level of "what Does" for the expression of truths that are not intrinsically narrative or temporal at all, but continuous and self-repeating, each one requiring and implying all the others. Thus for John "the sin and death" are inseparable from "the good and glory consummated thence," and he trusts that after stating the truths narratively, men will allow the eter-

[14] As with so much else in this study, I am indebted for my treatment of the trinitarian analogies in "A Death in the Desert" to Professor F. E. L. Priestley's lectures at University of Toronto. See Priestley's notes on "A Death in the Desert" in *Representative Poetry*, prepared by members of the Department of English at the University of Toronto ([Toronto, 1963] III, 418). A similar treatment appears in William Whitla's *The Central Truth: The Incarnation in Robert Browning's Poetry* (Toronto, 1963).

nity of "principles" to take over. He compares the historic focusing of the eternal truths, of the "star" of logical "firsts," to the operation of an optic glass. The reduction to historic fact is the kind of poetic enactment appropriate to a narrative style. But even if the historical events which John has witnessed never actually took place, he believes that the transcendent logic of a "love" behind "the will and might" would require the invention of the Christian story as a paradigm for the placing and timing of the eternal mystery.

To establish the logic of such a paradigm, John first relates theology to the faculty psychology that Browning had developed as early as *Paracelsus*, where power, knowledge, and love anticipate the three persons of the Trinity: "The love that tops the might, the Christ in God" (l. 265). Love (or Christ) should be at least as self-evident a value as the body's food or clothing. Even to the secular mind the myth of Christ as love should be comparable to Aeschylus' Promethean myth. Sophists may deny the imaginative relevance of the Promethean story, but even the pragmatist must concede "the indubitable bliss of fire." John defends the genius of the Christian dialectic by arguing that if "the indubitable bliss" of love were equally evident, God would be compelling man's assent. John's unformulated major premise is that all acts of faith presuppose free belief. It follows as a syllogism that since assent to a self-evident truth is not a free act, it is not an act of faith.

To anticipate and partly remove the difficulties of future generations, especially the problems of the nineteenth century, John argues that just as the prisoner in Plato's cave can logically infer from intermittent gleams the existence of a sun, so from revelations of power and love in their operations on his soul man can affirm the immanence of a greater "Love" in "Power," which John has already identified as "the Christ in God." Through analogical extension of what the nominalists accept as empirically "real," John can disguise the priority of his own commitments while establishing an implicit Christian "logic" that is independent of all historical verification. This logic must be judged, not by a "correspondence," but by a "coherence" theory of truth. Its integrity is more akin to the internal consistency of mathematics than to the "bridge-building" of physical science. Browning would deny that John's intuitive discernment of this logic is in any way irrational. Nor would he grant that we can apply the word "logic" to a religious revelation only metaphorically. Collard's treatise *The Essentials of Logic*, which Browning's father estimated highly and which occupied a prominent place in the poet's library, is emphatic on this point. One of its first axioms is that "when, in tracing back the evidence, from our most remote deductions, we arrive at the *intuitive* source, we discover it to be the fountain head of all ratiocination." [15]

St. John demonstrates why faith requires that as belief grows, miracles have to be withdrawn. The whole venture of faith is inseparable from doubt. Miracles, if they continued to abound after the rise of Christianity, would compel assent and, instead of helping to create faith, would destroy it. St. John does not know whether the disappearance of miracles is a change in the natural order or a change in the qualities of the perceiving mind. But to "unprove" the logic of this withdrawal is "to re-prove the proved." His deepest feeling is focused in punning contradictions which join similar grammatical forms with sharp conflicts of meaning. More important than a re-proving of the proved, which leads nowhere, is the use of men's knowledge, the living of their truth, which brings St. John to the central tenet of the ecclesiastic whose theology Browning presents in "Bishop Blougram's Apology." Since the best "proof" is a pragmatic living of the

[15] P. 48.

truth, the only "proof" that is relevant to faith is the probation or "proving-ground" of life itself. To re-prove the proved is a reversion, for when faith says, "I know," it is really a metaphor for "I assert." All of John's persuasive methods on behalf of Christianity, especially when they suspend syllogistic proof, help close the gap between acceptance of the "logic" of religion and the believer's subsequent emotional adjustment, the lag between Newman's "notional" and "real" assent.

The Christian who refuses to follow the analogical argument to its logical conclusion and who denies to God the highest of his own attributes lacks even Caliban's insight. But it is not enough for man to argue, like the savage, from might to will. He must take the third step and follow David in his ascent from will to love at the religious stage. The fact that man loves "and would be loved" is capable of two interpretations. It can affirm the validity of Christianity, the perfect chiasmus of the Cross, which makes the world the body of an infinite spirit that mirrors and subsumes man's love; or it can establish the projection upon God of a merely human attribute. This second possibility recalls Tennyson's question in *In Memoriam:* "Derives it not from what we have / The likest God within the soul?" (LV, 3–4). Does man's most godlike attribute of love proceed from a God of love who validates the "truth" of immortality, or is the God of love merely an anthropomorphic projection of a human state? If the latter, the "soul" is incapable of affirming the truth of anything beyond itself. St. John rejects the second alternative, not because it is inherently illogical, but because of its absurd consequences. His graphic analogy of the lamp swimming in its own oil marks a return to his strongest point, which is the pragmatic argument from consequences. Seldom before in Victorian poetry, except in *In Memoriam*, had the serious arguments against religion been properly advanced;

seldom before had they a chance, not to be refuted—for what arguments of the kind can be refuted?—but to be understood and explored.

John assumes that a God in whom might can coexist with will and love is a more perfect creator than one in whom these qualities cannot unite. If such attributes do not coexist in God, then man is more perfect than his creator, and faith is impossible. John establishes the thesis that "Man is not God but hath God's end to serve," not by appealing to religious authority, which would be a form of begging the question, but by once again pointing out the desirable consequence: *if* p, *then* q; q, *therefore* p. If man is less perfect than his creator, then God must possess all of man's perfections. John wants to define perfection as a combination of divine power and human love. To justify his definition, he first assumes that it is true, then tries to derive from it the fact of human imperfection, which has led him to define God as a coexistence of will and love in the first place. The reasoning, of course, is circular, and the conclusion is only a probable inference, not a necessary one. He commits the fallacy of affirming the consequent of a hypothetical syllogism. But even as he makes the formal error, the emotive force of John's rhetorical method helps hasten the acceptance of that Christian "truth" which a pragmatic "proof," far more persuasive than any syllogistic argument, has already recommended to him.

In the coda, Cerinthus' contemptuous dismissal of a society mystically incorporated in Christ enables Browning to fix in pictorial language the Christian philosophy of love. To St. John's opponent this philosophy is unintelligible, or at best immoral and obscene. In a monogamous society, a man should be the groom of only one bride at a time, yet the souls whom Christ would marry are multitudinous, and male as well as female: "Can a mere man do this?" But God's humanity is unintelligible only to those Gnostics who reject the religious mystery. By substituting a "transcendence" of Christian realism for the Christian transcendence of nominalism, Gnosticism produces a simplistic theology that is as deficient in material content as nominalism is in spirit. Browning makes this clear in a final comment, which he adds in his own person: "But 't was Cerinthus that is lost." The shift in tense reminds the reader that the Christian narrative is not a footnote to ancient history, but an event in which the modern world is still involved. Cerinthus is lost now, as he was then. He is eternally lost, because the Christian narrative gives time a new and permanent inflection, and its truth exists in an eternal present.

In his demonstration that the Incarnation occurred, not once, but always, Browning is trying to liberate himself from the historicity of faith. "A Death in the Desert" is his closest approach before *The Ring and the Book* to a workable notion of religious "myth." St. John puts the questions bluntly: Is the Christian narrative fact or fable? "Was this once" or "was it not once?" His evasive reply enables Browning to defend religion both against literal-minded believers, who accept every detail of the narrative as historic fact, and those higher critics, equally simple-minded, who discredit the Christian story as a "fable," by which they mean a lie. By judging the truth of Aeschylus' Promethean myth by empirical facts like the existence of fire, the former approach Christianity as they would a scientific treatise. The first group believes in the Christ child superstitiously, while the second throws out the Baby with the myth water.

The literal-minded fallacy is to reduce to the temporal order according to which theology has historically developed the logical order in which "might," "will," and "love" are eternally related. The fallacy of higher criticism consists in the opposite error of reconstructing Christian history accord-

ing to a self-repeating cycle of logical "firsts." The historic
approach of the literal-minded Christians slights the logical
element quite as much as the logical approach of the higher
critics slights the narrative element. Browning's own approach through St. John leads readily into both narrative and
logical vindications without confining him to either. But because the Christian narrative is not empiric "fact," as the first
group believes, Browning's main problem is to show how the
religious man can base his eternal happiness on something historical, knowledge of which is, at most, approximate. For this
reason, though he still is hostile to those higher critics whom
he attacks in "Christmas-Eve," and whose logical approach
neglects the historic elements, Browning is heavily indebted
for his most persuasive defense of Christian "myth" to the
more sophisticated higher critics, like David Friedrich
Strauss. Browning follows these religious philosophers in no
longer equating myth with falsehood, but with modes of
truth that can be apprehended only in terms of some total
allegorical structure, of a form in which the literal meaning is
different from the moral or mystical or analogical meaning.
His attitude resembles that of Browning's speaker in "Fears
and Scruples," who affirms his trust in an unseen friend.
When someone places the friend's traits in doubt and the
handwriting experts declare that his letters are apocryphal,
the speaker asks, in the last line, "And if this friend were
. . . God?" In rebutting the higher critics who try to read
poetry as science, Browning has St. John shift the emotive
and descriptive directions of "fable" in the way that Strauss
does when he opposes the concept of myth or unconscious
fiction to the usual dilemma: the choice between history and
intentional invention. The Christian fable depends for its
value on an illumination of greatness; its meanings must be
self-evident once they are pointed to, for they cannot be
proved by scientific means.

ᵽᵽᔑ 5 ᔑᵽᵽ

"Caliban upon Setebos; or, Natural Theology in the Is-
land" (probably written in the winter of 1859–1860) provides a kind of antimask to the solemn theological speculations of Browning's St. John. It is like a gibbering satyr play
that complements the more exalted ceremonial drama of
"Cleon" and "Saul." Caliban, a victim of necessity, circumstance, and sensation, is driven, like Cleon, by the sheer dialectics of his situation to posit its opposite. His systematic
ascent is closest in structure to David's and Cleon's, a passage
from sensual bondage to dawning ethical and religious consciousness. But whereas David's analogical argument includes
the lower stage in the higher, Caliban habitually explains the
higher stage by the lower. Though his principle of analogy is
valid, it uses the inductive methods of an empiricist whose
own experience is limited. "Caliban upon Setebos" is Browning's version of F. D. Maurice's principle, derived in turn
from J. S. Mill, that men are generally right in what they
affirm and wrong in what they deny. The benevolence that
Caliban denies is something that lies outside his experience,
and about which he can therefore say nothing. The chief
defects of his induction are all due to the "Idols" of his
"Cave," which reverse the usual practice indicated in Bacon's
analysis of the superstition by giving undue emphasis to the
negative instances of pain and privation. The suffering savage
is to be heard when he affirms the existence of evil; but when
he denies the existence of good, is he not simply saying that
he knows nothing about it? Browning's monologues show
how most men worship in this or that cave the particular
gods that attract them. Because the "enchanted glass" of
most perspectives is less fantastic or less grotesque, he can use
Caliban's "Idols" to exaggerate the biases that distort most
religious thinking.

Caliban's speech is Browning's most successful imitation of the verbal defects of the aesthetic man. At first his language is merely reactive and originates as a stammer from the mud, like Farinata's in *The Inferno*. Caliban concentrates an intense energy upon the enjoyment of viscous substances like mud and slush—as if these inanimate elements were responsive to his embraces and good to eat. He perceives in terms of "rock-stream" and "fire-eye," of "green-dense" and "dim-delicious," wholes which he has not yet separated into subjects and their properties. Unable to use generic words, he refers to the meteor as a ball of flame and to the lightning as a white blaze that cuts down trees. He also lacks the rational power to differentiate himself from his environment. In a monologue like "Johannes Agricola in Meditation" the speaker's repeated "I" remains a pronoun of surfaces only, so seldom does he "think" or analyze. Suppression of inwardness takes place *behind* the pronoun. It remains for Caliban to erase the first-person pronoun altogether at such moments, and to create in the third person a wholly new mode, strangely lacking in depth or inwardness. The references to Caliban in the third person are a sign that he cannot even identify himself. Words for God are normally employed in a categorical sense, but his are specific; for example, he calls Setebos "a cuttle-fish," with no sense of the figurative license usually implied in such comparisons. But even when Caliban's language is most infantile, his sprawling and rolling function like his later gestures of cringing and self-abasement as pantomimic performances, movements that enact his beliefs. One critic has noticed that Caliban shifts from the third to the first person whenever he feels himself becoming more powerful and godlike.[16] But this is only one aspect of a larger transition that occurs whenever Caliban, in searching beyond

[16] E. K. Brown, "The First Person in 'Caliban Upon Setebos,'" *Modern Language Notes*, LXVI (1951), 392–395.

Setebos for a god term, finds an overarching analogy between his present state and some higher life.

Though it follows logically from its premises, Caliban's cosmology owes its grotesqueness to its axioms. Caliban assigns a cause only to Setebos' creation of the world. The rest of Setebos' cruelties are all gratuitous. Even when he concedes that the god in his caprice may bestow favor, Caliban usually climaxes his examples with a negative instance: "pluck the other [leg] off" (l. 93); "leave him like an egg" (l. 93); "smash it with my foot" (l. 126). "Omnipotence" and its cognates "force" and "power" are prize words which most believers would ascribe to God. But Setebos' "power" resembles that of the God whom Johannes Agricola, in developing the nominalism of medieval theology, turns into an irrational despot. In Setebos, Caliban contemplates the horror of power divorced from love. The "jealousy" of the Old Testament God becomes the active hatred of a jealous tyrant. Because Setebos loves his errors, Caliban can make his god's gratuitous evil a parody of "grace." Unlike the Christian God, who appeals to man through his Son, Setebos is concerned only with the sense of release which the sheer act of cruelty affords him.

Caliban's idea of hierarchy enables him to define God in terms of an infinite regress of divine, human, and subhuman orders, which deepen his awareness of the ultimate mystery. But the logician surrenders his reason in worship of an irrational god when he omits the specifically human qualities, which are as far above himself as he is above the crabs. Caliban recognizes the danger of mistaking a sequential for a causal order when he is discussing crabs, which are at the next lower level (l. 102), but he cannot discern the truth and falsity of statements about his own level. When he cites examples of the human category, Prospero is just a lofty despot and Miranda a kind of lamia. A classification of man which omits the attribute of love is incomplete. This logical error generates a theological heresy, for Caliban's faulty induction creates his terror of his god.

Browning defines Caliban's essence by his name, an anagram for "cannibal," which implicitly contains his end. Yet within his limitations, the speaker turns out to be as searching as Job. His most savage quality is his irony, which produces excruciation as often as assurance and raises such unsettling questions as the mystery of evil's presence in a divinely created world: "But wherefore rough, why cold and ill at ease? / Aha, that is a question!" (ll. 127–128). This passion for the "truth" is what turns an ironic comedy into a dialectical poem. Almost at the beginning of his search, the logic of perfection drives Caliban to posit a grand over-all purpose which he calls the "Quiet"—"the something over Setebos / That made Him." The hierarchy of gods implied in the child's question "Who made God?" has appealed to many thinkers besides Caliban. William James concludes his *Varieties of Religious Experience* by suggesting that the world comprises many gods, of different degrees of inclusiveness. But Caliban can complete his ascent only by converting his own attributes, as they culminate in Setebos, into their opposites. Caliban's own bondage to necessity, circumstance, and brute sensation must become that embodiment of freedom, ends, and intellection which he identifies with the Quiet. Since its attributes are the opposite of his own, Caliban's logic forces him to discuss the ineffable Quiet mainly in terms of what it is not.

Because Caliban's theology is inductive, it magnifies in the name of all truth his own set of values, especially his worship of power. This idea of power comes to Caliban from two sources: the violence of nature and Prospero's personal authority. Setebos is the god of Caliban's mother, the witch Sycorax, and the merging of the speaker's early resentment of parental rulings with his view of Prospero's own authority as arbitrary is psychologically suggestive. If the magician is capricious in his exercise of power, then to Caliban the operations of his god's power will seem equally arbitrary, just as parental acts will often seem unreasonable to a child.

In mimicking Prospero, Caliban combines three kinds of pretension: verbal, sexual, and social—each disclosing warped perspectives. The verbal extravagance with which Caliban would imitate Prospero's "prodigious words" is symptomatic of his limitation. By abandoning his inventive diction for the showiness of Prospero, he tries to forfeit his own identity. Because he fortunately fails in this attempt, his style remains a marvel of strangeness that enables him, in a fantasy of sexual fulfillment, to mate himself with a "four-legged serpent," then without appearing to lapse into nonsense, to identify this snake with the beautiful Miranda. Instead of sublimating his lust for the girl, Caliban ascribes to Setebos his own sexual frustrations. Though his god can "make," in the sense of "create," the point of his pun is that Setebos is denied the sexual satisfaction of "making" a "mate." In its third and most concentrated form, Caliban's mimicry gratifies a desire to play the tyrant-leader, inscrutable and ruthless. As a cross between Setebos and Prospero, the Caliban of his disordered fantasy commands loyalty only because he is brutal enough to impose his will on the other animals. The regress, in which the slave-master relation is compelled to march backward in a set of identical steps, enables Caliban, as a microcosmic Prospero, to identify Ariel with a "pouch-bill crane," and the Caliban inside his microcosm with a blinded sea beast. Within the macrocosmic model of Setebos, the god's tyrannical power seems to depend upon the maiming of a sacrificial victim—the lumpish drudge he lames and calls Caliban. Inside this model is the smaller human world of Prospero in which a tinier Caliban lives, and within that, the microcosmic world of a tyrannical Caliban, in which an even smaller drudge lives, and so on down, like a set of Chinese boxes.

Caliban's insistence that "Who made them weak, meant weakness" (l. 172) recalls Browning's own doctrine of imperfection: " 'Tis the weakness in strength, that I cry for! my flesh, that I seek / In the Godhead!" ("Saul," ll. 308–09). The parallel seems less forced when we recall that the heresy of Sycorax is Gnosticism, the doctrine that Browning opposes in "A Death in the Desert." Of course, in developing his natural theology, Caliban is still strongly influenced by the Gnostic teaching that the world builder is the adversary of the true God. Browning is attacking Darwinian naturalism or perhaps, as DeVane suggests, the famous *Bridgewater Treatises*. But as an empirical theologian who conceives of Setebos to explain the cruelties of nature and who opposes the Gnostic doctrine that an anthropomorphic God is a contradiction in terms, Caliban is joining ranks with the orthodox Christians. He is proclaiming, like St. Paul in his letter to the Colossians, which is likewise directed against the Gnostic heresy, that in a creature subject to human emotions there can dwell "all the fulness of the Godhead bodily" (Col. 2:9). Caliban's merging of the monotheism of the Quiet with the sonship of Setebos is a major dialectical triumph. Except that Caliban still believes in a divine Father and Son who are opposed to each other, the true faith looks deceptively like the theology of the precocious savage.

But Browning cannot allow his speaker to discover the "truth." Caliban must subside into his old errors during the rest of the poem. He is right to say that God intended weakness, but wrong to think that God makes his creatures weak in order to force their obedience. In point of fact, as St. John argues, God makes man weak for the opposite reason—so as not to compel His creature to obey Him, but to love Him freely, as an act of choice. Caliban arrives at correct theses,

but for wrong reasons; and from the absurdity and pointlessness of his own creations he tries to establish the pointlessness
of God's. As soon as he and his work will be removed from
the scene, Caliban realizes, the vast machinery of nature will
have no further point: "No use at all i' the work, for work's
sole sake" (l. 198). In a world without purpose or direction
the whole creation reaches a zenith of magnificent absurdity.
Caliban and his achievements will perish while the ridiculous
performance continues. The god of nature, like a giant automaton, goes on spinning his senseless wheel, scattering "balls"
of "flame" and momentary sparks of life, but like Hardy's
"Vast Imbecility," producing everything absent-mindedly.
Ironically, Caliban, small speck of dust in the cosmic scale
and as such a symbol of man himself, is able to do what the
god of nature cannot: "I make the cry my maker cannot
make." Caliban's very achievement unfits him for life in a
world whose god, though indifferent to his own creation, is
jealous of any further improvements.

   "Such are the consequences of a natural theology."
Browning does not have to say this directly. He can allow
the point of view he imitates to reveal its own limitations. At
the very moment Caliban imagines himself to be imposing his
theological system on the world, his language keeps betraying him: "Those at His mercy,—why, they please Him
most / When . . . when . . . well, never try the same way
twice!" The phrases have a savage chop to them; they convey the desperation of a frightened slave whose god may be
placable, but whose only rule for pleasing his god is that
there is no rule. Reduced to despair, Caliban would seem to
be ready for spiritual development. If he could share Karshish's intuition of a God of love, he would be in possession
of the missing piece, and the other counters of his puzzle
would fall into place. As it is, he anticipates Thomas Hardy's
hope that, just as man in the course of the ages has evolved a

mind, so God may eventually develop, through man's insistence, a consciousness and moral sense. The idea of the
Quiet, who remains the symbol of this possibility, may seem
extravagant to many readers. But the concept finds its parallels in Shelley's Demogorgon, Byron's Arimanes, and even, in
our own time, in Paul Tillich's thesis of a "God beyond
God."

The closing sections abound in rich creativeness. The most
inspired of Caliban's speculations—the thought that the
Quiet will some day catch and conquer Setebos—alternates
with the mockery of "likelier He / Decrepit may doze, doze,
as good as die" (ll. 282–283). Caliban vaguely apprehends
what St. John discerns so clearly—the perfect symmetry of
the logical thinking behind Christianity. Since the Quiet's
divine order requires repression of Setebos' tendencies to disorder, responsibility to accept his god's repression involves
Caliban in guilt. This guilt demands redemption, which involves the sacrifice of a victim, which in turn allows the substitution of one victim for another. Though his blend of dishonesty and fear is never more repellent than in his parody
of Christ's personal substitution, Caliban's formal sacrifice to
appease an angry God anticipates the doctrine of atonement.
All that remains to complete his argument is the substitution
of love for hate, a step he can never take. Because he keeps
shaping his god in the image of Prospero, whom he tries to
thwart, the slave's frustrated plots and sensual lusts first create his guilt; afterwards he has to commit the blasphemies
that objectify this guilt. The blunt sarcasm of his gibe at the
god's decline is to this extent "infantile," like the crime of a
juvenile delinquent. But the prophet of millenial disaster gets
his apocalypse sooner than expected. With a rhythmic jolt
the prophecy turns back upon the joker, as the delinquent
cowers before a manifestation of God in the coming storm.

The closest Caliban comes to revelation is in the nightmare

of the close. But far from giving his life a new inflection, the revelation intensifies the terror of his past. Unlike David's direct impression of God's splendor, the power that descends on Caliban is a cross-surging of eccentric force. Whereas grace should bring the religious man closer to God, this show of transcendent force drives God and Caliban farther apart. Because Caliban has assimilated only experiences that demonstrate power, he has predestined his god to be a predestinating deity. His mind is incurably idolatrous and keeps moving in concentric circles. Without the synthesis of love that would provide the necessary communication between his thesis, the Quiet, and its antithesis, Setebos, opposition cannot yield to counterpart. His mind's circular, eddying motion arrests his dialectic and prevents Caliban from making any further advance.

Though Browning ridicules his speaker's attitudes, the sympathetic imagination that enables him to grasp their limitations from within should still have power to disturb the reader and intrigue him philosophically. Tenacious to the point of fanaticism, Caliban has a mind of great but brittle power. There is a sense in which his tough-minded exploration of life's comic and dreadful contradictions is a necessary part of religious thinking. If Setebos is God, then God is not good; if the Quiet is God, then God is not God. Since either Setebos or the Quiet is divine, God cannot be good and omnipotent at the same time. Such a being does not seem to care if his creatures blow themselves off this planet. He has a host of experiments going, and if this one fails, he will probably try again with something else: " 'Saith He is terrible: watch His feats in proof!" (l. 200). Shrewd in his criticism of causal logic, Caliban realizes, like Job, that there is no necessary connection between moral goodness and prosperity, and that the just man is often left crushed on the dust heap. The "irrationality" of a God who does not appear to run his universe on moral principles is the kind of paradox that has turned many believers into skeptics. They have not been able to bear the thought of a reconciliation that is capable of definition only in its own terms. But this same paradox has turned many agnostics into believers, for in Caliban's kind of answer they have felt a response as great as the question. The only way Browning can bring God and man together is by first driving them apart. It is the method used by God when he speaks to Job from the whirlwind. There is too much intellectual pretension and moral conceit in the world, and Caliban does right, though for wrong reasons, when, in speaking of himself in the third person, he obliterates himself before God's will.

By exploring the world's sinister design, his theological fantasies imaginatively discharge their terrors, even as they deepen his awareness of what Rudolf Otto, the German theologian, has called the *mysterium tremendum*—the ultimate mystery—which Caliban, like Fra Lippo, approaches with awe, fascination, and a sense of "creaturehood." Caliban's speculations, which are his defense against a world that is often unknowable but always terrifying to contemplate, raise once again the religious question in all its frightening complexity and timeless power. One feels that "Caliban upon Setebos" is born of Browning's own doubt, and that it has brought his own agnosticism back into the economy of fear and trembling and divine salvation. Most Christian answers to agnosticism seem not to begin to understand the agnosticism; they merely invoke a universal goodness in its place. In "Caliban upon Setebos," God does not understand that kind of goodness. Only one reality forbids Browning a feeling of resignation and denies him the experience of tragedy; and it is not a serene intuition of benevolence. On the contrary, this reality is a self-sacrificing principle, a love that accepts limitation and that first assumes the evil that it suffers in our stead.

This sacrificial love is not to be discerned in Caliban's absentee controller, the Quiet who allows a malignant Setebos to send hurricanes and cancer. It appears only in the crucified transfiguring figure of David's vision, the God who throws himself into the void between the Quiet and Caliban and who is most gracious to his human creatures when bearing their own suffering as the Son of Man.

☜ 6 ☞

Like "Caliban upon Setebos," "Bishop Blougram's Apology" (*ca.* 1850–1851) and "Mr. Sludge, 'The Medium'" (1859–1860) launch a speaker with certain defects toward the "truth." But just at the climax of the monologue, as a religious solution to his problem begins to dawn, there is a sudden return to the speaker's most striking aberrations. The intellectual sympathy that enables Browning to identify with such points of view engages the reader's own interest. By disclosing the speakers' limitations, this sympathetic identification also matures the reader's moral and religious attitudes.

"Bishop Blougram's Apology" attempts a systematic definition of "faith." Blougram first introduces the word as a blasphemous ejaculation to describe the wine he drinks, which is "cool i' faith" (l. 2). This is precisely Gigadibs' own condition, and it introduces the dialectic of belief and unbelief which the poem will treat. Just as Fra Lippo ingratiates himself with the officers, so Blougram tries to win his auditor's good will. He tries to implant in Gigadibs' mind the thought that Gigadibs really likes him. This is a daring strategy, which his auditor first resists. But instead of trying to prove that Gigadibs as an empiricist cannot logically dislike a more consistent empiricist,[17] Blougram first enacts this contradiction in his social gestures: "No more wine?"; "try the

[17] See F. E. L. Priestley, "Blougram's Apologetics," *University of Toronto Quarterly,* XV (1946), 139–147.

cooler jug— / Put back the other, but don't jog the ice!" By
emphasizing the material comforts which his own more systematic pragmatism affords, Blougram can gradually overcome Gigadibs' resistance. He keeps returning to this aver-
sion and converts it into his strongest rallying point: "So,
you despise me, Mr. Gigadibs" (ll. 13, 143, 970).

The Bishop introduces Goethe, Buonaparte, and Count
D'Orsay to prepare for the three stages of his argument. At
the lowest aesthetic level of "what Does" are Buonaparte, the
incarnation of power, and Count D'Orsay, the dandy and
fashion plate. He introduces Goethe (and later Shakespeare)
at the level of "what Knows," as prototypes of the ethical
man, the highest products of a secular culture. The Bishop
himself, a less worthy witness than Luther of "what Is,"
occupies the third religious stage. To force Gigadibs' own
advance, Blougram must first descend from his religious plateau to argue as an unbeliever. Gigadibs wants the Bishop to
sacrifice his beliefs to an imprecise ideal of human liberty,
which consists in doing whatever one likes. Though the
Bishop tries to sound as scatter-brained as Gigadibs, he is per-
fectly aware that democracy is naïve Christianity and that
free enterprise in the realm of ideas, when pushed beyond
rational limits, is lunacy.

The skeptic objects that because Blougram's worldly manner is not in keeping with a bishop's religious life, he remains
a comic figure. But the Bishop's beliefs are too secure—not
too frail—to be adequately expressed in external ways.
Blougram is so aware of this source of irony that he appropriately furnishes Gigadibs with the perfect illustration of
the danger of judging by appearances. The analogy of the
masquerade, in which the actor assumes the mask of death
only to be "touched . . . / The moment he had shut the
closet door, / By Death himself" (ll. 72–74), is one which
Gigadibs himself lacks the ironic power to invent. Gigadibs

thinks that Blougram would make an "unbelieving Pope," and there is a sense in which this is true. But the word "unbelief" must undergo systematic transformation. Although "unbelieving" can never remain a synonym for "atheistical" or "hypocritical," there is a sense, as Blougram illustrates later, in which unbelief is inseparable from faith.

The Bishop's cabin analogy makes Gigadibs' "all" or "nothing" appear ridiculous. Blougram dramatizes it as the absurd destitution of the traveler who peeps up "from . . . utterly naked boards" (l. 130) after having jettisoned all his possessions. By trying to bring everything aboard, Gigadibs ends up with nothing, while the Bishop, in executing his less ambitious program, climbs comfortably into his "snug and well-appointed berth." The comedy of skepticism lies in its audacity. Though temperate skepticism like that of Karshish is not necessarily absurd, Gigadibs' attempt to deny all values is self-contradictory in theory and impossible in practice. In expecting Blougram to infer from his embarrassing destitution the abstract truth of his "artist-nature," "imperial, plain, and true," Gigadibs is postulating a sentimental correlation between bankruptcy and spiritual good health. The Bishop's hoarding of material comforts would certainly be absurd if he were solemnly to declare in the name of religion that all life is vanity, like the Bishop of St. Praxed's. But such negation is the skeptic's attitude, not Blougram's. Because Gigadibs denies in practice the negations he entertains in theory, his own behavior is far more contradictory than the Bishop's. Blougram severs religious ideas from their traditional associations to help the biased Gigadibs jettison his "Idols." The absurdity of the naked traveler is too patently comic and encourages the skeptic to repudiate his speculative pose. Though Gigadibs regards the Bishop's enjoyment of his "sea-furniture" as a kind of criminal smuggling, Blougram's defense of expedience is designed to "remoralize" by accurately

naming a situation already debased by the secularist's in-
accuracies. This method of dissociation, whereby the Bishop
can talk blithely of expedience, is a striking rhetorical device.
It encourages intellectual exercise in Gigadibs, so that the
secularist will cease being the victim of his own naïve
rhetoric.

Gigadibs' charge that no dogmas "nail" (l. 154) the
Bishop's faith inadvertently redounds against him. The grammar is active, and the double sense of "nail" exonerates the
Bishop at the same time it indicts him. Gigadibs implies that
when an intelligent man professes to believe, he is being
hypocritical. But the fallacy hinges on the suppressed major
premise, the assumption that all intelligent men disbelieve.
Browning expects the reader to keep uncovering these hypotheses and to submit them to critical examination. When
Blougram admits that he does not believe absolutely, his
concession is a way of turning back on Gigadibs his miscon-
ception about faith. But the correction must wait till later.
Blougram will first "meet" Gigadibs "on his own premise,"
then correct his view of faith when they are "back on Christian ground."

The Bishop demonstrates that the skeptic's exchange of "a
life of doubt diversified by faith, / For one of faith diversified by doubt" (ll. 210–211) is intrinsically no more rational
than his own choice. Blougram's criterion for choosing is
pragmatic: he accepts the hypothesis that will produce the
most beneficial consequences. By cleverly realigning the
terms "dream" and "waking life," the Bishop can equate
the dreamer's impracticality with the skeptic and can use the
empiricist's "waking reality" to establish the practical genius
of the man of faith. The Bishop, of course, is right; the
choice is no more optional than death. To be consistent, a
skeptic's demand for logical proof should consign him to his
bed, where he should sleep, like Renan, with a revolver

under his pillow for fear of a revelation. The believer, on the other hand, "proves" his truths in the only way he can, by living them.

In using his pragmatic philosophy of religion to justify the comforts of his life as a bishop, Blougram may seem to be choosing an inferior way of arguing. But as Holloway observes of Cardinal Newman's rhetoric, such methods "are not mere verbal sleight-of-hand. . . . They really do draw our attention to certain facts and make these more vividly present than plain statement of them could do." [18] Moreover, the Bishop could defend himself by insisting that his choice of inferior arguments is a choice of the best means available. He is fighting on his antagonist's ground and must show Gigadibs that as an empiricist he cannot logically despise Blougram for taking even the most grossly empirical view of faith.

To demolish the validity of his opponent's "unbelief," Blougram examines the lives of Napoleon, Shakespeare, and Luther, who as prototypes of the aesthetic, ethical, and religious stages, respectively, cover the full range of possibility. Though Napoleon, as Gigadibs' most likely idol, rationalizes his lust for power with sentimental morality of the Carlylean variety, even he had the egoist's belief in himself, which constitutes a secular version of faith. Shakespeare, as the highest product of the ethical life, defines himself inwardly but still applies a material standard of success. Blougram first grants that he lacks the genius to imitate Shakespeare as a model, then uses this admission to reverse the proposition. Given Shakespeare's desire to "build the trimmest house in Stratford town," both Blougram and the poet are involved in the same contest of fitting out their cabins, and the Bishop beats Shakespeare at his own game. If Gigadibs is prepared to advance to the religious stage, the Bishop admits that this argu-

[18] *The Victorian Sage,* p. 196.

ment from utility "breaks up." The religious passion which transforms the life of a Luther or a David Friedrich Strauss is beyond him. Even if he unwittingly damns those higher critics who cannot sustain the tensions of his own dialectic, Strauss saves himself; and regardless of what happens after death, Luther finds "A real heaven in his heart." Either Gigadibs must ascend with Blougram to the religious stage, where the force of his arguments ceases to apply, or else he must concede victory to the Bishop, who has successfully demonstrated the pre-eminence of his own life at the first two stages. To postpone defeat, Gigadibs has only one choice left; he must follow Blougram onto "Christian ground," where the Bishop can now correct his view of faith.

Belief and doubt are dialectical terms, like the "good" and "evil" of Abt Vogler's argument, each requiring and sustaining the other. The kind of dogmatism with which Gigadibs confuses faith is discredited by the Bishop as the folly of certainty in matters essentially uncertain. His own pronouncements nicely balance belief and disbelief, qualifying one by the other and allowing belief only its necessary proportion of decisiveness. Such a method has its own dangers; and to defend or to explain its merits is only to weaken it. Its quality of disbelief is fairly cogent when expressed by Blougram or the Pope in *The Ring and the Book;* but Mr. Sludge, the medium, cheapens the method, and it is unendurable in Guido, in *The Ring.*

According to Blougram, the historical critics erroneously assume that all alternatives are mutually exclusive. It is as if a future biographer were to argue that since Blougram is English in his nationality, he cannot also be Roman in his religion, just as the Gnostic Cerinthus believes that if Christ is man, he cannot also be God. But even if the facts are reconcilable, the Bishop insists that those who demand "historic knowledge" commit a form of the genetic fallacy. They suppose that the actual story of Christ can take the place of a theological analysis of its structure and an appropriation of its eternal truth as a living force in their lives. Theirs is historic religion, not at the level of "what Is," but of what was.

Whereas Gigadibs begins by opposing faith to unbelief, Blougram comes to identify them: "faith means perpetual unbelief" (l. 666). The reader is probably accustomed to thinking of faith and unbelief as opposed, but by identifying them, Blougram is urging us to overcome a false separation of terms that are really dialectical. There is obviously a sense in which "faith" is not "unbelief." But by stressing their interaction, Blougram is urging us to think dialectically and to see quite literally "what all the blessed evil's for" (l. 654). He uses a pictorial analogy in which doubt is the "snake" beneath St. Michael's "foot." Then, to disavow the spiritual language—just as Fra Lippo mocks the Prior's Latin— he compares doubt to the snuff box that itches the nose without causing a sneeze. In this way Blougram shows that being a believer means living the contradiction of good and evil; so it also means not being a believer.

The Bishop defends his own beliefs by insisting that a passionate struggle of the intellect to submit to dogma generates more real intensity than the good breeding which acquits "God with grace" and which substitutes for the gracious God of Christianity the *savoir-faire* of Count D'Orsay. The beliefs themselves are less important than the consequences of disbelief: if he rejected the dogmas, there would be no limit to his doubt. The very nature of the Church involves the view that what it affirms is right. This conviction of infallibility certainly gives an initial advantage in argument to any hostile, intelligent, and skeptical mind. But the Bishop can hardly abandon the belief because of its intellectual inconvenience. Though Blougram's acceptance of the most preposterous miracles anticipates Newman's method in the *Apologia*, where his cogent arguments on behalf of controlled inquiry culminate in a surprisingly partisan defense of papal infallibility, the only possible final case against miracles is another postulate of faith: the dogmatic assumption that they do not happen. If the Church determines on something, then that something should be true; and it is arguable that the blood of St. Januarius liquefies because the Church wants to believe that it does, as much as for any other reason. But because the miracles enable him to instill fear and rule as lord of the "purblind mass" (l. 756), the Bishop's rhetoric in their defense is still a form of casuistry, a way of giving his inferior motives a specious covering.

The casuistry is, however, part of Browning's rhetorical technique: his divorce of the pragmatic motives of religion from its usual sanctions. He returns now to his cabin analogy to make the process clear to Gigadibs. Unlike Guido, in whom this rhetoric of dissociation is unconscious and in whom it produces a kind of schizophrenia that ends in disaster, Blougram is always in control of his method. The Bishop's defense of "the creature-comforts" is a controlled disintegration of topical assumptions, designed to restore Gigadibs' own beliefs on a firmer basis. Blougram never implies that such dissociation of expedience from piety is the ultimate in intellectual prowess; it is only a necessary first step to clarify for Gigadibs the pragmatic basis of religion.

The Bishop insists that since the historical origin of chastity can never provide an adequate analysis of its present influence over men, the very fact that Gigadibs is not unrestrainedly immoral proves that he recognizes the validity of Blougram's higher scale of values. If Gigadibs rejects this argument and maintains that he behaves chastely as a result of "certain instincts, blind, unreasoned-out" (l. 838), then he is acting in deference to popular opinion. Blougram deftly catches his opponent on the horns of a dilemma. Since the skeptic must either accept or reject the religious argument, he must either concede victory to the Bishop or accept all the disadvantages of superstition without any of the advantages of religion. It is in Gigadibs' interest to "win" by "losing": to concede defeat in the debate and thereby gain success in his life. By writing the journalist a note of introduction the Bishop dramatizes his own influence over the editors of the religious reviews. Even after winning the argument, Blougram keeps cavorting from form to form, flitting from literal to metaphoric "sheep," sliding from casuistic seduction to the final irony of the "Outward-bound," all with astonishing, but not quite incredible, ease. Whereas Gigadibs is butted and bickered by the "sheep" of popular opinion to which he weakly defers, Blougram is motioned by his religious flock "to the velvet of the sward" (l. 895). The irony reappears at the end when the literal and biblical uses of the word "sheep" converge. On his sheep farm in Australia, where he is urged to study his last chapter of St. John—"Feed my sheep"—Gigadibs will still be the slave of his flocks, while Blougram is the master of his.

Browning intrudes in the postscript to announce in his own person that the Bishop "believed, say, half he spoke" (l. 980) and "said true things, but called them by wrong names" (l. 996). A provisional, adjudicating irony is the best weapon to use against a skeptic like Gigadibs whose ideas are neither provisional nor ironic. Gigadibs is more dogmatic than the Bishop and can be demolished precisely because, having once succumbed to the notion that the religious man cannot be a pragmatist, he thinks it is necessary to stick to that idea. Imaginative skepticism and dramatic irony are weapons that the believer, no less than the skeptic, can use to advantage. They enable Blougram to keep his mind athletic and his "spirit on the stretch." By displaying the duplicity of every

thought, he can hold conflicting ideas in balance. The
Bishop's arguments are provisional and speculative and allow
him to turn against Gigadibs the readiest complaint of this
lightweight secularist by exposing his self-conceit and inconsistency for what they are. His chief aim is a constant, resourceful restoration of Gigadibs' ignorance. Blougram keeps
reminding the skeptic of the Bishop's own worldliness, while
altering the emotive direction of this worldliness. Terms like
"gain," "use," and "profit" become prize words at the same
time that their connotations change from the merely worldly
to the pragmatic. The rhetoric is not just verbal magic which
can transfer emotive force to suit the speaker's needs. The
readjustment of the empirical views of life and faith to a new
rhetorical end gives the Bishop's arguments clarity and complexity and makes his rhetoric art.

☞ 7 ☜

If Bishop Blougram's pragmatic philosophy of religion too
seldom illuminate his worldly analogies, the rhetorical art of
"Mr. Sludge, 'The Medium'" produces sustained casuistry
which not even Mr. Sludge's elevated critique of spiritual
truth can wholly surmount. Though there may be rhetorical
cunning in the Bishop's method of unveiling the pragmatic
analogies of his theology (which are all implicit from the
beginning), his worldly language, even at its most casuistical,
usually elucidates the religious beliefs behind them. Mr.
Sludge, on the other hand, passes in two distinct movements
from a dishonest attempt to shift blame from himself to society, to a more convincing defense of his frauds as events
which create faith. Sludge is a spiritual confidence man who
represents his trickery as the equivalent of miracles in a skeptical age. There are real resemblances between Blougram's
worldly expedience and his theology, even though his cabin
analogy may imply a resemblance that is fuller than it is. But

Sludge's paradoxical defense of "lying" to create truth compares things like art and deception, which, though they may accidentally resemble each other, do so only by chance. In other words, all of Mr. Sludge's analogies are really "false" analogies. As Holloway has shown in analyzing Newman's rhetoric, such analogies are "what Coleridge would call . . . metaphor[s]; and 'metaphors,' he goes on, 'are always allegorical, i.e., expressing a different subject but with a resemblance.' " [19]

Sludge first argues that his deceptions are a form of religious rhetoric which his "victims" force him to invent in order to "carry" to them as an audience. He hits upon the happy device of ascribing his defense to his dupes, whose most persuasive technique is to carry over to their own credulity the authority of others. This is a self-deceiving method which Sludge mocks by ranking their authorities in appropriately bathetic order, from Johnson and Wesley down to Mother Goose. The irony is implicit in the name of Sludge's patron, Hiram Horsefall, who shoes himself for his fall. He is already halfway to Niagara when he hires Sludge to push him over Horseshoe Falls. The medium deceives his victims because they want to be deceived. Whereas Blougram's will to believe makes him a cocreator with God of his own beliefs, Horsefall is the cocreator with Sludge of a truth that is wholly human in construction, the preposterous excrescence of a bored society rotating its pleasures in aesthetic parody of the religious process. Sludge's first name is David, but Browning's inversion of the biblical story leaves this society with only Horsefall as its Saul and with a mock David as its sole candidate for the position of religious sage. Instead of urging true claims to satisfy his love of Horsefall, this David loathes his patron and makes false claims that satisfy only his victims' love of themselves.

[19] *Ibid.*, p. 182.

After repeating the past arguments of Horsefall and other spurious apologists, Sludge moves, in the second half of his apology, to a direct defense of his deceptions. By conceding his minor offenses ("I cheated when I could, / Rapped with my toe-joints, set sham hands at work"), he hopes to win assent to his essential honesty. He keeps stumbling onto new truths, and as they carry away his imagination, he adopts a practice recommended by Cicero, the pretense of confiding in his auditor and of taking the reader into partnership: "Really, I want to light up my own mind." The multiplication of dashes becomes a kind of rhetorical barometer, measuring the sudden increase in emotional pressure. Sludge seems to be drawing on deeper experience which even he finds hard to comprehend.

There follows an ingenious application of the religious argument that God is present in all creation. Worms on grass blades give way, with a turn of the spyglass, to beings at the other end of the natural hierarchy. Like Pascal's two immensities, "the Name" comes close behind a "stomach-cyst" (l. 1117), and God permeates in an infinite regress the least of his creations. If the God incarnate lurks in every commonplace, then why should Sludge be rejected as too lowly for God's use? The problem is that Sludge's art is not itself an example of the principle he cites. His insistence that the step from the lowly to the lofty is everywhere at hand is close to Augustine's view that nothing can be trivial to the true Christian. But Sludge attempts an illegitimate progression from the lowly to the lofty. He has pledged himself, on the highest possible principles, to a breach of the highest possible principles. In citing true religious doctrines in support of false practices, he keeps committing a form of casuistry.

Somewhat in the way Matthew Arnold, in Holloway's analysis, uses the "value frame," [20] Mr. Sludge subjects the

[20] *Ibid.*, p. 215.

word "child" to systematic transformation, suggesting grounds for the attitudes his auditors are to adopt. At first the word signifies the infantile and puerile qualities that give the medium a fool's license. But by shifting its meaning, Sludge develops the term into a metaphor for faith. His "childship" is his susceptibility to mystery, that early-age wonder about the world that entitles him, as an heir of the Kingdom, to draw a much less rigorous line between super-stition and religion than would a more sophisticated believer. Sludge is greedy for a plenitude of aids, and is so "child-like" in his worship that he sees signs of God's favor everywhere. He believes he holds the "gold dust" of miracles and mys-tery, the exceptions to natural law that science cannot ac-count for. But just as he boasts of proving "the common-place" miraculous, he reanimates the dead metaphor of his spiritual "Kingdom" by describing it in charmingly absurd terms of coronets and eggnogs. He debases his own religious discoveries by associating them with grotesque capers like jumping to one's own height, cutting mutton with a broad-sword, and clipping nails while smiling.

Sludge's most persuasive argument is that, just as the Chris-tian narrative may have begun as a factual "lie" that evolved with time into a true religious myth, so the spiritualism that may have originated as a fraud has developed in his hands into a means of authentic revelation. To explain his art in terms of how it originated is to commit a form of the genetic fallacy. Sludge's rhetorical motive involves "lying" to tell the truth and requires the skillful medium, like the accomplished orator, to color the facts so that he can communicate better with his audience. Since the skeptic as well as the religious man "lies," it is simply a question of which mode of lying one prefers. Because God is supernatural, and not describable by the positive terms of nature, the religious man must dis-count all miracles, just as he discounts all of Sludge's tricks, for all spiritual metaphors make sense only insofar as we allow for figurative license in the analogy. What skeptics must discount in Sludge's spiritualism, they must also discount in theology. Either they accept both spiritualism and theology, or they reject both. Though spiritualism may be false religious promise, it is still promise. Where would religious zeal come from in a skeptical age, if it were not for the false demonstrations of the medium? If man eliminates illusion from among his religious motives, where does he find an equally urgent motive?

As Sludge keeps shifting the connotation of the term, "lying" is stretched to include aesthetic values. He redefines "lying" as mere "novel-writing of a sort," "Acting," or "improvising." The medium distinguishes between the falsity of his rhetoric in its debased form of magic, where his operations are "lies" from the standpoint of causal laws, and its essential moral truth in its power to move people in desired ways. This power is the pragmatic sanction of "lying," or "deception," just as it is Blougram's pragmatic sanction of expedience, and its function lies outside the realm of strictly true or strictly false propositions. If the disbelief of Sludge's critics is valid, everything beyond sense experience is disproved, including the skeptic's intelligence—a proposition which is nonsense; if the disbelief is invalid, nothing is proved except the impossibility of using such skepticism against Sludge, even as a speculative pose.

But the medium is so concerned with final causes that even in his persuasive definition of "lying" he forgets the extent to which he illegitimately manipulates efficient causes. When Horsefall refuses the five-pound note, Sludge cannot see beyond the discharge of his present anger. As he drops his artifice and returns to a level of blasphemous simplicity, Sludge debases his spiritual arguments by using persuasion, not rhetorically, but magically. Instead of inducing action in people, as David and Blougram do, he tries to induce motion in objects—things that are not subject to verbal manipulation. Whereas the Bishop keeps counterpointing his pragmatic advocacy of expedience against his most serious ideas, so that his irony and his doctrine are one, Sludge is only a superficial ironist. He lacks adequate resources behind his irony and keeps attributing to secondary causes the intention of the First Cause. Sludge also prostitutes his spiritualism by bringing it into the orbit of freakish capers which make him appear more skittish and eccentric than necessary. Like Chaucer's pardoner, another orator more eloquent than logical, he is carried away by his own exuberance. This wit lacks purpose of its own, but it serves Browning's end at every point. Sludge thinks he is a knave among fools, but his wit is altogether too active to save him from the charge of folly. He is a witty fool himself, a combination that enables Browning to turn Sludge's self-defense into indictment and make even his most persuasive arguments destructive.

ஐ 8 ஐ

To value Browning's achievement at the religious stage, we must first appreciate his limitations when he tries to consecrate the subjective impulse in "Rabbi Ben Ezra" (whose date is unknown) or the Epilogue to *Asolando* (probably written in 1888 or 1889). Whenever a monologue seems to have "designs" upon the reader, the speaker's attempt to persuade his auditor begins to turn into a form of direct persuasion by the poet himself. After he rids the speaker of his desire to persuade an auditor, who can function as the reader's "friend," Browning must take extreme care, as he does in "Saul," to command our own assent. Otherwise, his poetry of religious speculation is likely to become contentious. It is in danger of being consigned, like so much of his wife's verse, to the Victorian literature of forced sentiments and noble elegancies.

Because the spiritual victories are all won in advance, there is no dialectical movement in "Rabbi Ben Ezra." What matters in poetic argument is the habit of asking questions, and the difference these questions make in the life of the one who speculates. Rabbi Ben Ezra's affirmation that he can accomplish all things through God is simply the pretense of an ethical man who can do everything by himself and who mimics religious experience by pretending that God helps him. He recognizes the limitation of the aesthetic life in "Annulling youth's brief years" (l. 14). But in celebrating the doubt that makes the ethical man higher than the beasts, he is paying lip service to an uncertainty he shows little evidence of experiencing. The Christian dialectic is marked by one distinguishing feature, the difficulty which the doctrine of mediation has introduced by keeping man conscious of the truth that by himself he can do nothing. Though the speaker's religious beliefs would render the doctrine of incarnation untenable, he forgets that man can retain his religious freedom only by constantly practicing it.

One of the difficulties is that Rabbi Ben Ezra simply states the conclusions of other poems without suggesting the effort required to reach them. As a summary of Browning's own doctrines, the eighth stanza rehearses the doctrine of "Andrea del Sarto" ("Thy body at its best, / How far can that project thy soul on its lone way?"), and the tenth stanza presents the discovery made in "Saul": "I, who saw power, see now love perfect too." The twelfth stanza corrects the one-sided conclusion of "Andrea" by affirming Fra Lippo's thesis: "nor soul helps flesh more, now, than flesh helps soul!" But because the poem tries to establish its labels by fiat, its images strike the reader as consequences rather than as instigators of meaning. To find its doctrines presented as emotion we must turn to other poems. Though stanza xiv introduces "Prospice's" metaphor of death as the great adventure, there is nothing left of the absolute risk, because we sense that the

Rabbi can accomplish everything by himself. The limitation of his religious views is most evident in the twelfth stanza, where he demands the absolute knowledge of God that Browning finds incompatible with faith.

The speaker's closest approach to religious awareness comes in the metaphor of the Potter and His wheel, taken from *The Rubáiyát*. The wheel's stress gives shape and form to the human clay; the world tests and proves man and gives its product worth. But while the Rabbi finally concedes that the human cup is flawed, he turns theology into ceramics by trying to know the Potter as well as the Potter knows himself. He is still so confident that the Craftsman will perfect his flaws that he never abases himself before God, as David does. Even his final prayer is a celebration of the ethical doctrine of probation, of Keats's "vale of soul-making." The cup with foaming wine becomes a kind of wishing cup. Rabbi Ben Ezra has a superstitious way of apprehending the truth. The strength of his affirmations makes his belief a kind of overbelief; the more he protests his assurance, the less we believe it.

Every religious "truth" receives its value from the finder, but in the Epilogue to *Asolando*, as in "Rabbi Ben Ezra," we are invited to find nothing. In forcing his own beliefs upon us, Browning breaks the first rule of rhetoric. He fails to enlist the reader as an active collaborator. The poet has apparently neither the willingness nor the capacity to leave his most profitable messages for the reader to find and help develop. The dead lover of the Epilogue, in reply to the fears expressed by his beloved in the first two stanzas, uses the argument of the self-satisfied ironist in "A Toccata of Galuppi's." Because he has lived at the ethical stage, beyond the sensual bondage of the hedonists, "the slothful" and "the mawkish" (l. 8), he is confident of an eternal happiness beyond the grave. But since his moral circling—"fall to rise," "baffled to fight better," "Sleep to wake" (ll. 14–15)—is overeasy and primitive, it overleaps religious dialectic and indulges Browning's impulse to strident affirmation. In his vehement gesture of greeting "the unseen with a cheer," he is unduly confident of that eternal happiness which only a self-surrender before God, in the "black minute" referred to in "Prospice," can make viable. His raucous cry has less in common with the religious dignity of David or St. John than with Gerard Manley Hopkins' irreverent description of a man with his mouth full of cheese jumping up from the table. The absolute venture of "Prospice" is possible only if the way is more difficult than Browning pretends. Since what he hopes to gain by greeting "the unseen" is so certain, he does not risk or venture at all. The call to battle is a false alarm. He is simply making an exchange between fighting "here" and fighting "There," with no real transformation of his moral terms.

The poems that are most faithful to the Christian dialectic are those which enable Browning to turn the merely contentious assertion into speculative discourse. "To think" in the sense of "believe" is not to think in the sense of "ponder." What matters is less the doctrine than the life represented and the values discovered on the way. When a person like Rabbi Ben Ezra knows what to believe, he has no more thinking or speculating to do. For this reason I believe that the difficulties of Christianity improve Browning as a poet. When he writes the visionary climax of "Saul," which discards the rhetorical controls imposed by a speaker's attempt to persuade an auditor, the more closely Browning follows the Christian dialectic, the more successfully he can temper his prophetic powers with the consciousness of impotence. Without this consciousness all religiosity, Christian or otherwise, vanishes. Whereas Rabbi Ben Ezra and the speaker in the Epilogue to *Asolando* pontificate, David "thinks": he does not simply record his thoughts, but realizes them in the very act of uttering them. The Victorian sage must use his doctrines for the sake of the life that goes with them, for the sake of what is formed in the progressive act of thinking.

∽ 9 ∾

"Saul" is Browning's most comprehensive attempt to carry the reader through aesthetic and ethical contradictions to a grasp of Christianity at the religious stage. Because it begins with "lower" terms that are systematically elevated to religious status, the elements of its climax are all implicit in David's earlier arguments as bard and sage. Saul's conversion has in one sense already taken place in Section IV, where the austere agony and gloom of the gigantic figure spotlighted in the dark with his arms outstretched against the cross-supports of the tent—a symbol of Christ on the Cross—rises to a height of grandeur and strikingly anticipates David's final vision. Moreover, praise of Saul in Section IX implicitly contains the climactic revelation, since praise is the verbal equivalent of David's love, and this love equals the Christ principle that binds together spiritual father and son. Browning posits clear distinctions between "the wild joys of living" at the aesthetic stage and the communal life of the ethical man who "runs" to his fellow "to assist him and buttress an arch / Naught can break" (ll. 58–59). But because it uses natural, social, and rhetorical analogues to furnish the necessary empirical base for its religious truths, David's climax of "See the Christ stand!" is dramatic instead of melodramatic, and the logical culmination of an arduous but systematic process of ascent.

Even as bard and sage, before he discards his harp to assume his third, prophetic role, David uses a Longinian style to express religious elevation. Like much of Milton's rhetoric, it is a cross between the grand style of Augustine and

Longinus' fusing of the "sublime" with the awesome. His Miltonic mannerisms include the inversion of subject and verb ("Said Abner," "So sank he"); the inversion of noun and adjective ("care soft and grave," "habitudes kingly"); and his habit of framing a noun between two adjectives ("gold dust divine"). Even the incongruity of coupling rhymes like "enthroned" and "groaned" prepares for the dialectical relation David is trying to establish between suffering and salvation. Since everything bears upon this relation, steps from the lowly to the lofty are everywhere at hand.

As David transforms "the wine of this life," the hedonism of the aesthetic man, into the metaphor of the palm wine that invigorates and sustains the soul "on purpose of a life beyond life," he exchanges his role as sacred Pied Piper for his moral role as philosopher and sage. David's passage from the aesthetic to the ethical life brings Saul from his "Everlasting No" to a "Centre of Indifference." But the distance which still separates "God's throne from man's grave" (l. 198) is the distance between the ethical and religious stages, and one which David can bridge only by imparting his gift of spiritual vision to Saul. What David seeks to reveal is a perpetual "now"—a "new life altogether, as good, ages hence, / As this moment" (ll. 235–236). He seeks the grace of duration conferred upon the "good minute," a present eternally identical to itself and comparable to a simultaneous contemplation of all history. But this "new life" is not something he invents. Its revelation "comes upon him" from without, though in order to receive it, David, like the reader, must work at the height of his own creative powers.

The most authoritative criticisms of "Saul," those by W. C. DeVane [21] and A. W. Crawford,[22] are concerned almost exclusively with Browning's sources and the reason

[21] *A Browning Handbook*, pp. 254–257.
[22] "Browning's Saul," *Queen's Quarterly*, XXXIV (1927), 448–454.

for his delay in completing the poem after writing the original nine sections. The possible influence of Christopher Smart's "Hymn to David" is interesting, not so much as a specific source, but as an indication of Browning's kinship with a tradition of sublimity in literature which goes back through Blake and Smart to eighteenth-century poetic primitivism. Unfortunately, most of the orthodox critics of "Saul" are too tame and lack that adventurous confidence in the validity of their own perceptions without which no criticism worthy of refutation or assent can be written. Other critics, like Emily Hickey,[23] are merely appreciative and try to capture in their commentary something of the ecstasy that David feels. They indulge in a kind of reverential rhapsody that tells us more about their respect for the work than about those qualities in the work that are worthy of respect.

The most searching analysis of "Saul" is Roma King's somewhat unorthodox study in The Bow and the Lyre.[24] King's major criticism is that the wedding of David's highly emotional rhapsody to the drama of theological speculation is bound to produce an unequal union. He believes that the mystical elevation of the whole impedes the dramatic action of the opening and the free play of David's analogical arguments at the climax. King's fine attention to Browning's language is probably the most suggestive approach to "Saul." But we can approve of a critic's methods without agreeing with his conclusions. The rhetorical elevation of the opening may appear more appropriate than it seems to King if we assume that David is narrating the story shortly after his climactic vision. The continued excitement of surprise is still animating the speaker's voice and stimulating attention. The final revelation, which Browning probably wrote in 1852–

[23] "A Study of Browning's Saul," The Catholic World (Dec., 1911), 320–326.
[24] Ann Arbor, Mich., 1957, pp. 100–123.

1853, seems already implicit in the incantatory introduction written seven years before—odd when we remember the poem's history of composition. This is a theory F. E. L. Priestley has long argued. As he has shown in his lectures, the ending of "Saul" is obviously implicit in the original opening. Saul himself shows the suffering and the posture of the Crucifixion without conveying its meaning: the poem *has* to be completed by the meaning in the prophecy of Christ. What delayed Browning was not an inability to think of how the poem ought to end, but an inability to decide how much he himself believed in the ending.

"Saul" is not a dramatic monologue, if only for the technical reason that David addresses no specific auditor. It is, instead, a narrative account of the meeting between Saul and David, broken by frequent aria-like interludes and climaxed in Section XVII by the analogical argument in which David deduces from his own love for Saul the existence of a God of love who manifests himself in human form.

The climax of the poem unites intelligence with feeling through a rhetoric which combines the soaring statement of the sublime style ("I have gone the whole round of creation: I saw and I spoke") with a second, more discursive mode, which emphasizes serial predicates ("I saw and I spoke: / I . . . received . . . / And pronounced"). The rhetorical questions and shorter sentences are appropriate to the cautiously speculative mode that David now adopts as he discards the rapture of song for more meditative speech. But even his simplest statements seem to evoke celestial wonders to astonish the imagination: "I spoke as I saw"; "all's love, yet all's law." The reasoning by question and answer, recommended by Cicero, the supposed author of the *Rhetorica ad Herennium* ("Have I knowledge?"; "Have I forethought?"), and punctuated in each case by resounding exclamations, establishes the intellectual rhythm of a mind mov-

ing between analysis and revelation. There is a constant
eddying movement of advance and retreat. David has to circle through three rhetorical questions before he can affirm
that "God is seen God." The inexorable beat of the ana-
paests, momentarily freed of the reflective mid-line breaks,
carries David's vision of God relentlessly onward: "In the
star, in the stone, in the flesh, in the soul and the clod." But
the cosmic emotion, instead of dissipating into mysticism,
carries a strong charge of intellect and creates a forceful
stimulus for David's mind. For there is an immediate return
to freewheeling argument in the speaker's daring speculations
about his ability to surpass God in his love for Saul. The
passages in which Browning makes the reader participate
most actively, and forces upon him a sense of his own collaboration (as in the grand battery of questions beginning,
"What, my soul? see thus far and no farther?") are those in
which we are most aware of the intellectual content of the
poem.

Suspended in the "abyss," the empty space which engulfs
him when his ethical life breaks apart, David realizes that he
is wholly nothing in the presence of God. The sage's knowledge shrivels before "Wisdom laid bare," and even his forethought seems "blank" before the "Infinite Care." Though
David is nothing, and "the mere atoms despise [him]," he
must make the most desperate exertions to arrive at religious
truth. The resulting rhetorical effect is one which Longinus
praises—the elation experienced by an audience when it is
creatively participating in the speaker's own discoveries.

David uses the rhetorical figures of climax and repetition
to establish an attitude of "collaborative expectancy." When
"God is seen God" (l. 249), we participate on the level of
purely formal assent in helping round out the symmetry by
willing its perfection as an utterance. David invites us to
confer on "God," a term he first introduces with a purely

descriptive emphasis, the Word's full panoply of attributes. From logical reflection the dialectics of theology mount "the dream, the probation, the prelude" to find release on new plateaus of revelation: "Clear and safe in new light and new life." But each synthesis stimulates further speculation, which is in turn capable of more profound and complex intuitions. At each stage the progressive acts of discovery communicate, as in Donne's "Satire III," a sense of effort: they dramatize the cogency and rigor of the thinking. The dialectical movement catches the rhythm of a spirit subsiding from the passion of a "pain-throb" or a cosmic wonder ("I believe it! 'Tis thou, God, that givest") to a rhetoric of renewed speculation ("Why is it I dare . . . ?"; "What stops my despair?"; "Would I suffer for him . . . ?"). But intellectual and emotional power reinforce each other, and the mind returns from thought to vision in a progressive enrichment:

> I seek and I find it. O Saul, it shall be
> A Face like my face that receives thee; A Man like to me
> [ll. 309–310].

The principle of perfect love has corporate equivalents in a "pastoral" rapport between high and low, and in the marriage and funeral rites. But its most persuasive analogue is David's love of Saul; and just as Browning must actively involve the reader in the urgency of David's speculations, so David perceives that God's truth is not something he can receive passively, but rather an aid to his own activity. He must cooperate with God for Saul's redemption, in the same way that the skeptical reader must abandon his neutrality and make a conscious effort to respond to Browning's rhetoric if he wants to understand the poem.

At first David thinks of the divine and the human as two realities which stand face to face with each other. But "Each faculty tasked / To perceive [such a God] has gained an abyss," and in the course of his speculations David comes to realize that God's creation is not independent of what man creates. For, like Tennyson's love for Hallam in *In Memoriam*, David's own love for Saul opens his soul to a belief in a still higher love. Critics have attacked this analogical argument and maintained that no shepherd boy turned religious philosopher could ever have inferred on such grounds the necessity of a Christian Incarnation. They forget that, just as St. Paul proclaimed that his "strength" was made "perfect in weakness" (II Cor. 12:9), so David has already conceived the divine image in its two great forms that combine power and weakness, sublimity and pathos: " 'Tis the weakness in strength, that I cry for! my flesh, that I seek / In the Godhead!'". In his realization that God is not indifferent, but lives, suffers, and hopes with us, David already anticipates the truth of Christianity which made God descend in sacrifice for man. As the formal cause of David's vision, Christ does not exist in the future at all, but in a continuous present. David's argument is not anachronistic, since Christ's priority is "formal" rather than "temporal." The Incarnation, for Browning, is not just a historical event, but one which antedates the birth of Christ and continues constantly till the end of time.

David first establishes love as the essential human attribute and denies that, because he is unable adequately to express his love for Saul, he is essentially without love. He must be judged by what he wants to do for Saul, not by what he can do. But to establish this love by arguing that David exceeds God in his capacity to love is to curtail the principle of love for the sake of the principle, and to involve the speaker in a contradiction. The paradox consists in David's limiting love to its human forms. He resolves this difficulty in a causal enthymeme which concludes that because suffering and love are good deeds which he can perform on behalf of Saul, they are also deeds which God can perform. His unformulated major premise validates the analogy by affirming that all good deeds which man performs are also deeds which God performs.

Roma King objects to the poem's "vague theological system," and charges that it forces Browning to rely mainly on "sentimental emotionalism" for his effect.[25] The motive for the poem's apparent diffuseness is to give the impression of argument in process. The diffuseness is a way of engaging the reader in David's thinking by creating his discoveries out of the ideas and emotions he experiences at the moment. If the poet's theology is as vague as King maintains, then we could never be as deeply moved by it. On the other hand, Browning avoids the opposite danger of being suddenly too explicit or doctrinal. He demonstrates all along how the relations between God and David, Saul and Christ, are all implicit in David's praise of Saul and in other elements of the poem's dramatic design before being made explicit in the analogical argument.

Critics would be less willing to make King's second charge of "sentimental emotionalism" if they understood more clearly the literary tradition to which "Saul" belongs. The defense of the Word of God against the reason of man is not the sentimental vagary of an "emotional gnosticism" peculiar to Tennyson or Browning, but a defense of imaginative interpretation which goes back through Blake to the Cambridge Platonists. David's imaginative approach to God combines the Platonic experience of waking from "life's dream" to the "day-spring" of eternal life with the inner inspiration of a Nonconformist, which derives from the habit of basing religion on direct individual experience—a habit described by T. S. Eliot as the "Whiggery of the Inner Voice." To

[25] *Ibid.*, p. 108.

this union Browning also brings a powerful use of the creative imagination, which is probably his most immediate legacy from the Romantic movement. In a paradoxical argument from etymology, Christ is most David, not simply because He is a son of David, but because He is most beloved. This Christian apology is not to be mistaken for an indulgence in sentimental emotion. David's analogical argument has logical integrity as well as imaginative power; it is a splendid example of an inductive approach to religious experience.

Another of King's objections is that "Saul, initially presented with individuality, soon becomes merely an object for David to speak at." [26] If the poem is supposed to be an ordinary dramatic monologue, then we could say that it has been misnamed; to call it "Saul" would be like calling "Cleon" "Protus" or like calling "Andrea del Sarto" "Lucrezia." But "Saul" is not such a poem, and it would seem advisable to judge a visionary work in terms of what it accomplishes, not in terms of what its author usually achieves in other poems. "Saul" is one of those rare works in which Browning finally reaches the "pure white light" [27] without repeating the failures of his early subjective poems. As in "Abt Vogler," he is able to follow his wife's advice to "speak out of that personality which God made." In the later poem the visionary moment passes away, so that with Abt Vogler's return to self-persuasion the rhetoric of the monologue form can be preserved. But, in "Saul," Browning can sustain the "pure white light" only by going beyond the monologue form altogether.

[26] *Ibid.*, p. 105.

[27] Browning writes, in his second letter to Elizabeth Barrett, "You speak out, *you*,—I only make men and women speak—give you truth broken into prismatic hues, and fear the pure white light, even if it is in me, but I am going to try" (*The Letters of Robert Browning and Elizabeth Barrett, 1845-1846* [New York, 1899], I, 6).

T. S. Eliot identifies "the voice of the poet talking to other people" as the "dominant" voice in the dramatic monologue.[28] In "Abt Vogler" we cannot suppose that we are listening to any other voice than that of Browning himself. And if we can accept this in a monologue like "Abt Vogler," it should be doubly acceptable in the frankly visionary and prophetic climax of a poem like "Saul." When Roma King complains that "the poet's voice is so loud that we can scarcely hear David,"[29] he is objecting to rhetorical impurities in a literary form which, being more personal, is deliberately more rhetorical than a dramatic monologue. He is judging an oracular poem in terms of something it is not. Ironically, even the literary form by which King illegitimately judges "Saul"—that is to say, the dramatic monologue—will not only permit, but will often even require, the degree of rhetorical manipulation to which King objects in "Saul."[30]

[28] T. S. Eliot, "The Three Voices of Poetry," *On Poetry and Poets* (New York, 1957), p. 104.

[29] *The Bow and the Lyre*, p. 107.

[30] To further discussion on this issue, I have been trying since writing the section on "Saul" to define some common ground on which these differences between Roma King and myself might begin to disappear. There are, I think, many legitimate questions about "Saul" based on assumptions and methods differing from my own which would yield an appraisal of the poem similar to Roma King's. If we are to approach "Saul" as an autonomous work of art rather than a work of rhetoric (a plea by David to accept something, or an imposition by Browning on the reader), then we may soon find ourselves objecting to the kind of structural or stylistic flaw that disturbs Roma King. Is it possible that the differing assumptions of the New Critic and the rhetorical critic predetermine the different discoveries that each will make? To raise this question in the text would have destroyed the unity of my original argument. But reconsideration of the poem along more formalist lines has led me to conclude that "Saul" is not as perfect a poem, structurally, as others that Browning wrote. Though David has to gain momentum for the climax: "See the

Because Browning is so passionately engaged in David's speculations, he can communicate an additional enthusiasm to the reader. His rhetoric brings into play our critical intelligence and develops in us an analytic appreciation of religious argument. But David finally completes his dialectical advance, and this is why, for organic as well as technical reasons, "Saul" is not a dramatic monologue. I am not suggesting that "Saul" has no dramatic elements, but that the drama of its religious debate is transformed at the climax into a vision of transcendent truth, and that the voices of Browning and David seem to speak, for a moment, in unison. We feel that David's vision of Christ—"See the Christ stand!"—is something which Browning can now also see for himself. It is precisely because the poet seems too self-absorbed to communicate with anyone that the rhetoric at this point is so effective in communicating with the reader. Though the coda of "Saul" reverses the direction of the ascent, the "lower" terms of nature are so infused by the transcendent spirit that there is virtually no descent, as there would be in the coda of a religious monologue. The unuttered and the unseen are now the most alive, and the Christian solution allows David to celebrate a world that is totally responsive to divine control.

Christ stand!", the long thirteenth section, in which he develops the metaphor of the "palm-wine," leaves the poem broken-backed; it flaws the poem structurally. More significant than a modified view of "Saul," however, are the theoretical implications of this issue. Any poem seems to me to be many things; a pluralist might argue that different approaches are bound to disclose different "truths," and that such approaches are useful because for the purpose of their different inquiries each may be valid. Is is possible that "Saul" is really both an autonomous object and a series of rhetorical gestures, or really (but not exclusively) either of these things? For further discussion of this whole problem see Wayne Booth, "The Rhetoric of Fiction and the Poetics of Fictions," in *Novel*, I (1968), 105–117.

"Saul" affords a rare pleasure, which we cannot experience to the same degree in any of Browning's other works, of seeing the poet, like his speaker, soar magnificently to the "pure white light." Not even in "Abt Vogler" does Browning sustain his visionary inspiration undiminished, without betraying, as in "Rabbi Ben Ezra" or the Epilogue to *Asolando*, a disproportion between the urgency of his utterance and his power of mind. But a dramatic monologue like "Caliban upon Setebos" affords a different, and for Browning a much more characteristic, sense that no one ever triumphs completely, as David seems about to triumph at the height of his argument. The disparate pleasures that "Caliban upon Setebos" and "Saul" afford cannot be realized in the same work. One is the genius of the dramatic monologue, the other the genius of the visionary poem. If we are to rejoice in David's rhetorical flight into visionary truth, then we cannot at the same time delight in Browning's subtle characterization.

It is not hard to see why Browning, the frustrated visionary, chose "Saul" and "Abt Vogler" as two of his best lyrics. But to appreciate "Saul" it is not necessary to agree that Browning's true genius lay in visionary writing. Poems like "Rabbi Ben Ezra" and the Epilogue to *Asolando* are too often vitiated by that shrill, frenetic style which also makes his wife's poetry, since it is deprived of the discipline of a classical rhetoric, diffuse and shapeless. Browning will be remembered for his dramatic monologues, not for his visionary poems. "Saul" goes beyond the monologue convention, and in illustrating how the poet's words must become a study of the Word, it points toward the disinterested utterances of Caponsacchi and Pompilia. Only in such works, where the speakers are no longer trying to secure some personal advantage from their auditors, does Browning move with authority and ease in the visionary realm. With full awareness of the poet's radical limitations when he attempts similar effects in other poems, we may therefore say of "Saul" that it is one of Browning's most impressive attainments of the "pure white light," the rare discovery by Shelley's ardent disciple of his own genius in the master's mode.

PART III

THE UNION OF THE
SUBJECT AND THE WORLD

The Ring and the Book (1868–1869) enables Browning to write directly from his own experience. But because it first encompasses many points of view in the objective world, it also overcomes the limitations of his early subjective poetry. Browning has learned that as a mimic who portrays many one-sided and absurd attitudes in his dramatic monologues, he can display his own creative powers far more effectively than as a visionary poet. The subject whom *The Ring and the Book* unites to the objective world is a dynamic and histrionic being who dramatically portrays and ironically dissolves many points of view. If, as Browning believed, he had at last written "R. B.—a poem," a work in which he could present directly his own experience, it was because as an actor he was most himself when he was least himself. The only personality that counts in poetry is an accidental by-product of contrivance and disguise. As a representation of the final union of the subject and the world, *The Ring and the Book* is the culmination of Browning's Christian dialectic. It celebrates his creative personality, not by his ability to speak directly in his own person, but by his power to reproduce and criticize the internal nature of many points of view.

The dramatic monologues enable Browning to build the right kind of wall between his weaker, confessional nature and the personality he must create if, as a disciple of Shelley, he is to fulfill the poet's high didactic function and write "R. B.—a poem." But because Browning cannot hide behind the wall indefinitely, he keeps adding more of himself to his maturer monologues, till at the climax of a visionary poem like "Saul" he seems to be speaking directly in his own person. In writing "R. B.—a poem," Browning accomplishes in *The Ring* what he failed to achieve in his early subjective poetry. He is projecting, not the untransformed poet of *Pauline* with his confusion of unassimilated personal problems, but a mastered second self, which both Browning and the Victorian public can respect. By casting his heroine as a rescued damsel like his wife, his hero as a dashing deliverer like Browning the lover, and his villain as a version of Barrett the father, the poet imparts a ponderously formal, severely symmetrical design that turns the whole into a heavy myth, a kind of overgrown morality play. *The Ring and the Book* relates the characters to each other in a vast web of analogies which depend for their value on a revelation of greatness. Its doctrines are redeemed and illuminated by their biblical parallels. Though the overarching analogies by which Browning invites us to combine the different points of view remind us that no revelation in human terms is complete, the poet who mimics in progression a host of incompatible ideas and beliefs can gradually approach resultant certainty. The "truth is the whole" and must be progressively disclosed in some total form that can command our assent by the skill of its impersonations, the symmetry of its design, the sheer range of what it creates.

8

Dialectical Irony:
The Masks as Kaleidoscopes

Whereas Browning's dramatic monologues present many views about a variety of subjects, *The Ring and the Book* uses many points of view about the same events. Because it presents its characters in typical stances, like a play turned inside out to reveal "Action in Character, rather than Character in Action," its episodes have a schematic processional quality, a one-dimensional extension, and unroll like pictures on a film. A dramatic monologue stops the film of its speaker's life completely. But *The Ring and the Book* plays over and over again certain crucial episodes in a limited sequence of events. The analogy is that of a kaleidoscope, where the same pieces are shifted into new patterns at each turn of the instrument, without any alteration in the actual components. Like his early search for an objective form, Browning's kaleidoscopic technique is an attempt to permit inclusive perception of the center of truth around which many points of view organize and fulfill themselves. *Pippa Passes* had substituted for a linear dramatic action a set of interlocking scenes, with Pippa's songs at the center of each as the final cause of each of the conversions. Browning's ethical and religious monologues also tried to evoke at their climax the truth at the center of every person or event. By putting its masks

237

into motion and allowing the same pieces to fall into a bewildering variety of new designs, *The Ring and the Book*
tries to blend its dizzying play of color back into the "pure
white light," the divine truth that swirls through its masks in
a succession of temporary incarnations. The center of the
kaleidoscope, the "still point" of its changing configurations,
is the "central truth" of Caponsacchi, Pompilia, and the
Pope—the power of God and the mystery of his Incarnation.

If the characters of *The Ring* form a circle, with each reflecting something of the "central truth," but with only the
Pope, Pompilia, and Caponsacchi possessing it wholly, this is
not because Browning believes that all points of view are
equally false, but because he knows that only through participation of all the perspectives can we hope to approach resultant certainty. *The Ring and the Book* is certainly "relativistic," in that its main action can be seen from many perspectives. But as Hillis Miller observes, Browning "use[s]
point of view to transcend point of view." [1] For the observer who participates in an orderly development of such
perspectives, and for whom Pompilia and the Pope represent
the logic of this development, Guido is not just another
voice in a relativistic chorus.[2] Guido's villainy is an integral
motive, necessary to the development of Pompilia's virtue
and the Pope's wisdom. This dialectical irony, though it accounts for Guido's place in the design as a kind of "technical
equivalent" for original sin, is not to be confused with relativism. If we are looking for relativism, we must turn back
to Browning's aesthetic masks, which by fragmenting the

[1] J. Hillis Miller, "Robert Browning," *The Disappearance of God*
(Cambridge, Mass., 1963), p. 148.
[2] For a different interpretation see Robert Langbaum's excellent
discussion, " 'The Ring and the Book': A Relativist Poem," in *The
Poetry of Experience* (London, 1957), pp. 109–136.

complete Christian dialectic and isolating Kierkegaard's sensual man, view the development of a whole series of perspectives in terms of their limited distortions alone. Irony is incompatible with relativism and arises only when Browning tries to produce, through an interaction of religious, ethical, and aesthetic monologues, a dialectical movement which uses all the points of view together. Guido is ironic, not because his evil is just as valid as Pompilia's goodness, but because it is needed to produce the total development, in the same way that a disease may ironically "perfect" its cure. Browning keeps elaborating this point in his correspondence with Miss Wedgwood: "This good (of my lot) comes through—is evolved by—that prodigy of bad: hence its use, hence my poem, hence your blame, hence my kissing the rod, hence this word to beg you lay it on again and spare not!"[3] The Browning who wrote these lines sounds drunk with "inebriated" truths. But this dialectical revel contains a valuable insight into the nature of his art. Unlike most of his contemporaries, the poet who can "kiss the rod" and praise "that prodigy of bad" sees that "the essential advantage for a poet is not to have a beautiful world with which to deal: it is," in T. S. Eliot's words, "to be able to see beneath both beauty and ugliness; to see the boredom, and the horror, and the glory."[4]

៛ 1 ៛

Since Browning's first thousand lines expose to view all the pieces in his kaleidoscope, the only justification for the enormous work that follows is the skill with which he rear-

[3] *Robert Browning and Julia Wedgwood: A Broken Friendship as Revealed by Their Letters,* ed. Richard Curle (New York, 1937), p. 153.
[4] "Matthew Arnold," in *The Use of Poetry and the Use of Criticism* (London, 1933), p. 106.

ranges these pieces in a variety of new designs. Mere mystification is an art which Browning, like Shakespeare in the Prologue to *Romeo and Juliet,* is content to leave to second-rate writers. The opening inevitably destroys the kind of mystery with which even many inferior authors are able to envelop a courtroom drama. But the effect is to increase the more sophisticated pleasure of dialectical irony. This proceeds from the contrast between the essential simplicity of the pieces, as exposed to view at the beginning, and the fantastic chaos which Browning makes of them. Though the method's danger is that the work itself will lapse into chaos, as indeed it does in parts of the advocates' monologues, the more extensive and confusing the monologues, the greater the irony. This is the point Carlyle overlooked when he complained that *The Ring and the Book* "might have been told in ten lines, and only wants forgetting." [5] To be sure, almost nothing is left untold about the subject after the first thousand lines. But the rest of the poem arouses interest by its rhetoric. It is all a matter of how Browning "helps" the reader, how his selecting presence behind the very way in which he turns the kaleidoscope invites the reader to view the pieces and discover new dramatic ironies.

Browning's method is first to ingratiate himself with his British public; he assumes its literal-minded attitudes, then gradually discredits them. Book I opens with a narrator who is dramatized in his own right as a simple-minded nominalist. Incapable of rational selection, he can describe only the surface of objects and values the Old Yellow Book, the source of the story he will relate, merely for its "gold" of fact. To exercise his rhetorical powers, the narrator indulges in fatuous apostrophes: "But human promise, oh, how short of shine!" (I, 295). He speaks in the comically pedantic vein of Chaucer's Knight: "How history proves . . . nay, read He-

[5] W. C. DeVane, *A Browning Handbook* (New York, 1955), p. 346.

rodotus!" (I, 297). Only when he turns to address his British public directly does this dramatized narrator become one with the implied author. Browning retains "fact" as the prize word of his Victorian audience, but he shifts its connotation to include "fancy," the imaginative sense of fact as well as the crude residue itself: "Fancy with fact is just one fact the more" (I, 464). The "Fanciless fact" (I, 144) is the disorganized material in the Old Yellow Book, and "fancy" is the imaginative alloy that reveals the truth embodied in the gold. The British public is told that "fancy" is a "fact"; "fancy" is the "gold" which his audience has always supposed to be the opposite of "fact." This has a certain "shock-value," and to avoid absurdity, we are forced to give "fact" a broader meaning. Paul A. Cundiff believes that Browning knew that the squirt of acid replaced the alloy by a film of gold, while his fancy (alloy) still contributed to the making of the ring.[6] Fancy and fact remain distinct only until the final spurt of acid dissolves the alloy. The perfect ring that remains enables Browning to express his own values in the universal language of myth, and so to communicate through his masks—which present the particular truths of history—his knowledge of God's "central truth" to others.

Browning believes that each of the poem's phases is both false and necessary. Though mere truths of fact, comprising the crude "gold" of the ring, are false in isolation, they are necessary in fashioning the total product. Since truth involves its contrary as an integral part of itself, the ring requires not only the gold of fact but the gold's own opposite: the alloy of the poet's fancy. In Book I, Browning repeats the facts of the case three times in order to illustrate how he fashions the ring. When he first presents himself searching the square for the Old Yellow Book, Browning is, as we have seen,

[6] "The Clarity of Browning's Ring Metaphor," *PMLA*, LXIII (1948), 1276–1282.

feigning a consciousness not his own, a consciousness reduced
to a sensorium (I, 33–363). The original narrator supplies the
bare facts of the situation. But raised to the level of interpretation, his truths of fact must then become their opposites.
When the facts are repeated for the second time (I, 364–
697), they have turned into "truths of force," as Browning
calls them: acts of sympathetic imagination which judge the
right and wrong of the case. Though there can be no "truth
of force," open to moral valuation, in the absence of sensory
awareness, the exclusive claims of sensuous immediacy must
now be discounted. But if truths of fact at the first stage lack
"force," the "truths of force" at this second stage are still
merely "fanciful"; they are deficient in objective reference.
Browning therefore recounts the facts for a third time (I,
698–1389), combining the truths of fact and the "truths of
force" in a new fellowship. In asking whether "fiction which
makes fact alive, [is] fact too" (I, 705), Browning is not inviting us to identify truth with falsehood. On the contrary,
the fanciful in the sense of the false or the fictitious is something that the poet's use of fancy in the form of make-
believe is designed to expose and discredit. Browning insists
that every persuasion be entertained, or imaginatively re-
created, as if it were true. This is why, with the addition of
the alloy to the gold and the disappearance of the alloy in
the final wash of acid, fact, fully understood, must come to
include its opposite, fancy. Browning is not going to such
extremes simply to indulge his love of paradox. As the rest
of The Ring and the Book illustrates, the truth emerges only
out of the extensive interaction of such diametrically opposed elements.

In his rapid review of the main action Browning commands far more faith in his powers of divination than he did
as a seer in his early subjective poetry. We never for a moment doubt that the poet who can display such freedom and

power over many points of view in the objective world knows everything about Pompilia's innocence and Guido's guilt. To the first "Half-Rome," the witness for the defense, "a fact / Looks to the eye as the eye like the look" (I, 863–864). A "fancy-fit" inclines the witness for the prosecution, the "Other Half-Rome," to sympathize with Pompilia. Because between two runners he will arbitrarily choose the one who wears the pink scarf, his defense of Pompilia is equally absurd. The "Tertium Quid," who prides himself on his advanced relativism, is the most refined and dangerous product of the aesthetic stage. He represents his rejection of absolutes as intellectual enlightenment and tries to pass off the rationalist's "plague of squint" as universal truth. Next comes the testimony of the Satanic Guido, then of his victims, the "good beauteous priest" Caponsacchi, whom Browning has first introduced "in a glory of armour like Saint George," and the saintly Pompilia. The defense advocate "Wheezes out" his "law-phrase" and mixes Ovidian indecencies with his travesties of Cicero. The prosecutor is equally treacherous. He is a labile chameleon who parodies the artist's negative capability by defending Pompilia today, then accusing her tomorrow. The narrator tells us that following his condemnation by the Pope, the villain who "whined before" will "scream" as a "tiger-cat," and that after Guido's execution the poet will return in his own person to guide us back to earth.

Browning wants to show that by rapidly turning his kaleidoscope, he can blend the whirling "Red, green and blue" back into "the eventual unity" which makes "the miracle" (I, 1362–1364). Whereas Browning's early subjective poetry was unintelligible to everyone but himself, because it tried to present the white without the colors, the objective world of his monologues too often displayed the colors without the recomposition into unity. In uniting the subjective poet with the world, *The Ring and the Book* tries to satisfy the contradictory pleasures to be derived from learning that the truth is simple and absolute but that the way to this truth is complex and difficult. Both are legitimate sources of literary effect, but Browning's desire to realize the two effects simultaneously accounts for the great length of the work and its unpopularity with some critics. Rather than give us the "pure, white light" at once, Browning will take us through its highly colored distortions in the chaotic court records. Only the poet's sympathetic imagination can give intelligible shape to this material by trying to make manifest the central truth within.

Because this final truth cannot rise above the truth of Browning's original metaphor, he returns to his analogy of the ring. Imagination, as the alloy, is the organ, not of truth, but of meaning. It is not the cause of the truth's display but its very condition. The analogy by which Browning thinks is a suggestive one, for if imaginative meaning is the antecedent condition of the logician's true-and-false propositions, its opposite is not error but nonsense. As a master of metaphor, Browning is a master of human meaning. Since the truth can be won only by the imagination which creates such metaphors, the alloy itself is "justifiably golden," and when dissolved by the acid, makes visible both kinds of gold—the particular truths of fact and the unchanging truths of God and man.

Browning concludes the first book with an eloquent invocation to his "lyric Love, half angel and half bird." As in the coda of "Saul," his lyric exaltation is at its most intense. But instead of allowing his rapt emotion to dissipate into tenuous metaphors, as it does in his early subjective poetry, Browning identifies the universal design, Christ, with an individual bird, his wife. There are signs of burdensome forces which blanch the heavens of "their blue" and bare them of their "glory," and which even imprison the spirit in "the darkling earth." These motives reach a climax in a line that might literally be applied to the Christian Incarnation: "to drop down, / To toil for man, to suffer or to die" (I, 1399–1400). Like Hopkins' windhover, the bird foregoes its heavenly inheritance to work and suffer for all men, and its love is unchanging even after it has perished. The bird is wan and sorrowful, but it is also victorious and triumphantly white. "The red-ripe of the heart" is at once the blood of death and the transforming blood of new life. Even the last terrible "wanness," which seems "Deathwards progressing / To no death," like Moneta's visage in Keats's "The Fall of Hyperion" (Canto I, ll. 260–261), is redeemed by the preceding "whiteness," which sanctifies through sacrifice. Browning tempers the ecstasy of the opening into a subdued prayer— "Some intercourse / Of grace, some splendour . . . / Some benediction"—and even when the sense of flight is most vibrant there is a countervailing tendency to mortifying descent. This is the Christian dialectic of "stooping to rise." It challenges the British public's addiction to facts, which can proceed only from the higher to the lower term. Because Browning identifies the infinitesimally frail with the infinitely powerful, as in David's yearning to embrace the "weakness in strength," his lyric has its own persuasive genius and inventive charm.

∽ 2 ∾

In presenting the testimony of the first Half-Rome, Browning sacrifices sustained dramatic irony to the final shock of discovering that the speaker suspects Pompilia because he is a kind of Andrea del Sarto tortured by his wife's intrigue with his auditor's "Cousin." Only on a second reading, when there is a loss of such surprise, can we discover new dramatic ironies. Only then do we realize how completely the speaker suffers from a warped perspective. We see that his defense of Guido is really a superstitious rite performed before the chief "Idol" of his domestic "Cave."

To persuade his auditor, who has been prejudiced by his cousin's account, the first Half-Rome anticipates and refutes all the arguments against Guido before his interlocutor can state them. This is a form of *insinuation*, recommended by Cicero, and it gives the speaker an air of candor without damaging his case. But he soon destroys this advantage by committing a number of fallacies. Because Guido's cousin was unreliable, he proceeds to indict all cousins and to discredit the testimony of his auditor's cousin accordingly. On second reading, we discover that his sampling of cousins is more complete than we suspected. But at this point he would prefer to admit to a fallacy in logic rather than to the indignities of a self-revealed cuckold. When he indulges his literary imagination by casting Caponsacchi and Pompilia as a strutting Paris and a wanton Helen, first Half-Rome illegitimately argues from the accident of the priest's disguise to his essential lasciviousness (II, 709–710). The speaker himself would be the first to use the false wit of the argument from names if he were debating on the other side. For this reason he proves to be surprisingly adept at discrediting any attempt by the prosecution to establish Giuseppe Caponsacchi's chastity under temptation by linking him with the biblical Joseph (Gen. 39:7–12), who resisted the advances of Potiphar's wife (II, 1115). His own defense of Guido, which is far more preposterous, ingeniously converts the Count's lies into an argument from pathos, which he can indirectly transfer to himself. Instead of planting the evidence against his wife, Guido becomes the speaker's alter ego, the "poor soul" ferreting everywhere for new love letters (II, 1068–1072).

The speaker ascribes a rhetorical motive to Guido's deceptive use of Caponsacchi's name at the door of the Comparinis' home. He justifies this treachery as a "last experiment" to determine Pompilia's guilt or innocence. Though he acknowledges Guido's trick of language—"here's rhetoric and to spare"—he never recognizes that he himself is debasing rhetoric by trying to persuade his auditor of the basic honesty of this deception. After rapidly narrating the details of the murders, which he likens to a cleansing mountainwave, the speaker insists that the *arete* of the pagan hero, which he would substitute for Christian virtue, is to revenge his own wrongs. If Guido is found guilty, the first Half-Rome insists, pagan honor and civility will desert the world. Even if murder breaks the civil law, it confirms God's natural law that "the faithless wife shall die" (II, 1478).

3

The Other Half-Rome stumbles onto the right verdict, but because Pompilia's religious motives are beyond his comprehension, he defends her for wrong reasons. He keeps construing the biblical myth according to aesthetic categories, and reduces it to absurdity by mixing sacred and pagan analogies. He identifies Eden with the garden plot in which Pompilia's foster parents rear their daughter; he sees Pompilia herself, the apple of their eye, as a product of the Eden tree. Violante-Eve is prepared to pluck this apple as Hesperian fruit and to offer it as fit food to the Herculean Guido (III, 385–386). By forcing their daughter into sexual union with the Edenic serpent, and hence into ultimate death, her parents commit a gratuitous crime, which is their counterpart of original sin. The speaker recounts the enormity of Violante's crimes, which progress in kind from the "vulgar" and "abnormal" to the "prodigious" and "impossible." Even in confessing these sins, she disguises as a form of penance her real motive, which is to have the dowry pass from Guido to herself (III, 566–612). She goes to confession to receive religious sanction for what she wants to reveal in any case: that Pompilia is the daughter of a whore, and hence not entitled to the dowry. But despite this change in the biblical anecdote, Browning expects the reader to discern essential elements of religious truth, which are necessarily distorted through her limited perspective. Pietro's renunciation of his inheritance in favor of Guido never quite loses the resonance of Adam's sale of God's patrimony to the Archenemy. Through the *felix culpa* of renouncing Pompilia as their own child, the Comparini can regain their inheritance and receive back the rejected "daughter." Browning is already laying the groundwork for his religious analogies. For just as Adam and Eve regain their patrimony through the assistance of their offspring, the second Adam, so Pompilia, the adopted child, will plead with the Divine Father to readmit her erring parents to his breast.

As a witness for the prosecution, "the Other Half-Rome" is most convincing when he abandons his rhetorical indirection and tries to win sympathy for Pompilia by relating events directly from her point of view. After his *ad hominem* refutation of Margherita's testimony that Caponsacchi came to Guido's home the night of the elopement— "The woman's life confutes her word" (III, 1107)—he proves that Guido's own testimony is self-refuting. The Satanic scorpion that stands between Pompilia and heaven attributes "Love-letters" to a "wife who cannot write." Since he has obviously forged Pompilia's letters, he has probably forged Caponsacchi's as well. But even at the innocent's expense, "the Other Half-Rome" cannot resist the double-edged analogy which casts Guido as Vulcan surprising an unfaithful wife (III, 1450–1461). When more in control of his comparisons, he makes Guido parody the religious mystery of dying "into new life" by baptizing his worldly fortunes in the blood of the Comparini. By repeating Guido's charge that his use of Caponsacchi's name at the door proves Pompilia's guilt, the Other Half-Rome also argues convincingly for the opposite conclusion. If Pompilia had been seeing Caponsacchi frequently since her removal to her parents' home, a secret watchword would have been the lovers' signal, and she would never have responded to so open an announcement (III, 1606–1619).

σ⁊ 4 ⋀⋀

The judicious observer must in some way combine the simultaneous detachment and concern of the successful critic. But if the first Half-Rome betrays anxiety, which is a perversion of concern, "Tertium Quid" errs in the opposite direction: his indifference is a debased form of intellectual detachment. Priding himself as a spokesman for educated opinion, Tertium Quid ridicules the unfashionable idea of absolute truth, which he compares to a *deus ex machina* dropping to clear "things" in a play's fifth act (IV, 17). As a way of flattering his aristocratic audience, he keeps playing upon their class consciousness and apologizes to "His Excellency" and "the Marquis" for having to deal with "an episode / In burgess-life." As part of his casuistical defense of Pietro for defrauding the heirs of their estate, Tertium Quid introduces the comparison of the peasant in whose laneway His Excellency has discovered the precious sapphire. Since the auditor cannot very well deny his own right to the jewel, he cannot object to this defense of a thief on the ground that he has defrauded his victims without their knowledge. The casuist reasons that to condemn something because it began as a vice is like committing the genetic fallacy of rejecting a pearl because it originated as a grain of grit (IV, 310). To interest his aristocratic auditors, he represents Guido's crime as an example of aristocratic vice, as vengeance that has the appeal of style. He implies that class distinctions are inseparable from moral distinctions, and that the Count's nobility justifies in the moral realm what the sublime justifies in the aesthetic. Typical of this "finer vengeance" is "the writing traced / At Guido's instance by the timid wife / Over [his own] pencilled words" (IV, 769–772), which the speaker advertises as the kind of rhetorical cunning his aristocratic audience should admire.

Though he believes the priest would insist that Guido planted the letters which were found, he can imagine Caponsacchi's scoring a point by conceding that he and Pompilia exchanged letters. But Tertium Quid is equally adept in rallying his mental powers to Guido's aid by adapting Aristotle's stratagem of founding a defense upon mistakes. Suppose Guido proves "A murderer at the end"; it would have been unnecessary and a mistake for him to engage in such "woman's-work" as "Letters and embassies and weak intrigue" (IV, 1064–1065). Uniting a subtle intelligence with an incapacity to understand anything, the speaker immediately supplies Caponsacchi with a counterargument. He imagines that the priest's appeal to higher authorities would be an effective way of vanquishing all objections: "I must look to men more skilled / In reading hearts than ever was the world" (IV, 1111–1112). But to ingratiate himself with his aristocratic auditors, Tertium Quid must also add a ludicrous *ad hominem* defense of Guido, whose cowardice is to be excused by his marriage into the middle class.

The relativist fails to see his own limitations reflected in the court's attempt to please all parties. The outcome of its puppet play is the devil's slaughter of the Comparini family, when Guido appears with his horns, hoofs, and tail, and with slapstick bravura lifts up Pompilia, holds her disdainfully at arm's length, then drops her onto Pietro's knees: "Let us away, my boys!" (IV, 1391). The speaker unwittingly per-

petuates the court's permissive temper and implies that the
death from fever of the officer who finally arrested Guido is
an appropriate punishment for "the over-vigilant."

Tertium Quid's final argument takes the form of posing a
logical dilemma. If Count Guido hangs, then the nobility itself will suffer. But if he is freed, "What crime that ever
was . . . / Deserves the torture?" Since Guido must either
be sentenced or freed, either the nobility or the law must
suffer. Because Tertium Quid's aristocratic auditors will
never allow the nobility to be discredited, the only way they
can escape the horns of the dilemma without destroying the
law is to abolish the death penalty: "You see the reduction
ad absurdum, Sirs?" (IV, 1631).

But Tertium Quid's logical games have persuaded no one.
His contempt for "the two idiots" who leave him reveals that
his philosophy of mediation is only another species of relativism calculated to ingratiate himself with the nobility. The ultimate irony is directed at the "idiocy" of the chameleon
who, in borrowing his auditors' philosophy, discovers to his
horror that he is nothing in himself. Through a dishonest use
of ethical argument, he arrives at the conclusion that morality is relative, but then is forced back upon this further contradiction: How, in a world where no values are absolute,
can he affirm the absolute validity of any principle, including
his doctrine of a polite and cultured moral relativism?

〽 5 〽

Browning's dialectical irony becomes fully explicit only in
the twelfth book, which inverts the title of the whole and
recalls the title and structure of the first book. This circular
pattern involves the reader in an interaction of perspectives
that affect one another throughout. If it were not for the
privileged pronouncements of Pompilia and the Pope, who
are more than equal participants with the other characters,

there would appear to be no outside position from which the speakers could be judged. The same ironic cycle, with its interaction of "subperspectives," few of which are wholly right or wrong, would continue to run indefinitely. In approaching the truth as its limit, it would generate a dialectic that should ideally have no end.

To parallel the unreliable narrator of the opening Browning introduces letters from the two advocates and from an anonymous witness of Guido's execution. In his impotent heaping of details the witness betrays the unselective mind of the original narrator; and in writing to a client's friend, the defense advocate, still straining to seem overfine and eloquent, alludes preposterously to the execution of "His Blessed Memory / Count Guido Franceschini now with God" (XII, 241–242). Into the midst of his equally fatuous letter the prosecutor introduces the sermon by Don Celestine, Pompilia's confessor, who, like the Pope, enjoys the role of *primus inter pares*. As the summarizing testament, this sermon reaffirms Browning's own belief that, far from being able to reach the light through his own efforts, man must confess his nothingness and supplicate God's grace: " 'God is true / And every man a liar' " (XII, 600–601). To be sure, Don Celestine recognizes certain secular analogues of grace which may lead a Caponsacchi, or even a Fra Lippo Lippi, to religious truth. But he insists that man must prosecute his journey homeward, and not be satisfied with the idolatries that trap and enslave him at the aesthetic stage.

The prosecutor's rejection of this doctrine, which he dismisses as "Molinism / Simple and pure" (XII, 654–655), is merely another proof of Don Celestine's thesis that human speech is false. The prosecutor thinks he is being very astute in finding Don Celestine guilty of self-refutation. The monk is advancing as a truth the unreliability of human testimony, but this proposition cannot be true if the only truth is that all men are liars. The Fisc soon reveals, however, that behind this battle over logic is a fight over jobs. If man's words betray the divine Word, then lawyers are among the chief offenders. As a result of such indictments, the prosecutor realizes, he may "whistle for" his "fee" (XII, 663), like Judge J. M. Gest, perhaps, a critic of Browning's distortion of legal facts, who, as W. C. DeVane notes, seemed to have "some animus against the poet for his treatment of the lawyers." [7] To prove Pompilia an adulteress, so that her wealth will revert to the Convertites, the Church is involving the Fisc in the contradictory act of defiling God for religion's sake. In trying to refute Don Celestine's thesis that human speech is false, he vindicates it in a way he never suspects. When he boasts that he will turn "Noah's-dove" into an impure "raven" (XII, 727–729), the only impurity is a rhetorical one, and it resides in his willful distortions. Through his irresponsible language the Fisc once again becomes his adversary's most convincing proof.

Browning steps forward at the end of this book to lecture the British public in his own words, just as he had dropped his mask at the conclusion of the first book. We must not mistake his repetition of Don Celestine's charge that "human speech is naught" for an endorsement of relativism. It is simply a recognition that every dialectic is necessarily ironic, since the different points of view can seldom be considered absolutely true or false. They merely contribute to the resultant certainty which emerges from the interplay of all such attitudes. Tertium Quid's cynical assumption that all points of view are equally false is the constant temptation of those who engage in dialectic, but it is a temptation to which Browning never yields. He makes the opposite assumption that, since all the points of view participate in an orderly development, they are all valid. Though some perspectives

[7] *A Browning Handbook*, p. 342.

are more privileged than others, they are all necessary to a proper formulation of the total truth. Browning refuses to isolate any one advocate in the dialogue and to see the whole in terms of his position alone. Because the truth that they are blind to truth strikes most men as false, only the art of the dialectician, who takes the total interaction for his empire, can convince his audience that false is false, in a way that direct argument cannot.

On the one hand, the poet insists on his loyalty to "facts." In answering Julia Wedgwood's objection to his "scientific interest in evil," [8] Browning asserts that "the business has been . . . to explain *fact*—and the fact is what you see and, worse, are to see. . . . the minutest circumstance that denotes character is *true:* the black is so much—the white, no more." [9] Elsewhere the poet complains that Miss Wedgewood is "wrong about the proper treatment of facts. . . . They want explaining, not altering." [10] The critic C. W. Hodell has confirmed Browning's statement by insisting that "in few cases, indeed, does the Poet violate the ascertained fact of his sources, even in his freest range of creation." [11] Autograph notes for *The Ring and the Book* illustrate the extreme care with which Browning verified his statements. According to the catalogue of the Browning collections, on the first page of these notes "all the dates of events connected with the poem are set down, concluding with the Death of Pope Innocent XII in 1700; on the other side is an Almanack for January and February, 1698, the months of Pompilia's murder and Guido's Trial, with a note of the date of Easter-day, 1697, and of the phases of the moon during April of that year." [12]

[8] *Robert Browning and Julia Wedgwood*, p. 137.
[9] *Ibid.*, p. 144.   [10] *Ibid.*, p. 183.
[11] *The Old Yellow Book, Source of Browning's "The Ring and the Book"* (Washington, D.C., 1908), pp. 255–259.
[12] *Catalogue of the Browning Collections* (London, 1913), p. 40.

On the other hand, such dissimilar commentators as A. K. Cook,[13] Judge J. M. Gest,[14] and J. E. Shaw[15] have all challenged the view that Browning is consistently factual. W. C. DeVane points out that the poet has "given us, not history, but an idealized reading of life."[16] I think there is truth in both points of view. Hodell is right to stress Browning's debt to "the matters of fact" in the Old Yellow Book. As DeVane says, only "one who has read the Old Yellow Book almost as often as did Browning . . . [can appreciate] what a tremendous effort the poet made to transcribe the truth of small details from his sources."[17] But in his allegiance to truths of value as well as to truths of fact, Browning also demonstrates, as an over-all formula of dialectical irony, that the gold of fact which goes forth to "Suffice the eye" returns as a ring, which because it means something "beyond the facts," can show, in Browning's own words to Miss Wedgwood, "the incidental evolution of good thereby."[18] A "ring" which begins as the gold of fact is rounded into an object of value, his wife's wedding ring. W. H. Griffin and H. C. Minchin report that Browning "had in mind a simple and modern Castellani ring, which his wife had worn, and which he wore later fastened to his watchchain, with the letters AEI upon its flattened upper surface."[19] In turning at the end to address a special member of his audience, the rhetorician can thus be most universal at the same time he is being most particular. His "facts" depend for their value on an illumination of greatness; their real aim

---

[13] *A Commentary upon Browning's "The Ring and the Book"* (London, 1920).

[14] *The Old Yellow Book* (Boston, 1925).

[15] "The 'Donna Angelicata" in 'The Ring and the Book,'" *PMLA*, XLI (1926), 55–81.

[16] A Browning Handbook, p. 346.   [17] *Ibid.*, p. 338.

[18] *Robert Browning and Julia Wedgwood*, p. 144.

[19] *The Life of Robert Browning* (New York, 1912), p. 231.

is interior conviction. His "Lyric Love," though a specific auditor, is also a supernatural witness, and she restores the motives of secular prayer with which the first book concluded.

In a sense, then, Browning's poem is circular; it ends where it begins, with his own allegiance to "Lyric Love" and his authoritative judgments of each of the personae. The only reason for writing the enormous work that intervenes is Browning's belief that no truth has value as an abstract summation. When Browning repeats Don Celestine's charge that human speech is false, he is not, like Carlyle, advocating a gospel of silence in twelve volumes, nor is he trying to invalidate all human testimony. Though committed to absolute truth, Browning insists that this truth depends for its meaning on the progressive phases contributing to its development. On the one hand, *The Ring and the Book* must first be read as "poetry of experience," to use Langbaum's term. The reader must first pre-empt each point of view vicariously and re-create it sympathetically. But *The Ring and the Book* cannot be read simply as "poetry of experience." Browning invites us to re-create each point of view sympathetically, not so much that we may then approve of it, but for exactly the opposite reason: so that we may then more effectively discount its limitations from within. The poem's structure is designed to deepen the inner conflicts which Browning's theory of truth requires for its progressive disclosure and fulfillment. *The Ring and the Book* is less "poetry of experience" than poetry of experiment. Its invitation to examine many points of view is an invitation to perform a dialectical experiment, requiring alternation between sympathy and judgment, and between appreciative insight and critical vigilance. Each reader must become an actor and a spectator in turn. In this respect the truth is like the poetic imagination, as Coleridge defines it. It depends on the way rather than the whither. One must read the whole poem to understand this view of truth, for either in advance of its dialectical deduction, or subsequent to it, the truth has no probative power. It is not at either time a "truth of force," but only an inert "truth of fact." [20]

[20] Among his contemporaries, Browning's view of truth is closest to J. S. Mill's. Compare Mill's insistence that (1) the truth is the whole, and (2) the truth must be held as living doctrine, not as inert or dead dogma. See "Of the Liberty of Thought and Discussion," in *On Liberty:* (1) "Popular opinions . . . are often true, but seldom or never the whole truth. They are a part of the truth. . . . The exclusive pretension made by a part of the truth to be the whole, must and ought to be protested against." (2) "When the mind is no longer compelled . . . to exercise its vital powers on the questions which its belief presents to it, there is a progressive tendency to forget all of the belief except the formularies, or to give it a dull and torpid assent." See *Prose of the Victorian Period,* ed. W. E. Buckler (Cambridge, Mass., 1958), pp. 259, 263, 265, and 269.

9

Legal Rhetoric:
Count Guido and the Advocates

Count Guido, the villain of the piece, is a Duke of Ferrara on a gigantic scale. His rhetoric mingles the same complacent wit and cunning with a cruelty which is perpetually flickering in the background, and whose manifestation enables Browning to insinuate all that is false or demonic in the speaker. But Guido has deeper introspections than the Duke of Ferrara, and his two orations, insolent and calculated as they are, engage issues much vaster than the tenuous conjurings of "My Last Duchess." Guido's legal rhetoric is public, grand, and fatal; and though his manner is at first as imperturbable as the Duke's, the scale of his passion is more titanic. Count Guido is a mythical Satan, dragon, sufferer—a melodramatic agent in some cosmic drama which reduces and simplifies his emotions, then magnifies them to a height of epic pain and wrath.

Most of Guido's legal arguments in his original appeal before the court correspond to Cicero's divisions of the classical oration in *De inventione*. Guido begins with an *exordium* designed to bring his judges into a proper condition to receive the rest of his speech (V, 1–139), then adds a *narrative* of events leading up to his marriage (V, 140–566). In place of a clear *partition* of his argument, Guido simply

258

turns to a consideration of his "profit or loss" in the transaction. His proof of his wife's deceit takes the form of an induction calculated to command the judges' assent to certain
undisputed facts (V, 570–1306). His *refutation* uses the
same inductive methods as his *confirmation* and shifts blame
for the murder to the judges themselves (V, 1307–1865).
The *peroration* includes the three parts analyzed by Cicero:
a summing-up, in which Guido reminds his judges of what
he has proved; an *indignatio*, in which he tries to incite
hatred against his adversary; and a final *conquestio*, calculated to arouse pity for himself.

Since Guido's case is discreditable, his *exordium* takes the
form of an *insinuation* which by indirection tries to steal into
his judges' favor. The *insinuation* leads directly into his
statement of the facts: he has married a prostitute's daughter
who has committed adultery with a priest and who wants to
pass off her bastard as Guido's heir. But the defendant builds
a form of the genetic fallacy into his very accusation. His
explanation of Pompilia's behavior in terms of her origin as
"the mongrel of a drab" (V, 88) should alert the reader to
further fallacies. Guido freely admits to the three murders,
but then proceeds to defend his "irregular deed" by insisting that what is important is not the "fact" but its "truth,"
which he equates with his righteous indignation. His argument gives point to Browning's criticism of Miss Wedgwood's distaste for "fact." [1] It leaves the emotive meaning of
"truth" eulogistic but weds it to a much narrower conno-
tative one: the sentimental justification of his own feelings as
of moral value.

Guido begins his proof, or *confirmatio*, by ridiculing the
accusation that Pompilia was forced to "co-embrace with
sulphur, snake and toad" (V, 636) as though he were a
practitioner of black magic. Because these fantasies carry

[1] See above, p. 254.

over to the charge that his brother made love to Pompilia, Guido can safely challenge the more serious accusation at the same time. He uses a method of dissociation, and analyzes ideas for love of the rhetorician's art. But sometimes his analogies carry him away, as in the metaphors from falconry. His conceit that Pompilia is the egg from which is hatched a cockatrice instead of a swan sounds at first like deft indictment. But in arguing that Pompilia is no pigeon, but a hawk, Guido is turning himself, as her owner, into a hunter of innocent game. He instinctively sees himself as a hawker who "twists" off the "neck" of his "bird" when it disobeys, and as a sadist who wants to cut off a third of his wife's ring finger for smiling at Caponsacchi. His depravity is comically irrepressible. Reinforced by rhetorical questions and searing antitheses ("Daughter? Dirt / O' the kennel! Dowry? Dust o' the street!"), the denunciations grow steadily more vicious ("by-blow bastard babe," "nameless strumpet"). At last even his carefully wrought antitheses disintegrate in the bleats of his sham despair: "but—oh—ah—assuredly / A Franceschini and my very wife!" (V, 774-775).

In an *ad hominem* appeal to the "Idols" of the court, Guido insists that his only motive in failing to kill the offenders when he first discovered them was his reverence for the law. He adapts Aristotle's method of arguing from degree by pointing out that though the court would justify his killing of his wife while there was still only partial proof of her guilt, it illogically protests when the proof is complete and all chance of reformation has been lost. If the judges grant justification when there is less reason, they should grant it a fortiori when there is more. By admitting to the earlier forgeries, Guido wins assent to the genuineness of his forgery of the love letters, which must be credited as his most important circumstantial evidence (V, 1141-1162). But in inventing a jocular reply from Rome in response to his suit for a divorce, he forgets Quintilian's advice that the fictions he devises must be probable. It is incredible that an ecclesiastical court would mock Guido's state or tell him that Caponsacchi is secretly visiting Pompilia at her parents' home. Nor would Rome degrade the Church by insinuating that its priest is better versed in Ovid than in St. Thomas. The rhetorical method is a good one and marks the transition from Guido's *confirmation* to his *refutation*. But because the fictions are preposterous, Guido never succeeds in shifting the blame from himself to his judges, or in giving his accusations against Caponsacchi the authority of the court's own testimony.

The *peroration* includes the traditional *indignatio*, in which Guido arouses hatred against "The perjured priest" and "that thief, poisoner and adulteress" called Pompilia. He also adds a *conquestio* in which he tries to arouse the judges' pity by pleading the destitution of his mother and his heir, Gaetano. In his summing-up he reviews all his strongest arguments, hoping that what is insufficient when presented separately will sway his audience when arrayed together. He insinuates that by disregarding the authority of the archbishop and the governor, who have upheld his case against Pompilia, the judges are inviting personal ruin. By adapting Aristotle's stratagem of reasoning from relative terms, Guido also argues that if Pompilia was guilty, then he is innocent, and that if Pompilia was innocent, the judges have already committed an error in punishing her (V, 1898). Since she is either guilty or innocent, Guido concludes that either he is blameless or the judges are wrong. He implies that the only way his accusers can escape from the horns of this dilemma is by acquitting him. But Guido forgets that the partial guilt of Pompilia, even if it were established, would not imply his own total innocence. In ironic anticipation of a favorable verdict, Guido ends by forgiving his captors for the suffering they have inflicted on an innocent man. This is once again an argument from pathos, and an effective way of shifting responsibility to his judges.

↝ 1 ↜

Guido's later appeal before the cardinal and priests, after the Pope has condemned him, is only ostensibly designed to sway his auditors. His real audience is now himself, and though his oration vindicates the Pope's verdict, it has for him the subtler satisfaction of substituting for the court's moral absolutes a complex rhetorical morality that seeks desperately, but without final success, to justify Count Guido to himself.

The logical divisions of his first oration now break down into a tissue of confirmation and confession, charge and countercharge. His *exordium* (XI, 1–27), instead of putting the cardinal and the priests in a proper condition to receive the rest of his speech, is an attempt to escape seeing the facts as they are. He thinks the announcement of the Pope's decision is only a trick designed to coax from him the real truth. But in denying his guilt, Guido unconsciously admits it in the most damaging way. The irony of his being as innocent as "Innocent my Pope and murderer" establishes Guido's blame, in a joke at the Pope's expense that redounds against the joker.

Guido contends that in sentencing him, Christianity is renewing the obsolete Mosaic law and using a form of persuasive definition to alter men's attitudes without changing their beliefs. By calling "Law" the "gospel" and "justice" "mercy," the Church is introducing a change only in the emotive implications of its names, not in the substance of its doctrine. Guido identifies this rewedding of descriptive and emotive meaning with casuistry, and extends it to the Church's dishonest labeling him a wolf. But in insisting that

he is harmless as a sheep, Guido indicates that he would at
the same time bare his teeth, and "gnash, tear, / Foam, rave"
(XI, 448–449). He is simply reversing the rhetorical technique for which he has attacked the Church. Instead of shifting the emotive meanings by changing the labels, Guido is
retaining the eulogistic name of "sheep," but shifting its descriptive content to coincide with his own vulpine temper.

The ritual that Guido mistook for a puppet play acquires
real religious significance, and Christianity proves a very earnest business. Like the mass of men, he has been playing the
game by aesthetic rules. When the rules are changed during
the middle of the game, why should Guido, rather than another man, be punished? He recognizes that the religious life
is not simply a subdivision of the aesthetic life, and therefore
not just a matter of "surface, mask and make-believe" (XI,
625). But running the risk of rejecting his "Faith in the present life" for the "Either / Or" of religion is a commitment
Guido can never make, partly because he misunderstands the
nature of the commitment. He introduces Gigadibs' false distinction between "Entire faith, or else complete unbelief."
Guido fails to see that unbelief is inseparable from the most
active faith, which demands a life of crisis and choice. For the
ingratiating appeals of his first oration he now substitutes a
fierce indictment of the clergy. In a kind of eulogy in reverse, he blasts the hypocrites for playing a worldly role till
necessity requires that they change their costume and pretend to be adherents of the religious life. The real deception
is that of the temporizers who always adjust their attitudes
to their audience. The Count, on the other hand, is what he
is because Guido is Guido, not because the priests are
priests, and he refuses to shift positions. He has a fierce
loyalty to his perverted values and believes that his dedica-
tion to them inverts the disinterested persuasion of the saints.
Because the neutrals are in many ways less admirable than

Dante's Ulysses or the Brunetto Latinis, he thinks his rhetoric of "Pure Impurity" makes the rhetoric of the temporizers
impure by comparison.

Guido boasts that his management of Pompilia just missed
being a masterpiece. Imbued with aristocratic pride and all
its reliance on noble style, the Count wants to know where
his aesthetic morality went wrong. Ironically, the artist in
crime, who never hoped to achieve "perfection" on his fatal
mission, seemed about to attain it. Though he admits that he
should have spared two of his victims, the sheer formal symmetry of "king, / Queen and knave in a sequence" (XI,
1602–1603) required that he kill all three together. Here he
is literally following the aesthetic creed with a vengeance,
and his adherence to the creed damns Guido irrevocably.
But it is almost as though the criminal unconsciously willed
his defeat. Though he knew his accomplices needed the
proper papers to escape, he failed to supply them; and though
his knowledge of anatomy was flawless, he bungled the
operation by failing to kill Pompilia outright. In wounding
her, he supplies her with her most potent argument from
pathos. Her ethical proof is also infallible, for the assassin
permits her to hold God's hand and forgive him before the
world. According to Freud's account in *The Psychopathology of Everyday Life*, Guido's bad luck would be interpreted as the expression of unconscious motives. Because
these motives require his arrest to complete the irony of his
design, they resist his conscious goal of wanting to escape.
Boredom, as the final contradiction of the aesthetic life,
leaves Guido "Sick, not of life's feast" (XI, 1903), but of
the means of achieving that end. Because the Count cannot
find release in the normal ethical solution, he tries to ration-
alize his execution by pretending it is a form of suicide, the
only way of escaping the despair that awaits him at the aesthetic stage.

Guido's peroration summarizes his strongest arguments against religion. He is convinced that the Church condemns him for failing to apply the proper rhetoric. An act is commendable or criminal depending on whether the defendant labels it murder or sacrifice. If he had tried to persuade the court that he was sacrificing Pompilia to "the Unknown God" or "the Genius of the Vatican" (XI, 2029–2030), Guido believes, he would have been invoking the magic formula. Even if he had urged such a preposterous motive as doctrinal concern about the heretical upbringing of his son, he believes his judges would have forgiven him. There is exquisite irony in the appeal of this master casuist to the "Idol" of his own "Cave." The murderer tries to convince himself that his only fault has been his chief attainment: his power to debase the rhetorician's art.

But as Guido begins to speak from a deeper level of himself, he abandons this complicated rhetorical morality in favor of a new and blasphemous simplicity. The panegyric to his wolflike nature is appropriately couched in Augustine's "grand" style. It uses highly wrought like endings— "Deformed, transformed, reformed, informed, conformed" (XI, 2063)—and an alarming number of parisonic members—"annoying and annoyed," "Malignant and maligned" (XI, 2067–2068). Park Honan has shown how Guido develops the wolf metaphor beyond what is consistent with an attempt to win from his auditors some personal advantage.[2] The more passionate he becomes, the more luridly his vulpine temper is projected against the darkness of his mind. As he strips off the sheep mask entirely, the wolf imagery reveals that the factual side of Guido has no connection with his professed, ideal side. He has the violence of a whirlwind that keeps blasting out his venom in torrents of denunciation. The reader may respond with certain satisfaction to

[2] *Browning's Characters* (New Haven, 1961), pp. 307–309.

the thunderous clash of forces, colliding powerfully before discharging themselves in dazzling blasphemies: "Be holy still, / And stupid ever!" (XI, 2077–2078). But when his fine intelligence begins to break the "truths" apart, nihilistically and skeptically—in this case showing that there is no connection between piety and intellect—it is usually to his own embarrassment. This technique is a kind of rhetorical schizophrenia. When carried to extremes, it calls Guido's own sanity into question. If we think his magnificent rhetoric, regardless of what is exaggerated or defiled, indicates Browning's approval, then we ought to find even more "approval" instead of "excitement" in the much finer speeches of Shakespeare's Iago or Milton's Satan. By reducing the emotional distance between the reader and the speaker, the long-sustained "inside" view presented in Guido's two monologues may reduce the moral distance as well. But Browning's sympathetic imagination is a dialectical weapon. It discloses the internal contradictions of the point of view that it portrays. Appropriately, Guido's language is like a tray of surgical instruments which can be felt cutting and laying bare the rotten flesh beneath.

The atheist's worship of natural instinct is one-sided and absurd. Its incongruity lies in its fated incompleteness. If all values are relative, then how can Guido proclaim the value of anything, including the integrity of his own "wolf-nature"? The atheist's freedom to mock everything, if taken seriously, demands universal extension. Guido thinks he can "surge by death into a visible flow / Of rapture." But this very exaltation is the atheist's heel of Achilles, for if Guido cannot repudiate the ecstasy of hating, he cannot repudiate everything. Dialectical logic requires that "the wolf" become his opposite; after exhausting his hate, Guido must "grow / Into the man again" (XI, 2060–2061). The atheist who cannot deny his own humanity cannot negate everything, and if he cannot deny everything, what happens to his much vaunted atheism? Browning's own philosophy is a condemnation of the limited point of view masquerading as total truth. He shows that it is impossible to deny the value of life and yet continue living to deny it. The clash between theory and practice is ironic wherever discerned. Guido's surprise at being condemned to die is inconsistent with his point of view. If everything is an object of the atheist's destruction, then his own life must obviously be included.

But since villainy is integral to the total dialectic and necessary to the development of Pompilia's virtue, Browning can still present the atheist's disorder as an inverted form of order. Guido's household at Arezzo is a travesty of the divine household in which obedience to the Church and its Bridegroom brings payment for service. At Arezzo, Pompilia's only payment for domestic servitude is the tyrant's threat of punishment. From Guido's side of Arezzo comes the principle of punishment as payment, and from Caponsacchi's side the principle of reward as payment. Both principles meet in the same person, Pompilia as servant and sovereign. She first appears at Arezzo as her husband's slave, but at the end of Book XI she is the sovereign to whom Guido must make his last appeal. Like Christ, Pompilia is the perfect victim to cancel the gratuitous, and hence "perfect," sin of Guido, in which the rest of society shares. The guilt is a corporate one and emerges from the very conditions of dominion and subjection implicit in all social and religious hierarchies. Guido's inability to find his place in society makes him feel guilty, and because this guilt is inseparable from all such hierarchies, it is analogous to "original sin." His guilt precedes his crime; and because his murders are offenses to "justify" or "defy" the guilt, they are a social analogue of the Fall. Once he commits the crimes that dramatize his guilt, Guido is "publicly" committed, and must preserve allegiance to his satanic counterorder. Though his primal impulse to rebel ironically "perfects" a religious cure, Guido's sheer assertive striving makes shipwreck of Christian ethics. From the standpoint of the total dialectic, his titanic will is self-destructive and immoral, and must be treated ironically. As a result of his crime Guido, like the first transgressor, must see himself under sentence of death. This is why the vast blasphemies of his two monologues have an "inevitability," both moral and stylistic, which, however noisy and declamatory, is just as ruinous as the Fall. Guido's death cannot be conceived merely as a natural process, and it is appropriate that it should be a kind of "capital punishment" to match Adam's.

2

If Guido's rhetorical excesses become, at the end, an enriching element, and even a component of psychological realism, the speeches of the two advocates are always monstrous and grotesque. By glorifying family life at the expense of social life in general, the defense attorney makes a festive burlesque of the trial. His oration is a form of subversion by antics and includes both social and rhetorical clowning. It is as though a Lord of Misrule were asking to be called a minister of justice. The pretension of his colleague, the prosecutor, who is equally guilty of trying to seem overfine and eloquent, is aggravated by an affected diction and use of Latinisms. Browning's blank verse commands greater sweep and volume in public utterance than any other verse form. It is a broadcasting megaphone that enables the advocates to consolidate their debasement of rhetorical tradition. By enlarging stupidity and inflating conceit, Browning can make their travesty of the classical oration roar and resonate in a full-dress circus of vulgarity that no ancient sophist could hope to rival.

Archangelis is so entranced by the portentous sound of his language that he refuses to interest himself in its meaning. His alliteration in parallel syntactic units is as freakish as the verbal capers of Euphuism: "So, liver fizz, law flit and Latin fly" (VIII, 124). The small, flat words contrast with the extreme artifice of the figure. In planning to rebut the prosecutor's charges by inane repetition of the formula "*Inanis est responsio*" (VIII, 175, 184), he keeps committing a form of the vice he decries. But he freely admits that he would introduce any number of damaging concessions if they also included further morsels of Latin wisdom, calculated to appeal to his ecclesiastical judges. When such Latinisms do appear, the mincing lilt of his lines robs them of their force and gives them a grotesque air. Though Quintilian warns against repeating the adversary's charges unless one means to ridicule them, Archangelis proceeds to compromise his own client. He rehearses as a gem of deductive reasoning the prosecutor's argument that Guido's charge that Pompilia wrote the letter is inconsistent with the fact that she could not write. Archangelis seems less concerned with his own defense of Guido than with the prosecutor's melodramatic perversion of the argument from pathos: "He eludes law by piteous looks aloft" (VIII, 227).

Most of the speaker's digressions express a form of professional anxiety, which is the perversion of concern. Their failure at rational selection proceeds from the frantic hope that Archangelis will deal with all the facts even if he cannot identify the relevant ones. He pictures himself as an alchemist who refuses to submit to experimental verification but who, "buoyed" aloft by words, will offer his auditors a "spiritual display" (VIII, 390). Archangelis believes that his demonstrations are securely beyond the accidental testimony of witnesses, which might crudely wreck at a blow his carefully wrought designs. This contempt for evidence gives point to Browning's own statement to Miss Wedgwood that the facts "want explaining, not altering." [3]

The defense attorney hopes to justify the murder by showing that Guido's honor was at stake. He will expand the term "honor" to cover all of Guido's vices, first assuring its eulogistic worth by calling it "a gift of God to man" (VIII, 459). If chastity is present in animals and insects, where it would be less natural, it must be present in man, where it is more natural. The absurdity of this argument from degree resides, not in its illogic, but in the incongruity inherent in its notions of chaste insects and bees, especially when Archangelis attempts an etymological argument from the name *castae apes* (VIII, 497). The amplification is itself an example of another rhetorical vice, the needless telling of what is already understood and accepted. Archangelis does not have to establish that adultery is wrong, only that Pompilia has in fact committed it.

In compounding precedents from pagan and Mosaic law, the defense operates on the irrational assumption that the same codes still apply. As a result, Archangelis' agility at argument is marked by an insane kind of logical consistency. He either reaches conclusions that represent the *reductio ad absurdum* of a sequence that has lost direction (the proof, for example, that a Christian should multiply vengeance), or else, in a desire to be inventive, he unwittingly provides the prosecution with all its subtlest arguments. As Archangelis climbs down the ladder from a lack of honor to contempt, from contempt to injury, from injury to indignation, the *sorites* begins to work less as a logical model than a Procrustean bed (VIII, 601–624). The more the series looses

[3] *Robert Browning and Julia Wedgewood: A Broken Friendship as Revealed by Their Letters,* ed. Richard Curle (New York, 1937), p. 183.

direction, the more notorious becomes his citation of authorities, in an effort to restore meaning.

Archangelis continues to use and pervert almost every effect known to classic oratory. The Ciceronian device of pretending to recollect himself by shifting to "the dubious act you bade excuse" (VIII, 975), and his subsequent attempt to anticipate and forestall Bottinius' arguments, add further touches of pedantry to what is already a travesty of Cicero. Archangelis recognizes that he should follow Cicero's practice by dismissing the arguments from "aggravation" as irrelevant to the main issue (VIII, 1144–1146). But having quite properly declared that he will collect all such "aggravations" in a body and dispose of them in a single proposition, he proceeds to contradict his own precept. He solemnly itemizes and refutes each of the subordinate charges in turn.

Dazzled by the Latin treasures discovered en route, Archangelis jolts crookedly from one irrelevance to another. His refutations are even more grotesque than the charges themselves. To rebut the accusation that Guido has violated domestic sanctity, he argues that since the home is not as sacred as the church, criminals who cannot be granted the right of sanctuary in God's house cannot be granted the same right in their own. But Archangelis is arguing from the abuse of the right of sanctuary, not from its proper use. To refute the fantastic charge that Guido was disguised as a rustic the day of the murder, Archangelis cites the religious authority of St. Paul, who escaped from Damascus in a basket let down from a wall, and who was disguised in a cloak. The fifth accusation, that Guido killed his wife while she was under the law's protection, is more serious, for it involves the vested interest of the judges themselves. Since no logical rebuttal occurs to him, Archangelis decides that this is the moment to meet the charges in a block, lumping together the fifth and sixth "aggravations" in a climactic *indignatio*. He will pretend that, as the law's chief defender, Guido is personally affronted that the court should accuse him of a legal violation. But his self-damaging correction—"Our stomach . . . I mean, our soul" (VIII, 1393)—identifies the advocate's real values. The persistent references to food and drink in his figurative language remind us of his ever present sensuality. Into his projected peroration the glutton uncorks his breathless recital of meats and sauces, mingling in with a superb disregard for relevance, family and dinner plans.

Archangelis discloses in the postscript that the chief weapon in his rhetorical arsenal will be the *ad hominem* argument. Because he has "to plead before these priests" he will "latinize" and "Cicero-ize," and "poke at them with Scripture" (VIII, 1745–1746, 1753). He anticipates the mimicry of his little son, who will imitate his father's legal travesties as another advocate of the poor. This is Browning's way of reminding us that Archangelis is not just a farcical rogue in a theatre of the absurd. His mockery of almost every classical rhetorical device indicates more than an extravagant aberration, exorcised in the ritual of his son's birthday feast. The sinister note is heightened by his eulogy of the banquet, which is given the same importance as his skill as an advocate. By envisioning his travesty of today as the son's folly of tomorrow, Archangelis is trying to set up his holiday license on an everyday basis. His oration is all uproar and commotion, but behind its clowning is a carnival view of the world which Pompilia and the Pope must finally expel with sanctified social and religious power.

〽 3 〰

If Archangelis thinks that everything is relevant, and in his plodding refutation of the six immaterial "aggravations" seems unable to initiate a fruitful line of inquiry, the prosecutor's overactive mind suggests to Browning an imbalance in the other direction. The defense advocate has a well-stocked memory, but he seems incapable of making logical connections. The Fisc, on the other hand, is good at making connections, but he is so inventive that we may wonder what he is connecting. He contemptuously rejects the "fragmentary studied facts." Unlike Browning, who in his correspondence with Miss Wedgwood insists that he is explaining the facts of the Old Yellow Book as he finds them, the Fisc creates the truth out of his own metaphors. It is almost as though Browning, in the second of his "two buffoon lawyers," as he calls them,[4] were defending by contrast his own artistic method. Whereas Archangelis seems to say everything about nothing, the Fisc appears to make metaphoric nonsense out of everything.

The exordium likens the prosecutor's art to painting. Though a painter should first study his models carefully, the Fisc insists that only a "spirit-birth" incapable of being literally described can create "the main central truth / And soul o' the picture" (IX, 100–101). His theory that the sudden illuminations of creative genius are the result of unconscious prior work is a persuasive one. But the Fisc proceeds to suppress half of what this theory involves; namely, the need for conscientious prior study. The theory is opposed to Browning's own practice during his many years of preparation for this poem, during which he read the documents in the Old Yellow Book eight times. Because much of the orator's necessary selection is done by his conscious mind beforehand, the Fisc's reliance on a subliminal creative self superior to the conscious self issues in bizarre romantic fantasies. He keeps discovering connections, not between a material cause and its effect, but between persons or events and what Aristotle and the scholastic philosophers would call their "final" cause. In-

4 *Ibid.*, p. 146.

stead of closing with the opposition in a logical encounter, the Fisc pictures himself behaving like an innocuous Duke of Ferrara grandly sweeping aside the drapery covering Pompilia's portrait.

> But shall I . . . play my proofs . . . ?
> Much rather let me soar the height prescribed
> And, bowing low, proffer my picture's self!
>
> [IX, 154–159].

Browning's criticism of this contempt for proofs is also his critique of Miss Wedgwood's objection; he would dismiss as irresponsible fantasy the evasion of the poet who, ignoring the facts, proceeds to spin the truth out of his own imagination.

The Fisc models his oration on the epic poets. Frozen into a variety of antique postures, he appeals like Homer and Virgil for aid to sustain him: "A great theme: may my strength be adequate!" (IX, 191). The formality with which he apes the convention of beginning *in medias res*—"I dare the epic plunge" (IX, 217)—illustrates the complacency with which he hearkens to the sound of his own voice. The Fisc is always ready to sacrifice the truth to a pun, and in making Caponsacchi the "levite," "Calm in his levity," bear the altar "bell" away (IX, 341–342), he is preparing for the erotic reduction of the priest to a strutting lord of the barnyard, "the very phoenix of such fowl" (IX, 350). He alludes to Pompilia's "melting wiles" and "vernal pranks," not because the logic of the case requires such innuendoes, but simply because he has read about such wiles in literature. His mimicry of epic includes his affectation of heroic epithets: "if Pompilian plaint / Wrought but to aggravate Guidonian ire" (IX, 265–266). Since he only half understands his classical sources, most of his allusive gems harbor an irony against him and poke fun at his panoply of literary terms.

Like Archangelis, the Fisc spends most of his energy exhausting for form's sake a whole spectrum of possibilities
which he admits are immaterial. He doubts that Pompilia
drugged her husband, but to show that he could defend her
if she had, he compromises her position by conceding the
point he later denies. Though he tries to dignify the crime
with quaint circumlocutions, his classical allusion to "Helen's
nepenthe" (IX, 626) is damaging, for it likens the escape of
Caponsacchi and Pompilia to the elopement of Paris and
Helen. The Fisc turns Pompilia into a sorceress or witch—a
siren more intriguing and seductive than even Guido could
imagine. He concedes that Pompilia has her faults, that her
love letters may be genuine, and that she may even have
been actively amorous with Caponsacchi, not because he has
to grant these points, but simply because the concessions
gratify his taste for romantic speculation. They enable the
bachelor who knows nothing about love to see love in
everything and to pour down on his judges a cascade of
words in which every obvious or absurd opinion is supported by comical quotations from Roman law or the ro-
mances. The Fisc is a cherub of the disengaged intellect, a
child with "pure eye and pippin-cheek, / And brow all pre-
maturely soiled and seamed" (I, 1197–1198). He is a
buffoon without morals or faith, who can only probe or
prance intellectually.

In his summing up, instead of consolidating his strongest
arguments, the prosecutor introduces the novel hypothesis of
Gaetano's virgin birth. Since not even the Pope makes such
claims for his saint, the judges are sure to dismiss these fantasies as wild attempts to exonerate an adulterous priest (IX,
1352–1366). The peroration includes the traditional *indignatio*, which takes the form of scurrilous defamation of his
colleague Archangelis, whom he sees as a glutton and a
swine. But his climactic vindication of Pompilia betrays her

by its very ingenuity. Instead of crediting the Pope's absolute belief in her innocence, the prosecutor makes the facts more complicated than they are. To leave himself a case to argue, he believes he must vindicate Pompilia on the grounds that she has tried to save Caponsacchi and to make Guido repent. But he damages Pompilia's cause by adducing as her greatest triumph her clever simulation of death when she was only wounded. The Fisc's error lies in remaking Pompilia in his own image, in his making her "wily as an eel that stirs the mud" (IX, 1419). His self-congratulation on the careful logic of his oration is the complacent reflection of a fool who is so obtuse that he unwittingly betrays his cause at every turn. This irresponsibility with language is a counterpart of the moral irresponsibility that later leads the Fisc to defile Pompilia in order to secure her property for the Convertites.

The pedantries of Browning's orators have seldom been equaled for bombast and falsity. The poet himself is a master of language, but he knows that the figures of rhetoric, when devoid of all sustaining content, are mere paper ornaments, and he delights in setting fire to them. If too often repeated, however, any device for winning attention becomes wearisome. Though Browning's destructive parody of the advocates is at first diverting, we soon become inoculated against the intended effect. A tissue of casuistry may be highly successful in a much shorter monologue like "Andrea del Sarto." But when such linguistic satire becomes the staple of a longer work, variety and forward movement inevitably suffer. To be sure, some objections to the legal comedy fail to appreciate that Browning is seeking more than one general effect in *The Ring and the Book*. To reconcile the claims of purity with truth to life's impurities, he must dramatize the tortuous complexities of the advocates before he ascends to the radiant simplicities of Pompilia and the Pope. But the lawyers' antics do not, it seems to me, achieve the purpose Browning told Miss Wedgwood he intended: to "let [the reader] breathe a little before the last vial is poured out."⁵ Though the advocates' arsenal of rhetorical weapons, arrayed in a competitive world of self-seeking and greed, is an important ingredient of Browning's dialectical irony, their deployment, by itself, provides little comic relief.

By extinguishing the light by which we live, any debasement of the human word debases the Divine Word as well. I think that, like Pope in *The Dunciad*, Browning is offering the advocates' abuse of words, not as an efficient, but as a formal, cause. Their rhetorical vices crystallize a pagan society's impulse to subsume the Word in itself—a debasement in which most of Browning's post-Romantic public shares. This common guilt enables the poet to invest two portentous fools, who could otherwise never be more than figures of gruesome farce, with powers for evil of truly epic magnitude. The problem is that Browning, unlike Pope, commits "the fallacy of imitative form." *The Ring* renders, but too seldom irradiates, the stupidity it decries: it never quite succeeds in the difficult art of making sheer fatuity interesting.

⁵ *Ibid.*, p. 153.

The Rhetoric of Religion:
Caponsacchi, Pompilia, and the Pope

Despite many pagan anachronisms in the allusions to the St. George and Perseus legends, we can discern in the climactic orations of Caponsacchi, Pompilia, and the Pope, the elements, broken and reassembled, of a biblical myth. This mythic action is more privileged than the partisan rhetoric of the other points of view, for the testimony of this holy triumvirate is addressed to God, and its motives are therefore disinterested. The basis of their myth is a metaphoric identification of Pompilia's foster parents with Adam and Eve. In yielding to the wiles of the Satanic Guido, the Comparini are admitting into their domestic Eden a son-in-law who is a demonic parody of Christ, the second Adam. The hero of this myth is the Messianic deliverer, Caponsacchi, whose crusade to right the wrong choice made by the first Eve issues in his rescue of the second Eve, Pompilia, his victory over the Edenic serpent, Guido, and his redemption of what is at once a society and a bride. In "A Death in the Desert" Browning had shown that if Christianity is in disrepute, it is because myths are taken only factually or figuratively; they are not read in their proper mode. Like the advocates, who are too "sophisticated" to accept as inclusive the total wealth of meaning in the literal action of the poem's story, Browning's Victorian public finds it difficult to read a mythic form in which all levels of meaning are implicit. As prelude to its climactic rhetoric of religion, *The Ring and the Book* has therefore had to include extensive preparations in the first two books, where Browning has introduced elaborate metaphors of the ring's gold and alloy to educate his public in the lost art of myth-reading.

⌒ 1 *⌒*

Throughout his oration Caponsacchi is addressing a twofold audience—the judges, who become less important as he proceeds, and God, before whom he is making a profession of his faith. With his conversion to Pompilia's cause, his very rhetoric undergoes "conversion." Though he follows the main lines of the classical oration, his legal rhetoric takes the form of the Platonic dialectic. It systematically matures a sensuous delight in women into worship of beauty in general and a transcendent desire for union with God.

Caponsacchi opens with an *exordium* in which he departs from the usual practice by first attacking his judges before commending the good he sees in them. After the announcement of his subject, in which he promises to "Burn [his] soul out in showing . . . the truth" (VI, 149), he merges the traditional *confirmatio* and *reprehensio* in his account of Pompilia's rescue. The priest's "confession" of his masquerade as a worldly cleric, which he intermingles with his refutation of Guido, sounds increasingly like a "profession" of his faith. The *peroration* begins with a disavowal of rhetorical motives: "I have done with being judged" (VI, 1859). Caponsacchi makes clear that his immediate purpose of trying to see Pompilia, or even of avoiding future miscarriages of justice, is subordinate to the conversion of his audience and his continued worship of God. Of course, Pompilia's divine attributes are implicit from the beginning, as is evident in the *exordium* from Caponsacchi's invocation of her as a saint. There is a certain rhetorical cunning in his gradual disclosure of this motive through the different stages of his adventure. But the attempt to gain some personal advantage is always subordinate to this disinterested celebration of Pompilia, which begins and ends his monologue. It is through her passionate and directed love that energy comes—the energy that signifies the greatness of heavenly fate, the customs and metaphysics of the redeemed life. Because a sense of Pompilia's divinity pervades the whole, and because the imagistic bridge of moon, sadness, and beauty aids in the priest's conversion to her cause, much of Caponsacchi's rhetoric is a form of prayer. Its end is present in its beginning and its answer implicit in its address: "not by the grandeur, God— / But the comfort, Christ" (VI, 2095-2096).

Caponsacchi divides his *exordium* into two parts: an introduction, in which instead of trying to win the judges' good will, he attacks them, and an *insinuation*, in which he mocks the judges' innuendoes of an adulterous liaison between Pompilia and himself. He begins his *confirmatio* with an attempt to show how the erotic courtship in which Conti and Guido abetted him implicitly contained his pure courtship of Pompilia following his conversion. To illustrate how the erotic motive was transformed, he first symbolizes the idea of sexual temptation in terms of food. His indulgent uncle had told him that although he was a priest, he would not have to fast, and Canon Conti threw candied fruit at Pompilia as a seductive overture from Caponsacchi. Pompilia as the second Eve and mediator is paralleled by a kind of demonic Eve, the servant Margherita, who is a mediator in a bad sense. She bears forged letters from Guido representing Pompilia as an adulteress who will gratefully take the crumbs from Caponsacchi's table (VI, 566). In representing her mistress as "a dish for any duke" (VI, 595), Mar-

gherita is inviting this clerical Adam to partake of sensual
fruit. But the golden apples that the Herculean priest plucks
are not sensual, and we find that Pompilia is starving, not for
sex, but for actual food. After his account of their second
meeting, the food imagery comes to signify hunger for
divine truth. Only Caponsacchi's "thirst" for God explains
why he has "recognized [his] food in her" (VI, 124).

Caponsacchi makes Canon Conti and his uncle, the
worldly bishop, serve his own rhetorical ends. He uses the
Canon as a lightning rod to draw the sensuality from himself
and ground it in his own bluff ribaldry. Caponsacchi portrays his uncle as a casuist who sees the priest as a modern St.
Paul with influence among the slaves, but with insufficient
converts among men of influence like King Agrippa (VI,
319–320). By repeating the judges' former suspicions as
those of the indulgent bishop, Caponsacchi can equate them
with dishonesty and make their intimations appear more
favorable to his own side than to theirs.

To confound the rationalists Caponsacchi has Pompilia
speak in paradoxes that present her deliverance as part of a
mystery. She appeals cryptically to "some kind of sake"
(VI, 765), whose identity is at once unclear to her and yet
as certain as the fact that she is alive. Instead of appealing to
St. George to rescue her at once, she merely hints at his role
as helper, then consecrates his intervention by calling it the
offering of bread from the altar cloth. This imagery of
courtship is as crucial to *The Ring and the Book* as Fra Lippo's sensuality is to the religious dialectic of the earlier poem.
Priestly and aristocratic classes, celestial and worldly orders,
draw sustenance from each other. The only mistake of the
bishop and the judges is to explain the higher in terms of the
lower. The motives are not positive but dialectical, and love
dialectically approached cannot be reduced to sexual terms.
Browning is writing a myth of Platonic ascent. Though sex,

to be sure, is a component of this process, it is not its substance. Pompilia's "riddle" is partly her way of resisting the genetic fallacy. She knows that the content of the forged letters is not her own "theme"; eroticism is only a metaphor for the myth of deliverance her hero is about to enact.

Pompilia's rescue becomes the great spiritual experience of Caponsacchi's life. Because she raises the priest to her own level, more comes out of his adventure than he contributes to it. Only this consecration into "another state, under new rule," makes the Church's asceticism a cogent demand: "Leave that live passion, come be dead with me" (VI, 1001). Caponsacchi's way is that of paradoxical religion, which bases its relation to an eternal happiness, not upon continued existence, but upon sacrifice and death. As in "Prospice," death undergoes careful redefinition. To rescue Pompilia, even if it means disgrace or death, is to "Soar to the sky" (VI, 952). Because the eternal has itself entered time, Caponsacchi's spiritual conversion is conceived as a dying to sensuality in an "ecstasy" that "outthrob[s the] pain" (VI, 973). Since their dying together—metaphorically for the priest but literally for Pompilia—is also symbolically a sexual union, we can see how systematically Browning transforms the rhetoric of erotic courtship into divine worship, and why his myth of transcendence requires, for purely dialectical reasons, the kind of restrictions implicit in the hero's ordination into priestly celibacy.

The intellectual conversion of Caponsacchi had already taken place: "I dare to say I have confronted these / In thought" (VI, 943–944). But only Pompilia can solve for him the remaining problem of love. His complete conversion occurs when he substitutes for the sensuality of a mistress the Pure Mediator whom he identifies with the Second Person of the Trinity, the love which unites the power of God with His knowledge. The seductive lure of Eve to the first

Adam is now replaced by the dignified figure of the maternal lady imbued with the properties of an absolute order. We respond to Pompilia's virtues because of the values Caponsacchi discovers on the way toward affirming her possession of those virtues. In his dialectical ascent he must supplant the Edenic apples and the golden fruit of the Hesperides with the "rosy shame" of "the virgin-band" and "victors chaste," as they rise "Into immortal nakedness" (VI, 968, 970–971). Caponsacchi has always recognized the power of the Father, "God above," who has authorized his priest to interpret to the world "The mystery of this murder." Because he has also "thought long and hard" about this mystery, Caponsacchi has already gained that knowledge of God which Browning attributes to the Holy Spirit. But the third motive, the love which should logically lead to a communion of the knowledge with the power, is still absent. Pompilia, by making love a presence in the world, completes the symmetry of this design. She can take the role either of the Virgin Mary or the Christ principle, exemplifying in both cases love's mediatory power in rounding out the Christian Trinity.

Because Caponsacchi does not want to threaten the divine by placing excessive demands upon the virtues of its spokesman, he keeps advertising himself as "A poor rash advocate" (VI, 1963), a priestly Antony whose plain, blunt truths do not require his polishing. He affirms the anti-Donatist position that efficacy lies in the rite of divine advocacy itself: "And God shall argue for the Lady!" (VI, 1706). Even if performed by an unskilled orator like himself, the office of pleading Pompilia's case is a holy one and must be effective. But if he escapes the error of the Donatists, he must also avoid the Pelagian heresy of his judges. By playing down Guido's original sin, the court had initially slighted the mediatory role of the deliverer in the redemptive process, just as the Pelagians had slighted the role of Christ. Caponsacchi shows that Guido's treachery is dialectically necessary. It is the "negative form" that defines its opposite, the dark background against which Pompilia's virtue stands out in relief. On the other hand, despite the black colors, Caponsacchi does not want to imply that human nature is intrinsically evil. To defend himself against the third heresy of Manicheanism, he dramatizes the utter impotence of Guido and Judas, who are bound together in "one spot out of the ken of God" (VI, 1953). Even more vividly, in the imagistic detail of Guido's "wraith" going "to nothingness" (VI, 935) and the metaphor of Franceschini the "opprobrious blur" (VI, 1526), he affirms that evil is only an eclipse of the heavenly truth. With this repudiation of the substantial reality of evil, Caponsacchi completes his deft avoidance of the three heretical positions—the Donatist, the Pelagian, and the Manichean, which are inseparable from all problems of God's Word and the human word.

In his summing-up Caponsacchi argues that if he is punished for saving Pompilia, Guido should be punished a fortiori for destroying her. Nor can the judges logically use his priesthood to disallow an intervention they would otherwise commend, and at the same time repudiate that priesthood now as a means of keeping Caponsacchi and Pompilia apart. By abasing the judges in bearing witness to her sacrificial role, Caponsacchi completely transforms the traditional *conquestio* of classic oratory.

The concluding prayer is a form of religious courtship. Pompilia is no longer simply a woman or even a saint: she is the orator's absolute audience realized. Her martyrdom makes the victim the sovereign and brings the highest and lowest rungs together. The paradox that first shall be last is congenial to middle-class society. It supplies Browning's myth of bourgeois England with an ideal of lowly social election as opposed to aristocratic ideas of nobility. Pompilia's martyrdom as the "final" cause of the oration implicitly contains the future. The priest's first invocation to her in the exordium is thus an invocation to the end that is felt to precede, formally as well as temporally, the stages leading to its attainment.

Critics have recognized that of all the speakers in *The Ring and the Book*, Caponsacchi comes closest to being Browning's surrogate. J. E. Shaw, among others, has argued that in playing St. George to Pompilia-Elizabeth and outwitting her Guido-like father, Browning himself was acting Caponsacchi's part.[1] But if, as Betty Miller believes, Browning refused to abdicate the role of knight and was uxorious in his attachment to Elizabeth even after marriage,[2] then this myth of deliverance may be his way of imaginatively prolonging his submission to her. Elizabeth apparently wanted Browning to abandon these vermiform attitudes and assert his mastery in marriage. But the poet yearned to be Caponsacchi's faithful knight. He wanted to court in terms of the infinite so that he could court eternally. In view of Elizabeth's illness and her father's tyranny, it was perhaps the very unlikelihood of marriage that led Browning to court Miss Barrett in the first place. Renunciation and possession had to be fused into one attitude, just as Caponsacchi's faith in courting his princess had to be faith in the impossible. Only by invoking Kierkegaard's religious category of the "absurd" could Browning discover his surrogate in Caponsacchi, the heroic, faithful knight, whose ordination in priestly celibacy both justifies and requires the adoration of his princess in perpetual repetition. Through eternal courtship Caponsacchi is forever winning Pompilia while forever

[1] "The 'Donna Angelicata,' in 'The Ring and the Book,'" *PMLA*, XLI (1926), 55–81.

[2] *Robert Browning, a Portrait* (London, 1952).

losing her. Because Browning could find satisfaction only in such a state, he is right to call his "lyric love" half-angelic. His love for Elizabeth, like Caponsacchi's for Pompilia, is in the region of the infinite, since his worship of her is logically prior to any specific forms of courtship. Elizabeth, to be sure, would have welcomed more persuasion, but, technically at least Browning's worship is on the side of the "divine." Caponsacchi's persuasion is essentially a rhetoric of martyrdom. (Though the word "martyrdom" originated in the law courts, it means "bearing witness" and presupposes a supernatural audience.) Under the guise of testifying before the judges, Caponsacchi, as Browning's surrogate, is bearing witness mainly to God himself.

2

Pompilia's oration conforms to Aristotle's temporal classification of the three kinds of rhetoric. Her legal oratory consists of her defense of Caponsacchi, which is designed to justify a past action, and her plea on behalf of her son, which is directed to the future. But as a panegyric addressed to God, her oration is not calculated to win any personal advantage. It takes place in an eternal present which bridges the gap between the rhetorics of past and future, of forensic and deliberative oratory. After an *exordium* (VII, 1–179), consisting of an *introduction* and *insinuation*, Pompilia adds a *narrative* (VII, 180–904) in which she first recounts the murder, then the events preceding her elopement. The *confirmatio* (VII, 905–1695) establishes Caponsacchi's innocence. It takes the form of a history that fills in the events between the time of the elopement and the murder. By returning to Guido's knocking at the door, the point in the story where Pompilia had dramatically broken off at the beginning of the *narrative*, the *confirmatio* completes the time scheme. The *peroration* (VII, 1696–1845) begins with a summing-up, in which Pompilia reviews the main characters and reveals their inner motives. In place of the traditional *indignatio*, which excites ill will against the enemy, Pompilia forgives her husband and ends with a *conquestio* designed to arouse pity for Caponsacchi and her son.

The *exordium* skillfully adapts Aristotle's ethical and pathetic proofs to convince the judges of Pompilia's innocence. Isocrates cites as an extreme example of the pathetic argument the custom of bringing a defendant's children before the jury. Pompilia in a much subtler version of the same kind of proof keeps bringing her infant son metaphorically "before" the judges. Her main ethical proof is her habit of confronting the situation with scriptural analogies. These have the effect of making Caponsacchi and herself essentially biblical characters. In renouncing Pietro and Violante as her earthly parents, Pompilia affirms her role as the second Eve. Because her child, like Christ, is not the natural son of his presumed father, she is able to adopt a scriptural parallel that gives her account of her adventure with Giuseppe a biblical resonance. Pompilia devotes the second part of her *exordium* to an *insinuation* in which she disarms her critics by formulating their own suspicions as Guido's. Instead of a direct *ad hominem* refutation, Pompilia must escape the charge of libel by stating Guido's accusations in ridiculous terms and by having others discredit these charges for her.

The *narrative* contrasts the peace of the Nativity scene and Pietro's plans for their domestic happiness with the swift descent of the holocaust (VII, 267). In retrogressing chronologically, Pompilia heightens Guido's treachery by having him step melodramatically from behind the altar at his wedding (VII, 441–444). In applying the lesson he had learned with so much difficulty in overcoming the rhetorical and dramatic failings of his early poetry, Browning makes Pompilia treat the characters, not simply as psychological puzzles, but as rhetorical subjects whom she places in dramatic relation to an audience. He treats Pompilia herself in a similar way. By introducing erotic caricatures of her behavior, he makes her virtues seem by contrast active and dynamic. Guido, of course, in his first oration carries the main burden of preserving the erotic potential of Pompilia's elopement. But even her defenders, "the other Half-Rome" and the Fisc, keep her virtue vibrant by constantly reminding us of the sexual temptations. Pompilia acknowledges that her husband's guilt preceded his crime. Because she would not allow him to ease that guilt, she admits that she might have kept Guido from the greater crime if she herself had appeared to commit the lesser one (VII, 694–695, 717–719). Though it is psychologically improbable that Pompilia should perceive now what she was too ingenuous to discern at the time, her defense of Guido is Browning's way of emphasizing the mercy as well as the integrity of his saint. By involving the reader in the dynamic motivations of sainthood, the poet can render psychologically convincing one of the most difficult of all states to dramatize.

The mythic action which Pompilia develops is remarkably close to the Pauline logic whereby the sins of the world represent a guiltiness in everyone. She appeals in vain to Conti and the guilt-ridden Guillichini, whose lame excuse echoes the very language of Everyman's false friend in the morality play (VII, 1306–1308). The criminal negligence of church and state, betrayed by the Archbishop and the Governor, respectively, involves the rest of society in the sins of Pompilia's foster parents, the first Adam and Eve. A second Adam, Caponsacchi, and a second Eve, Pompilia, must serve as substitutes when mankind is atoning for its common crime.

After completing her narration of events preceding the elopement, Pompilia can begin the *confirmatio:* her proof of her deliverer's integrity. Once again she uses a form of *insinuation*, rejecting the efforts of smirking detractors to implicate the priest in a sexual crime. For Pompilia, as for Dante's Guido and Cavalcante, there is no hereditary salvation. The gossips who charge her with adultery because her mother was immoral are committing a form of the genetic fallacy. The passage from *narrative* to *confirmatio* is also a transition from Pompilia's attempt to gain some advantages for Caponsacchi to her visionary utterances as a saint. Though she is at first reluctant to state the difference, she finally admits that while she has always spoken the truth, she formerly amplified the facts so that they would "carry" better to her judges. There may have been falsity in overplaying her "pathetic proofs," but she insists she had an honest purpose in assuming these attitudes. Judges amenable to the legal rhetoric of Archangelis and the Fisc "Could only take the truth in through a lie" (VII, 1197). It was the only means of translating the truth into an effective medium of communication. But in "speaking truth to the Truth's self" (VII, 1198), Pompilia is now presenting her case to God and appealing to her auditor to "lend credit to [her] words." Though this pretense of speaking only to God might be an effective trick of legal rhetoric, which even the advocates could use to advantage if they were ingenious enough to think of it, it is, I believe, part of Browning's own strategy against the reader, not of Pompilia's against her judges.

The "conversion" to religious rhetoric takes place when Pompilia affirms the unity of God and the world the morning after she has longed for death. In reciting from *The Ring and the Book* in later years, Browning seems to have read most often from Pompilia's monologue. This is not surprising if, as many critics think, Browning has transformed Pompilia into the memory of his own wife, who had died in Florence in 1861. Like his "lyric Love," Pompilia treats life in its lowest forms—even the dripping shag of weed—as an entry into spirit. Because the rhetoric of religion makes possible the ultimate communion with God by means of the objective world, in a way that Browning's early subjective poetry does not, Pompilia's sympathetic identification with flies and birds and all natural creation is systematically treated, on the model of the Christian Incarnation, as a necessary step. Her holy intimacy with the "Wrath of God" humanizes everything it treats and sanctifies even the inanimate "fire" as a "Servant of God," a "thou" which "befriend[s] His child!" (VII, 1395–1396). Idealists like Paracelsus and Sordello must first reverse direction and learn the "Downward Way," before they can see in "A broad yellow sunbeam" a "sudden drawbridge" let down "From heaven to earth," which they can then use as a ladder in climbing, like Pompilia, to a unifying transcendent term (VII, 1225–1226).

Pompilia first prays that Caponsacchi "will come"; then she invokes God in language that contains the answer to her prayer: "God the strong, God the beneficent, / God ever mindful in all strife and strait" (VII, 1385–1386). If God answers to her definition of him, then he must grant her request. Because the answer to every prayer is implicit in the address, the rhetoric of religion is necessarily circular. The appearance of her deliverer strikes Pompilia, not with amazement or surprise, but with a sense of fulfilled expectation. M. H. Abrams has shown how the "correspondent breeze" functions as a metaphor in Romantic poetry;[3] and when Caponsacchi comes to Pompilia like a wind bearing before it as dust or feathers all evil and false report, he infuses the whole scene with a spiritual power. Once again the imagery reinforces the idea that good alone is an efficient cause, while

[3] "The Correspondent Breeze: A Romantic Metaphor," *English Romantic Poets*, ed. M. H. Abrams (New York, 1960), pp. 37–52.

evil is merely Augustine's *causa deficiens*. Guido is only an
eclipse of goodness, like darkness temporarily obscuring the
sun—a metaphor which is reinforced by traditional Platonic
and Christian associations of religious truth with light. Pompilia can unite man's soul with the world by illustrating how
God "grew likest God in being born" (VII, 1691). Like
Dante's *Paradiso*, her *confirmatio* integrates the spirit into
history by ending, not with beatific vision, but with the specifically Christian act of Incarnation.

In the *peroration* the different characters in the drama pass
in review before Pompilia for the last time as she delivers her
judgment on each. She pardons her parents and even pleads
with God on Guido's behalf. She believes that by purifying
his victim, her husband has made her better able to redeem
him through her martyrdom. Pompilia recognizes that her
own sainthood is a dialectical term that implies its contradictory, damnation. Guido is the hell-fire, the symbolic neg-
ativity, which is the metaphysical ground of her own being.
He is less a psychological fiend, a "fact" of nature, than a
figure in a myth, a Satanic dragon in a children's fairy tale.
Because Guido's "Pure Impurity" inverts the priest's integrity, it can even save Pompilia by "rightly" ruining her
(VII, 1736).

The *peroration* concludes with praise and thanksgiving.
Instead of commending the good she finds in her judges, as
she had at the beginning of the *confirmatio*, Pompilia now
reserves her praise for God alone: "Why should I doubt He
will explain in time / What I feel now, but fail to find the
words?" (VII, 1760–1761). In death she will plead her
son's case, no longer before the judges, but before the perfect auditor she now awaits. Since Caponsacchi's deliverance
of Pompilia is a form of grace, perfecting nature, she can
apply the private vocabulary of love to the ultimate experi-

ence. She knows that when she calls the priest the "lover of [her] life," God will know how to discount the inadequacies of such language. He will approve her delight in the sheer forms of heavenly courtship for their own sake.

Pompilia's vision of heaven is not just of a romantic stage setting: a place perfumed with balsam where she will dress in flowers and meet her soldier-saint. "Marriage on earth seems . . . a counterfeit" to the martyr, because it has been transformed for her by a transcendent power. Caponsacchi's love, which in some way pervades seed, flower, and balsam tree alike, is the "god term" under which the other elements are subsumed. Pompilia draws her words for Caponsacchi's divinity from three realms: from natural metaphors of light, flowers, and seeds, from military descriptions of her "soldier-saint," and from the priest's religious rhetoric, which "reverberates the truth" and flashes "the word God gave him, back to man!" (VII, 1796–1797).

> Through such souls alone
> God stooping shows sufficient of His light
> For us i' the dark to rise by. And I rise
> [VII, 1843–1845].

The final understatement overcomes the radical failure of language to say explicitly what is in the full heart. When she calls the priest the "lover of [her] life," Pompilia disavows the sexual analogies. She avoids a conventional erotic form while preserving the conventional intention in all its power. As an expert in the art of charging ordinary words with extraordinary meaning, Pompilia can use a rhetorical device like understatement to achieve exactly what she pretends not to achieve. Her last three words, "And I rise," gain a compression of substance which amounts to a triumph of form: they achieve the fullest possible meaning consonant with the simple words this saint must use.

≈ 3 *≈*

Like a Platonic dialogue, *The Ring and the Book* first sets up several voices representing different ideologies—the first Half-Rome, the Other Half-Rome, Tertium Quid, and so on—with each one trying to discredit all the others. Only in the monologues of Caponsacchi and Pompilia does Browning establish a set of mythic postulates to supersede these competing rhetorics. The ideal "end" of this dialectic is found in the Pope's intellectual formulations. The priest's heroic deliverance, like the myth at the end of one of Plato's dialogues, is the statement of these concepts in terms of anecdote or fable. But the Pope's "transcendence" of the myth is at once a step up and a step down. It is a step up because it ascends from the impurity of mythic images to the purity of conceptual formulations. But it is also a step down, for it descends below Caponsacchi's and Pompilia's level of motivation. As the only soliloquy in *The Ring and the Book,* the Pope's speech is more likely than the other monologues to approximate a pure appeal to God, especially when it approaches a form of prayer. But the Pope is for the most part an "I" addressing its "me." He is presenting his privileged intuitions to his rational self, the young student Antonio Pignatelli, who lacks the pontiff's direct access to the truth. The most authoritative exposition of the poem's "philosophy," the Pope's soliloquy is a kind of "still point" at the center of *The Ring,* as though it were in a state of suspended animation. But because it lacks a motive beyond ideas, the soliloquy's animation *is* suspended. Its pure ideas lack the dynamism of myth, just as Caponsacchi and Pompilia do not develop a systematic critique of their ideas. If the Pope's logical formulations must pass instantaneously into the saint's religious motivation, mythic power must flash back in turn as a new organ of knowledge. A complete rhetoric of religion depends, not on the ascendancy of either Pompilia's spiritual imagination or the Pope's theological intellect, but on their constant interaction in a costly but noble state of tension. What is thought must be experienced, and what is experienced must attain the exactness of thought.

Though the Pope is his own auditor, he adapts the divisions of the classical oration, partly to persuade himself, but also to defend his decision before God. He opens with an *exordium* (X, 1–162), which consists of a brief introduction that acknowledges the importance of his place in history and a repudiation of the many injustices which the papacy has formerly committed in God's name. This repudiation takes the place of the traditional *insinuation*, in which the Pope can forestall indirect criticisms of his office by vowing to redeem past wrongs. The *narrative* (X, 163–235), which states the facts of the case, makes clear that the Pope has already reached his verdict that Guido is guilty. The arguments which follow are only an attempt to justify what he has intuitively discerned. By reversing the normal order of *confirmation* and *refutation*, the Pope can first review the different characters in turn (X, 236–1238), and in support of each of his verdicts rebut the arguments against him. The Pope's *confirmation* (X, 1239–1929), which sets forth his theology, constitutes the final justification of Caponsacchi and Pompilia by giving their religious imagination the necessary place in his scheme. After summing up his judgment of the others, the *peroration* (X, 1930–2135) excites the Pope's *indignation* against Guido. His reversal of the customary *conquestio* mocks the sentimental appeal used by the moral relativists in trying to win sympathy for their cause.

The Pope first repudiates the errors committed by earlier pontiffs in "God's name." Pope Stephen wanted the world to believe in some connection between his dismemberment of his predecessor and a solicitude for fish, an association he supported by referring to learned authorities. The comedy of "unpoping" assumes that a pontiff is only his name and the role that name implies. The ceremony produces the kind of animated-cartoon world in which the next pontiff can depose again the Pope, Formosus, whom John and Theodorus "repoped" after Stephen had "unpoped" him. Innocent concludes that what matters is not what man can *make* but what God can *do*. To uphold his office, the pontiff resolves to "think, speak, act, in place of Him— / The Pope for Christ" (X, 168–169).

In defense of the verdict he has already reached, the Pope begins his refutation by anticipating three fallacious arguments against a conviction. Those who oppose the death sentence because of the acquittal of other criminals who are just as guilty as Guido are trying to compound a wrong in order to create a right. A second objection, that if Guido is convicted, his friends will rise against the papacy, is a mere appeal to force. The third argument, which opposes a conviction on the ground that it will render Guido useless to the state, proceeds from an abuse of Aristotle's argument from consequences. This same argument would assume that if a man is good, his last deed will be good. It would insist that if the Pope's last act is his conviction of an innocent man, he cannot be a just pope (X, 341–346). But Innocent would reject this assumption. Because all human words betray, God does not judge in the way his rhetoricians do. The center of truth is a kind of wordlessness, whose validity is guaranteed by the divine Word. Legal wordmen must turn from their rhetorical words to Christ, "the Truth," who "is, too, / The Word" (X, 376–377).

After refuting the arguments advanced by the populace on Guido's behalf, the Pope directly discredits the Count's own defense. Through base comparison of Guido to an "ambiguous fish" (X, 486), the Pope constructs a logical dilemma. On the premise that the shell is part of this fish, the analogy would rank him with other vermin. On the assumption that the shell is detachable, the comparison would render the creature vulnerable by stripping him of his armor, of his legal "case" and his shell. Innocent's conclusion that Guido is either vulnerable or is vermin is inevitably imposed by logical and pictorial aptness. It seems to follow deductively, as it were, from the symbolic satire he creates.

Having vindicated his verdict negatively, the Pope can now try to incorporate the spiritual intuitions of Caponsacchi and Pompilia into his own theology. Since this *confirmatio* is also Browning's, it occupies the same position relative to the rest of *The Ring* as the climax of "Saul" does to all of Browning's dramatic monologues. It is the "final cause" of his myth as a whole, not simply because its speculations are directed toward the future, but because they are continually present in the rest of the work and can be felt implicitly to contain its "end."

Innocent's auditor is no longer his rational self but the transcendent God. The vibrant "I-Thou" structure encourages in the Pope a purely formal incentive toward the idea of a perfect audience, before whose "measureless" extension he can assess the insignificance of his own life as an "atom width" (X, 1310). In adapting the argument from design, the Pope maintains that even in a Platonic system the sufficiency of God's power and knowledge in creating man and the world should be self-apparent. But only Christianity can illustrate how God also outstrips man in His capacity to love. The Incarnation is what makes Platonism accessible to man; only the "tale" of Christ provides the final access.

What is so profoundly rhetorical about Plato's metaphysic is its idea that the divine element in the world is a persuasive power, not a mere coercive force. The Pope follows Plato in rejecting the argument *ad baculum* and in reading into God's creation a persuasion of his audience through love and knowledge: "why live / Except for love,—how love unless they know?" (X, 1327–1328). Though the idea of a loving power immanent in the world originated with Plato, the Greeks stressed the role of knowledge, and it remained for Christianity to perfect the other aspect of the doctrine. The Pope believes that Christianity's permanent appeal lies in the genius with which it recasts the idea of a loving power immanent in the world as an anecdote or story able to "carry" to a human audience the doctrine of persuasive agency that Plato had divined in theory. Innocent sees this planet merely as the stage for God's "transcendent act." The Incarnation is a paradigm for the placing and the timing of that eternal "act" as it sweeps down out of Plato's heaven to gather in the whole of human history.

The power and knowledge that Plato had deified left God "eminently real," and the world merely "derivatively real." Only the Incarnation can make the "strength" and "intelligence" part of the objective world. By adding the third ingredient of "love without a limit," it perfects the symmetry of Plato's design. Because it substitutes a persuasive force, love, for Plato's second-rate God of the world, a mere icon, Christianity culminates in the concept of a gracious God who invites man to cooperate with Him for his own redemption. The realization of love's power in the world must be repeated constantly till the end of time; the truth the Incarnation represents has no past or future, but only a continuing present. Browning's early subjective poetry, with its Platonic inspiration, finds only inadequate intimations of the divine in the real world. But Christianity proclaims that because the objective world is the "scene of [God's] transcendent act," it is just as necessary to God as God is to the world. Browning's most significant contribution to religious thought is the consistency with which he conceives of the world in terms of the metaphysical category of love, or persuasive force. By making this doctrine of love central, Browning has pushed further the fine effort on the part of the early theologians to exercise their religious imagination. He has perfected that element of Christianity which represents, in A. N. Whitehead's view, "the only fundamental metaphysical doctrine [that has] improved upon Plato." [4] In striking reminiscence of David's analogical argument in "Saul," the Pope reasons that if a condition is present where it would be less natural, it must also be present where it would be more natural. The supposition that God can outstrip man in knowledge and power, but not in man's most godlike attribute of love, is illogical and blasphemous. Since God's love is revealed in suffering, the pain must be a way of making man "love in turn and be beloved" (X, 1381).

Though he never states whether the Christian story is "fact" or "imaginative sense of fact," the Pope speaks as though the historical evidences of Christianity were a matter of indifference to him. This quality of disbelief is entirely consistent with sanctity; but it allows for and encourages agnosticism and the possibility of error. The Pope would like to bypass the baffling ontological questions by accepting the pragmatic formula that whatever works is conceptually respectable. He might be hard-pressed to show how the mythic dodges of the higher critics, with their symbolic "fictions," could ever fit into a rational conception of theology. But his skepticism is a qualitative mode of belief rather than a mere denial of dogma. He believes that when religion, like science, deals with ultimate things, it uses imaginative models, not "facts." Religious arguments are based on assumptions about what is worth living and dying for; these are rooted in the imagination, and only the imagination can

[4] "The New Reformation," *Adventures of Ideas* (New York, 1933), p. 215.

nourish them. Whereas science studies the waves' motion and makes acoustical charts of the sound (X, 1402), religion is like the poetic child who hears only the roar of an angry sea (X, 1400). By using various myths to impose meaning on the world, both science and religion use rhetoric to adapt the "truth" to their particular audiences. It is not a question of eliminating rhetoric, but only of which model to choose.

The Pope is less concerned with theological disputes over words than with the quality of life that belief in God makes possible. What matters is, not a battle over names in To-kien Province, but the heroism of a priest in Italy.

> Where are the Christians in their panoply? . . .
> The helmet of salvation, and that sword
> O' the Spirit, even the word of God,—where these?
>   [X, 1566–1570].

What can never be refuted by logomachy is the underlying vision of Caponsacchi's life. All such polemics try to formulate this vision conceptually. But to use Browning's revealing phrase from his letter to Elizabeth Barrett dated April 18, 1845, the mystery is "too large to be taken in the hinge of a syllogism."

Skeptics who play the word game like to infer from the evil of the human agents the absence of a benevolent God. But their logic fails to disturb the Pope, who once again introduces his anti-Manichean metaphor of darkness as eclipse of light. The clouds are no longer simply Augustine's *causa deficiens*, but a necessary imperfection. They are part of God's design in softening the blaze of his truth so that he can now more effectively transmit the light to a weak-eyed observer. God's allowance for "weakness," by supplying "incentive to humanity," is synonymous with the Christ principle. By descending to their level, "that which men think weakness within strength" is really its opposite, the perfect power that completes the symmetry of the Christian scheme. The sacrificial principle which culminates in the Crucifixion ensures the worshiper's collaboration with God: "How can man love but what he yearns to help?" (X, 1652). Christ's "weakness" means that his Crucifixion is not just a historical event. The "divine instance of self-sacrifice / That never ends and aye begins for man" (X, 1657–1658) is a miracle in which men must continually participate, a mystery they must constantly renew. The Incarnation is a continuing historical process, a progressive movement of Spirit into flesh and flesh into Spirit, in which each must dialectically become the other. The Messiah who, in Christian theology, created "the first things," and thereby introduced a distinction between nature and supernature, is also the Son of God who makes them "new." His "weakness" is therefore both a condition of separation and a means of overcoming that separation. The principle of "weakness within strength" which rounds out the Pope's theology finds its supreme embodiment in Christ's threefold function: creative, mediatory, and redemptive.

Like Browning's St. John, the Pope insists that difficulty is inseparable from the whole religious venture. In demolishing religious myths that deified immorality and power, Euripides was laying the philosophic groundwork for Christianity's appeal to man through the most powerful rhetorical motive, love. Even if Euripides lacked the religious genius to anticipate the dialectic that made persuasion immanent in the world, the Pope believes that it is better to see some light at midnight than only darkness at noon. It might be supposed that Christianity would be easier to believe in after the persecution of the early Christians had ceased. But at high noon the "world's gross torch" merges with "heaven's white" (X, 1830–1831). Without the black foil of Nero's cross, it is even more difficult to believe in a Christian age than in Eurip-

ides' pre-Christian Greece. Though the obstacles are pro-
portioned differently to Euripides and Innocent, the difficulty of acknowledging his own insufficiency requires of the
Christian an even greater effort than it does of the pagan. If
whoever passes his probation, therefore, is "last," in the
double sense of least privileged and latest, he "proves first
indeed" (X, 1827).

The Pope wants the coming generation to live more dan-
gerously, for only when prepared to die is man at last alive.
His call for "Faith, in the thing," as well as "faith in the report" (X, 1866), corresponds to Newman's insistence that
real assent to religious truth must accompany notional assent.
While religion is being apprehended as truth by the theological intellect it must also be appropriated as living "reality" by the religious imagination. The Pope's own dogmas
must return to the spiritual intuitions of Caponsacchi and
Pompilia, which in turn require new theological formulation.
Though the mass of men cannot keep pace with this process
of the spirit and are incapable of following the progressive
disclosures of truth from age to age, the Pope foresees that
in periods of transition there will always be a few Christians
who, instead of slinking "Worm-like into the mud," will rise
to the new height. The Church has to keep up with the advance of truth. This is the Church's calling, but as the Pope
recognizes, it is an impossible vocation, for the truth is always outstripping the Church, overtaking and anticipating
its dogma in the discoveries of a Caponsacchi or Pompilia.
The truth, in other words, has to be found in the doing, and
exactly what this means the Church can never know in advance. A knight of faith like Caponsacchi must let his life be
directed, not from behind by the safety of received doctrine,
but by the danger of love ahead. His religion is not a set of
static formulas from which all the quest and questioning
have been drained away, but a process of learning to be vul-

nerable—to the love and demands of Pompilia, and even to a Guido's hate.

Caponsacchi and Pompilia have been betrayed by the Church for the Church's good. Their intuitions, enkindled with the light of thought and elaborated by reflection, will permit in turn the attainment of more profound intuitions. This is the rhythm of the spiritual process, which returns from thought to life in a progressive enrichment. The Incarnation is a forward-moving process; and saints like Caponsacchi and Pompilia point the way to a new epiphany of the Word. Their "real assent" is the rediscovery of the unchanging truth, of the essence that inspirits the Christian story— the essence whose temporal manifestations must be revived from age to age to "Correct the portrait by the living face, / Man's God, by God's God in the mind of man" (X, 1873– 1874). The Pope's artistic metaphor incorporates as the cornerstone of his theology a rhetorical principle that makes every man a conscious collaborator with God in the discovery of "some truth / Unrecognized [as] yet, but [still] perceptible" (X, 1871–1872). The disparity between "the portrait" and "the living face," far from perpetuating the fideist's ultimate divorce of faith from reason, sets up a dynamic dialectic. The theological intellect, instead of illegitimately absorbing the intuitions into itself, recognizes that experience of "the living face" is its own necessary origin and the point to which Christianity must always return for renewal.

Pompilia's vicarious atonement is intrinsic to the idea of corporate guilt. Though the Pope believes that only the exceptional individual can redeem society, he hopes that even while the new century ushers in the "impatient antimasque" of a post-Christian era, experimentalists like Caponsacchi will still be present to guide the age. The burden of the Pope's prophecy is that the Christian cycle must repeat itself in every generation. But his religious speculations are not the theology of an age of belief. Like so much of Browning's best religious verse, they probe the turbulent voids beneath theology. Wild beasts like Guido will reappear and forever incite anew the search for a curative victim. The principle of mortification, which culminates in the Crucifixion, has its human counterpart in the martyrdom of saintly victims. Their sacrifice is dramatically a catharsis, and philosophically a term of mediation between the temporal and eternal orders. But despite Christ's perfect martyrdom, in which Pompilia and Caponsacchi share, the Pope implies that this process of guilt, atonement, and redemption must repeat itself indefinitely. These repetitions are intrinsic to the nature of spiritual development. The guilt may be expiated, but even the sacrifice of the Pompilias and the execution of the Guidos can never remove it. Far from denying evil, Browning must retain it as a necessary part of his Christian dialectic. There is even a strange similarity between the functions of Christ and Guido. Whereas Christ limits while enlarging, Guido's limitations are confining. His disorder has its own order, though it exists only by the sufferance of God. Browning has thrown the Pope's philosophy of imperfection out like a lifeline to all skeptical minds in all the ages to come. Like the Christ principle of "weakness in strength," Guido's evil is the necessary condition of spiritual development. It is a catalyst that miraculously precipitates a chain reaction of partial cures. But between Christ's absolute victory and its imperfect repetition in the historic cycle, the Pope implies, some kind of tension must always exist, till the possible and the actual meet at infinity. When it insists that it has already reached the truth and that its dialectical pilgrimage is at an end, the doctrine of the Church becomes one of the great heresies of the human mind.

The peroration is the moment of motionlessness, when the

axe has been raised to its full height over Guido and is just about to fall. By bringing together in a body his less crucial judgments, the Pope can announce his most important verdicts separately. Instead of using the *conquestio* of classic oratory to arouse sympathy for himself, he mocks the pathetic proofs of the moral relativists who would sacrifice religion to culture.

> That in this case the spirit of culture speaks,
> Civilization is imperative.
> To her shall we remand all delicate points
>
> [X, 2071–2019].

The voice of culture, whose soft guitar music is an aesthetic travesty of the Sanctus et Benedictus, introduces the Virgilian analogy of a Papal Priam on the verge of tears. But the *indignatio*, which Innocent discharges against Guido with the force of a thunderbolt, dispels the illusion of a sentimental pope. In hurling back Guido's rallying cry *"Quis pro Domino?"* he lifts the words from a local, feudal context to a universal level (X, 2100). The soliloquy which begins with a pageant of mock justice ends with a symbolic enactment of God's justice. Instead of accepting the earlier argument that Guido's execution will endanger the Pope's afterlife, Innocent is now afraid to face God if Guido lives. This reversal is his most dramatic way of emphasizing the justice of his sentence. If Guido is saved as a result of Innocent's verdict, Guido will then merit God's forgiveness. Innocent believes that the ultimate mercy is to encourage Guido's atonement by attempting to convert him through the severity and swiftness of the papal judgment.

⁂ 4 ⁂

Unlike the young subjective poet, who had tried to communicate the truth instantly and as a whole, Browning discovers that the "pure white light" is the end product of a long and arduous dialectical ascent. Only by celebrating his power and freedom in portraying many points of view can Browning unite the objective authority of the dramatic poet with the subjective poet's ability to write "R. B.—a poem."

If we think of *The Ring and the Book* as three concentric circles, with the Pope's soliloquy at the center as its "final cause," we can see how its rings repeat the three stages of Browning's prior development in the dramatic monologues. Like the early masks, the monologues in the outer ring (Books II through V and Books VIII, IX, and XI) expose the reader to the rhetoric with the most partisan bias, a rhetoric bound indissolubly to Kierkegaard's aesthetic stage. By unscrambling the elements presented in these monologues, the first and last books transcend the limitations portrayed in the outer ring. They narrate the events in logical sequence and educate the Victorian public in the lost art of myth-reading. If taken literally, the central action of the elopement lends itself to the reductive analysis of the advocates. But in *The Ring and the Book* Browning is not merely writing his religious myth. In spinning out his metaphors of gold and alloy in Books I and XII, he is also writing his own "philosophy of myth." The work can reveal its true nature only if it reveals a motive beyond the legal game. In the monologues of Caponsacchi and Pompilia, which together with the first and last books constitute the middle ring, the courtroom oratory moves beyond the legal words to the Divine Word at the center of each person and event. The action of Books VI and VII resolves the contradictions of the aesthetic life by dealing with experience at a higher ethical and religious stage. This myth of deliverance, death, and redemption is still rhetorical, in the sense that it adapts the pure ideas of the Pope to an audience more receptive to situations than ideas. But its disciplined arrival at religious truth comes only through a systematic transcendence of the reductive methods of the outer ring.

By locating the Pope's monologue at the philosophic center, Browning reminds the reader that the ingenuous simplicity of Pompilia's faith, which can have little to do, in an illiterate girl of seventeen, with the free play of the mind, is inadequate by itself. Only the intellect can refract into many emotions the primary egoistic ones. The richest and fullest faith is that which combines the private immediacy of Pompilia's truths with the public clarity of the Pope's pronouncements. Only the universal language of theology enables him to communicate her intuitions to the world. Though the rational imagination must absorb such intuitions, it can never be confined to them. Religion must be recomposed beyond the simplicity of myth and, like the Pope's faith, should include within itself the torment of a doubt that is perpetually overcome. Like the rationalism of Dante's Virgil, Innocent's intelligence wins its most impressive triumph when, at the height of its powers, it acknowledges its limitations. Only the Pope's reason can prepare him to confront a motive which, since it is beyond ideas, cannot lend itself to statement in philosophic terms. Hence the inner and middle rings are as closely fused as Newman's "notional" and "real" assent. The two are only abstractly separable; and the one always calls us back to the other. To dislodge the Pope's ideas from the center would be to turn Browning into a misologist. But to minimize the role of myth by dropping the middle circle would be to forget that pure ideas are themselves only a preparation for myth. It is a great advantage for Browning to base his myth on a religious form whose reason is in mystery rather than in logic, but which is no less rational as a result.

The poem's dialectical method requires that all points of view be portrayed but that they all be superseded in turn.

To be grasped as a whole, the "truth" must first express itself in all the forms of human folly. If it were possible to discard the outer and middle rings as extraneous layers, Browning would hardly expect his readers to be any more attentive to the vast processional structure of his poem than casual viewers at the continuing performance of a Hollywood spectacular. But the genius of *The Ring* is that the final spurt of acid dissolves the alloy. The gold does not simply supersede the outside rings, but fuses and transforms them. This is why Browning's religious myth is complete in a way that his early subjective poetry was not. The rhetoric of religion redeems the sensuality and the particular truths of legal "fact" by including them in a new fellowship. Though parts of the poem are inferior to his earlier work, I believe that *The Ring* is still Browning's most sustained achievement. Because it raised him to eminence in the popular imagination, it is not surprising that Browning himself regarded the poem as his masterpiece and invited Miss Wedgwood to think better of the work, if only "for precision in criticism." [5] Though skeptics like Tertium Quid and atheists like Guido may possess limited truth, dialectical logic reveals that their conclusions are partial, because the opposite principles are also valid. Each individual suffers from a lack of proof insurmountable by all dogmatism. But the points of view of many men, when taken together, also attain a truth invincible to all skepticism. By reviving a mythic mode to resolve in the fullness of its own dynamic life all the limitations of the aesthetic, ethical, and religious stages, *The Ring and the Book* repeats Browning's rhetorical evolution, bringing it to its logical "end" in the monologues of Caponsacchi, Pompilia, and the Pope, who may be regarded as the summarizing representatives of the whole development.

[5] *Robert Browning and Julia Wedgwood*, p. 194.

Conclusion:
The Dialectical Temper

The distinctive feature of Browning's rhetoric is its dialectical temper, which forces the reader to discover the astonishing (and often disturbing) life of the ideas. We value Browning for the authority and brilliance, often the sheer excitement, of his thinking. Though this emphasis on rhetoric and "content" is especially helpful at a time when other elements of Browning's work are being stressed, I argue that the poet's doctrines are less important than the life represented and the values found along the way. The Victorian sage must use his doctrines for the sake of the discoveries that go with them, for the sake of what is formed in the progressive act of thinking.

The young Browning is one of the "subjective poets" who, according to his Introductory Essay to the *Letters of Shelley*, seek the truth "in their [own] soul[s]." In its extreme form, Browning calls subjective art "a deformity." Because "the world is not to be learned and thrown aside, but reverted to and relearned," Browning finds that as a subjective poet he must become his opposite; he must make the objective world an inseparable part of himself. In order to understand points of view other than his own, the poet has to play a series of roles and pretend to be what he is not. By

308

breaking the illusion of identity between himself and his roles, the dramatic monologues enable Browning to understand and criticize many points of view. Far from destroying his ethical identity, such "negative capability" is the necessary condition of his moral growth. Different and recurrent attitudes—sensual and ethical, skeptical and dogmatic, emotional and reflective—must keep contending for mastery and must keep finding their claims rebuked. In order to advance from the lower aesthetic to the higher ethical and religious stages, the poet has to reveal the limitations inherent in most ideas and beliefs.

Browning uses this dialectical method for two purposes: to portray persons who are comic or bizarre and to reveal their internal contradictions. If the objective world is more in focus in the comic use of this method, the poet's own attitudes are more important when he is portraying and dissolving limited points of view. In the first case the dialectic is an instrument of comic creation; in the second it is a means of transition and growth. It demands and justifies a distinction between lower aesthetic and higher ethical and religious stages.

Even in portraying the lowest aesthetic stage, Browning is producing more than a gruesome farce. By imitating many points of view, the poet overcomes their individual grotesqueness. He allows the religious philosophy of Johannes Agricola, which takes its rigid mold too soon, to contribute to the maturing of a David or St. John. Even Browning's villains, marionettes of pathos whirled powerlessly through disaster like Guido Franceschini, are used to perfect his total design. They enable the reader to grasp from within the speakers' own points of view the contradictions of the aesthetic life and to attain a higher degree of truth in contemplating the ethical freedom of Fra Lippo or Childe Roland, characters who are responsible for their own behavior. What elevates the Duke of Ferrara or the court lady of "The Laboratory" above the Fu Manchus and mad scientists of melodramatic fiction is the genius with which Browning can reproduce all that is bizarre in their sensual masquerade. Because they find temporary release in the ethical solution of Childe Roland's perseverance or his charity toward his fellows, Browning shows that aesthetic motives are not ultimate but dialectical. The Bishop's greed, the Duke's pride, and Johannes Agricola's lust for power are outrageous and funny. But because Browning the moralist is the very opposite of grotesque, he cannot, in his soul, believe in their final reality. He keeps submitting to comic analysis beliefs more profound and attitudes more subtle: the psychological complexity of Andrea del Sarto or the rhetorical cunning of Mr. Sludge and Bishop Blougram. Because nothing escapes his dialectical scourge, his attempt to arrange all these attitudes hierarchically redeems each melodrama and accords them their necessary place in an "ultimate" order.

Browning's ability to entertain and renounce many points of view in his dramatic monologues draws increasing attention to the poet himself. His range of creation emphasizes a disparity between his true and his assumed nature. By shifting attention from the characters to their creator, his constant rehearsal of new parts enables him, like a versatile actor, to display his own powers far more effectively than he did as a subjective poet, when he tried to express them directly. The dialectical pattern, which develops by opposition and union, reveals that Browning can be most himself when he is least himself. By assuming a number of dramatic masks, he discovers that the only sincerity that matters in poetry is the unintentional by-product of contrivance and disguise. In a way denied to the confessional poet of *Pauline*, the mimic who imitates many points of view can make focal a creative personality that manifests its power and freedom in portraying large segments of the objective world.

After his many experiments in the monologue form, Shelley's disciple is at last in a position to achieve what he told
Miss Barrett in a letter of February 11, 1845, he was "born
to begin and end—'R. B.—a poem' "—that is to say, a work
in which he can reach the "pure white light" and write directly of his own experience. Since Browning can approach
this "light" only by personifying many points of view, *The
Ring and the Book* represents not only itself but also the development of his monologues as a whole. Its triad of outer,
middle, and inner "rings," and its three religious champions
incorporate the trinitarian principle characteristic of the entire development of the monologues. Guido sends forged
letters to Caponsacchi on three occasions, and on the third
occasion Caponsacchi comes to the rescue. Pompilia appeals
to three deliverers—Conti, Guillichini, and Caponsacchi—
and in the early morning of the third day Guido overtakes his
wife. Three days elapse between Guido's crime and Caponsacchi's appearance before the court. Even in *Sordello* and
Paracelsus this trinitarian pattern represents a radical aspect
of Browning's faculty psychology, in a purely secular sense.[1]
It pervades the dialectic of subject and object and their
final union in a higher form. It also appears in the triad of
aesthetic, ethical, and religious stages. In R. P. Blackmur's
words, "The deep skills of imagination, by which insights,
ideas, and acts get into poetry, thrive best when some single,
pressing theme or notion is triplicated. It is not a matter of
understanding, but of movement and of identification and of
access of being."[2]

As the culmination of this dialectical movement, *The Ring*

[1] Once again, I am indebted for this treatment of the trinitarian
pattern to Professor F. E. L. Priestley's exposition and to William
Whitla's *The Central Truth: The Incarnation in Robert Browning's
Poetry* (Toronto, 1963).

[2] "Wallace Stevens: An Abstraction Blooded," in *Language as
Gesture* (New York, 1952), p. 250.

and the Book unites the faculties of the subjective and objective poets, achieving that combination which Browning discerns in the most "perfect works." It brings under the "harmonizing law" of the seer what the Introductory Essay to the *Letters of Shelley* calls the "positive yet conflicting facts" of the objective poet, who alternately assumes and abandons a series of roles. Unlike Browning's early masks, the monologues of *The Ring and the Book* are not simply a means of self-protection. On the contrary, Browning uses them to celebrate the triumph of his own creative power over every content and every form. By allowing him to remain aloof from satisfaction at any level of insight, the monologues become his avenue to the "pure white light." They enable Browning, in his quest for the infinite, to pass beyond the limits of his medium.

Though a poem like *The Ring and the Book* resolves in theory its author's problems, it does not necessarily follow that it is his best work. Browning's union of the subject with the world coincides with his attainment of literary perfection in the monologues of Pompilia and the Pope, and in a poem like "Saul." But other "resolutions" seem too easily achieved. I have tried to show why poems like "Rabbi Ben Ezra" and the Epilogue to *Asolondo*, though they theoretically solve the poet's problems, are still inferior to monologues like "My Last Duchess," "The Bishop Orders His Tomb," and "Andrea del Sarto." These last three poems are the most perfect Browning ever wrote, not because, like "Saul" or *The Ring and the Book*, they resolve anything, but because they are among the most memorable presentations of the aesthetic stage in literature. My analysis of Browning's rhetorical art, by trying to give a systematic account of his development, may modify a reader's response to an individual work like "Saul." In illustrating the kind of rhetorical relevance that the postscript of "An Epistle . . .

of Karshish" has, it may even change his opinion of a particular poem. But such evaluations are ultimately a matter for each reader's response. Though I have included such judgments where appropriate, my main aim, like John Holloway's, has been "to provide and elucidate the subject-matter for responses, not to control them." [3]

In fact, in view of his ability to modify his readers' aesthetic, moral, and religious attitudes by revealing the limitations inherent in most ideas and beliefs, I think we may safely leave such control to the poet himself. For Browning's most original contribution to the kind of comprehensive rhetorical theory that this age of new grammars and stylistics seems to be evolving is his systematic application of *Sordello*'s doctrine that by involving the audience as his collaborator, the poet, while still controlling responses, can impart "the gift of seeing" to his readers. The plots of Browning's plays, like the action of *The Ring and the Book*, are not undramatic; they are merely dramatic in a special sense. They constitute a series of revelations, like changing patterns in a kaleidoscope, which have the effect of shifting attention to the reader's own experience. Browning presents different points of view without predicating any relations among them, even though his selecting presence can be felt behind the order in which their limitations are revealed. Because *The Ring and the Book* offers shifting perspectives on the same events, the cumulation of effect from book to book forces the reader to make connections. Whereas the early subjective poetry proceeds from cause to effect, the dramatic monologues reverse this process. They work backward from the desired effect on a silent auditor, who serves as the reader's surrogate, to the source of that effect in Browning's shaping of the poem.

The more consistently the poet invites the reader to par-

[3] *The Victorian Sage* (New York, 1953), p. 19.

ticipate in the creative process, the more persuasive he becomes. The difference between the stridency of "Rabbi Ben
Ezra" and the ecstatic affirmations of "Saul" is not in religious commitment or belief, but in rhetorical involvement, in
the degree to which "language gains the force of gesture," to
use Blackmur's phrase. Whereas "Rabbi Ben Ezra" simply
records antecedently defined beliefs, "Saul" achieves what
F. R. Leavis has so finely discerned in T. S. Eliot's best religious verse: "Enormous labor [has been] expended by the
poet in undercutting mere acceptance, inhibiting inert acqui-
escence, and circumventing, at every level, what may be
called cliché; a tendency, that is, to abet the reader's desire
to arrive without having travelled." [4] The more successful
poem engages the reader in David's own experience. Because
it makes the reader a collaborator with Browning in the discovery of important truths, David's rhetoric fortifies rather
than obstructs our "sense of gesture." The typical modern
reader can accept the doctrines of Browning the sage only
when their possibilities are dramatized for him to share. In
poems like "Cleon" and "Saul" these doctrines produce excruciation as often as serenity. The problem with "Rabbi
Ben Ezra" is that the reader has to provide most of the irony
and drama for himself. Instead of suppressing the problem of
belief and working out the irony implicit in the attitudes,
Browning is more interested in the doctrines and ideas than
in the life represented and the values discovered on the way.
The sage can never relinquish the responsibilities of his
poetic craft. He must eliminate authoritarian assertion and
use his rhetorical art to give authority to his beliefs.

Early masks like "Soliloquy of the Spanish Cloister,"
which, by failing to incorporate a silent auditor, omit the
rhetorical motive altogether, create at best a brilliant impres-

---

[4] "Approaches to T. S. Eliot," in *The Common Pursuit* (New York,
1964), p. 287.

sion, never a complete dialectical action. By continually enlisting the reader as coauthor, the monologues of Browning's
maturity move toward a climactic truth with a decisiveness
and assurance not to be found in the earlier masks. As their
compressed debate between opposites in personality and
ideas approaches a truth beyond the arguments, Browning
invites us to leave his private theatre of the mind for David's
prophetic visions or Caponsacchi's splendid ascent from sensuality to worship of beauty, to transcendent desire for
union with God. As Helen Gardner has argued, "It is not
the poet's business to make us believe *what* he believes, but
to make us believe *that* he believes. He must convince us that
he himself is convinced." [5] As mask and man converge,
Browning can finally speak convincingly in his own person.
Unlike the early subjective poems, *The Ring and the Book*
does not invite us to discard the particular truths of fact, but
to treat the objective world as the necessary entry into ultimate communion with God.

In Hegel's words, "The truth is the whole." But it is no
longer the undifferentiated whole of the young subjective
poet, who had tried to leap directly into his omniscient role.
The "pure white light" can be reached only by acts of sympathetic imagination that reproduce in successive monologues a series of gradual approximations to truth, each of
which, not being total, is inevitably tainted with bias and
falsehood. The truth requires for its comprehension just
those dramatic and dissolving views of reality that enable the
poet to encompass in the fullness of his own dynamic life the
whole range of aesthetic, ethical, and religious stages. As
Browning affirms in his essay on Shelley, by "climb[ing] that
mighty ladder, of which . . . the world dares no longer
doubt that its gradations ascend," the poet combines the
faculties both of subjective and objective poets; in this way

[5] *The Art of T. S. Eliot* (London, 1949), p. 68.

he unites the "natural to the spiritual" and "the actual to the ideal." Though only God comprehends the total truth, Browning can approximate absolute knowledge by multiplying his points of view. He can render continuous his homecoming as a visionary poet by re-enacting his entry into the objective world. This is the law of his poetic development, that he should first voyage abroad to experience what is foreign to his own nature. He must repeat this voyage and incorporate its movement in successive poems. Only then, after a long apprenticeship in the monologue form, can Browning come home again to write "R. B.—a poem."

The vast web of analogies by which *The Ring and the Book* tries to unite its different perspectives reminds us that no revelation in human terms is complete. The closer we come to the "pure white light," the farther away it seems to recede. Only in his "grey ultimate decrepitude" is the Pope "sensible of fires that more and more / Visit a soul, in passage to the sky, / Left nakeder than when flesh-robe was new" (*The Ring and the Book*, X, 389–392). The total truth is like physical death. This is its excitement, promise, and terror, that no one can experience it without being destroyed. But by first descending from his Shelleyan heaven, Browning has done all that a Christian poet can hope to achieve. He has helped rebuild "the great world's altar-stairs / That slope thro' darkness up to God." The dramatic monologues are the steps of Jacob's ladder leading the poet back from the objective world to the "pure white light." Because the Incarnation is the dialectical movement of a divine being, sweeping down out of eternity to gather in the whole of human history, the poet who has traced the essential nature of this development in his own career can at last participate in the central Christian mystery. In writing a myth to "Suffice the eye and save the soul beside" (*The Ring and the Book*, XII, 867), he can even re-enact, from the human point of view, the Incarnation's paradoxical union of God and the world. By making spirit immanent in nature, as something that realizes itself only when it becomes its opposite, the Incarnation validates the whole dialectical venture—the mutual antagonism between subject and object, and their final union in a higher form.

Index

Numerals in italic type indicate the main discussion.

319

Milton, John
  his religious elevation, 171
  his rhetoric, 221-222
  his Satan, 100, 266
Minchin, H. C., 132n, 255
Monsignor, the bishop (*Pippa Passes*), 51-52
Monteiro, George, 94
"Mr. Sludge, 'The Medium,' " 55, 203, *212-217*, 310
"My Last Duchess," 50, 71, 73, *92-104*, 111-112, 133, 152, 258, 274, 310, 312

Negative capability, 129, 243, 309
  in *Pauline*, 13
  source of the poet's power in *Pippa Passes*, 47-48, 52
  see also Sympathetic imagination
Nero, 91
New Bearings in English Poetry, 166
Newman, John
  his doctrine of "notional" and "real" assent, 189, 301, 306
  his rhetoric, 142, 207, 210, 213
Nominalism, 65, 160, 191, 195; *see also* Gnosticism *and* Manichean heresy

Ogniben (*A Soul's Tragedy*), 54-56, 71
Old Yellow Book, 240-241, 255, 273
Ossian, 26
Other Half-Rome (*The Ring and the Book*), 243, *247-249*, 293
Ottima (*Pippa Passes*), 48-49
Otto, Rudolf, 202

Pacchiarotto, 57
Palma (*Sordello*), 29, 33
Paracelsus, 8, *14-21*, 48, 290, 311
Pascal, Blaise, 214
Paul, St., 184
  Acts of the Apostles, 178
  Epistle to the Colossians, 198
  Epistle to the Corinthians, 227
Pauline, 8, *10-14*, 112, 236, 310
Pelagian heresy, 283-284
Perrine, Laurence, 101
Phene (*Pippa Passes*), 49-50, 52
Piaget, Jean, 66

Pied Piper of Hamelin, 222
Pippa Passes, 8, 40, *45-53*, 54, 56, 58, 237
Plato, 179
  his dialogues, 293
  his intellectual supremacy in the dialogue form, 167
  his metaphysics, 296-298
  myth of Platonic ascent, 281
  parable of the cave, 187
  his "philosopher-king," 36
  Platonic elements in St. John's gospel, 185
  his Socratic dialectic, 115, 155-157, 279
  see also Cambridge Platonists
Poetry of Experience, The, see Langbaum, Robert
Pompilia (*The Ring and the Book*), 2, 173, 243, 245-254, 264-265, 267, 269-270, 272, 274-276, 278-285, 286-292, 293-294, 301-303, 305-307, 311-312
Pontormo, 93
Pope, the (*The Ring and the Book*), 2, 208, 238, 243, 262, 272, 275-276, 278, *293-304*, 305-307, 312, 316
Pope, Alexander, 95, 277
"Porphyria's Lover," 75-77, 79, 112, 114
Pound, Ezra, 91
Priestley, F. E. L., 15, 173, 186n, 224, 311n
Prince Berthold (*Colombe's Birthday*), 42-44
"Prospice," 116, *124-126*, 127, 185, 218, 220
"Protus," 91-92
Psychopathology of Everyday Life, The, 264
Punctuation
  elliptical questions, 26
  exclamation points, 11, 224
  multiplication of dashes, 106, 214
"Pure white light," the subjective poet's goal, 2, 149, 232, 311-312, 316
Pym (*Strafford*), 41-43

Queen Kate (*Pippa Passes*), 50, 53
Quintilian, 261, 269

Stevenson, C. L. (*Ethics and Language*), 83n
Strafford, 40, *41-44*, 45
Strauss, David Friedrich, 192, 208
"Sun-treader," epithet for Shelley, 14, 65, 149
Sympathetic imagination, 13, 33, 47-50, 52, 76, 84, 88, 121, 131-133, 136-138; see also Negative capability

Tamburlaine (*Paracelsus*), 15
Taurello (*Sordello*), 29, 33-34, 36-37
Tennyson, Alfred, Lord
In *Memoriam*, 189, 227
his Ulysses, 86, 124
his view of man as the tragic accident, 181
Tertium Quid (*The Ring and the Book*), 243, *249-251*, 293, 307
Tillich, Paul, 200
"Toccata of Galuppi's, A," 133, 135, *136-139*, 145-146
Trinity
anticipated by faculty psychology of *Paracelsus*, 19, 187
Browning's conception of, 19
trinitarian pattern of Caponsacchi's conversion, 282-283

trinitarian patterns throughout Browning's work, 311
see also Christianity
"Two in the Campagna," 116, *120-123*

Ugo, the Intendant (*Pippa Passes*), 51
Ulpian ("The Bishop Orders His Tomb"), 107

Valence (*Colombe's Birthday*), 42-44
Vane (*Strafford*), 42-43
Varieties of Religious Experience, see James, William
Victorian Sage, The, see Holloway, John
Virgil, 274, 304, 306

Wedgwood, Julia, 239, 254-255, 259, 270, 307
Wimsatt, W. K., 83n, 108
Whitehead, A. N., 298
Whitla, William, 186n, 311n

Yeats, W. B., 141
"The Second Coming," 169
on the "tragedy of love," 122
his view of sanctity, 127